EZRA, NEHEMIAH *an* ONE

Also available in the Old Testament
for Everyone series by John Goldingay

Genesis for Everyone, Part I

Genesis for Everyone, Part II

Exodus and Leviticus for Everyone

Numbers and Deuteronomy for Everyone

Joshua, Judges and Ruth for Everyone

1 and 2 Samuel for Everyone

1 and 2 Kings for Everyone

1 and 2 Chronicles for Everyone

EZRA, NEHEMIAH
and ESTHER
for EVERYONE

JOHN GOLDINGAY

Published in the United States of America in 2012
by Westminster John Knox Press, Louisville, Kentucky

Published in Great Britain in 2013

Society for Promoting Christian Knowledge
36 Causton Street
London SW1P 4ST
www.spckpublishing.co.uk

Unless otherwise indicated, Scripture quotations are the author's own translation.

British Library Cataloguing-in-Publication Data
A catalogue record for this book is available from the British Library

ISBN 978–0–281–06132–7
eBook ISBN 978–0–281–06781–7

First printed in Great Britain
Subsequently digitally printed in Great Britain

Produced on paper from sustainable forests

CONTENTS

Contents

CONTENTS

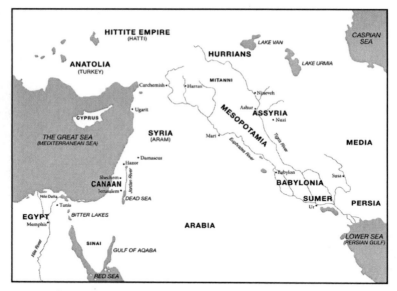

© *Karla Bohmbach*

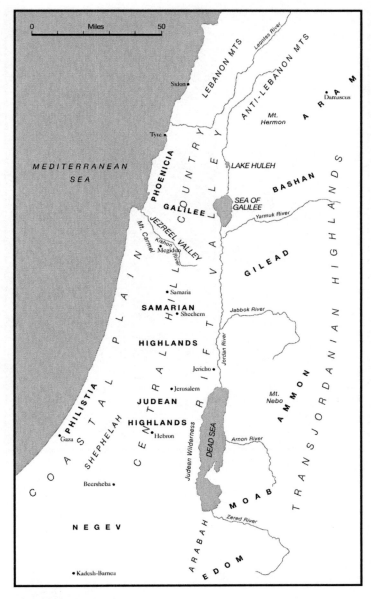

© Karla Bohmbach

ix

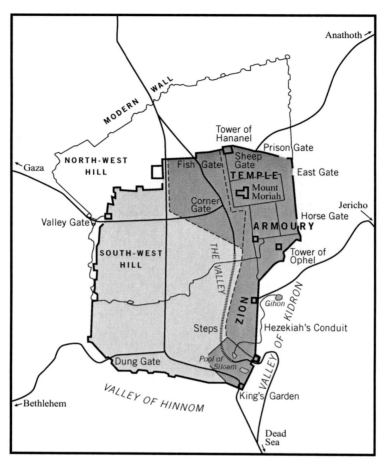

© *Westminster John Knox Press*

ACKNOWLEDGMENTS

The translation at the beginning of each chapter (and in other biblical quotations) is my own. I have stuck closer to the Hebrew than modern translations often do when they are designed for reading in church so that you can see more precisely what the text says. Thus although I myself prefer to use gender-inclusive language, I have let the translation stay gendered if using inclusive language would make it unclear whether the text was using singular or plural—in other words, the translation often uses "he" where in my own writing I would say "they" or "he or she." Sometimes I have added words to make the meaning clear, and I have put these words in square brackets. At the end of the book is a glossary of some terms that recur in the text (such as geographical, historical, and theological expressions). In each chapter (though not in the introduction) these terms are highlighted in **bold** the first time they occur.

The stories that follow the translation often concern my friends or my family. While none are made up, they are sometimes heavily disguised, in order to be fair to people. Sometimes I have disguised them so well that when I came to read the stories again, I was not sure at first who I was describing. My first wife, Ann, appears in a number of them. Two years before I started writing this book, she died after negotiating with multiple sclerosis for forty-three years. Our shared dealings with her illness and disability over these years contribute to everything I write, in ways you will be able to see but also in ways that are less obvious.

Just before I started writing this book, I fell in love with and married Kathleen Scott, and I am grateful for my new life with her and for her insightful comments on the manuscript, which have been so careful and illuminating that she practically deserves to be credited as coauthor. I am also grateful to Matt Sousa for reading through the manuscript and pointing out things I needed to correct or clarify and to Tom Bennett for checking the proofs.

INTRODUCTION

As far as Jesus and the New Testament writers were concerned, the Jewish Scriptures that Christians call the "Old Testament" *were* the Scriptures. In saying that, I cut corners a bit, as the New Testament never gives us a list of these Scriptures, but the body of writings that the Jewish people accept is as near as we can get to identifying the collection that Jesus and the New Testament writers would have worked with. The church also came to accept some extra books such as Maccabees and Ecclesiasticus, that are traditionally called the "Apocrypha," the books that were "hidden away"—a name that came to imply "spurious." They are now often known as the "Deutero-canonical Writings," which is more cumbersome but less pejorative; it simply indicates that these books have less authority than the Torah, the Prophets, and the Writings. The precise list of them varies among different churches. For the purposes of this series that seeks to expound the "Old Testament for Everyone," by the "Old Testament" we mean the Scriptures accepted by the Jewish community, though in the Jewish Bible they come in a different order as the Torah, the Prophets, and the Writings.

They were not "old" in the sense of antiquated or out-of-date; I sometimes like to refer to them as the First Testament rather than the Old Testament to make that point. For Jesus and the New Testament writers, they were a living resource for understanding God, God's ways in the world, and God's ways with us. They were "useful for teaching, for reproof, for correction, and for training in righteousness, so that the person who belongs to God can be proficient, equipped for every good work" (2 Timothy 3:16–17). They were for everyone, in fact. So it's strange that Christians don't read them very much. My aim in these volumes is to help you do that.

My hesitation is that you may read me instead of the Scriptures. Don't do that. I like the fact that this series includes much of the biblical text. Don't skip over it. In the end, that's the bit that matters.

An Outline of the Old Testament

The Jewish community often refers to these Scriptures as the Torah, the Prophets, and the Writings. While the Christian Old Testament comprises the same books, it has them in a different order:

Genesis to Kings: A story that runs from the creation of the world to the exile of Judahites to Babylon
Chronicles to Esther: A second version of this story, continuing it into the years after the exile
Job, Psalms, Proverbs, Ecclesiastes, Song of Songs: Some poetic books
Isaiah to Malachi: The teaching of some prophets

Here is an outline of the history that lies at the background of the books (I give no dates for events in Genesis, which involves too much guesswork).

1200s	Moses, the exodus, Joshua
1100s	The "judges"
1000s	Saul, David
900s	Solomon; the nation splits into two, Ephraim and Judah
800s	Elijah, Elisha
700s	Amos, Hosea, Isaiah, Micah; Assyria the superpower; the fall of Ephraim
600s	Jeremiah, King Josiah; Babylon the superpower
500s	Ezekiel; the fall of Judah; Persia the superpower; Judahites free to return home
400s	Ezra, Nehemiah
300s	Greece the superpower
200s	Syria and Egypt, the regional powers pulling Judah one way or the other

Ezra and Nehemiah

In Hebrew manuscripts of the Old Testament, Ezra and Nehemiah form one book, and there is logic in treating them together. They tell one unfolding story, and Ezra himself appears alongside Nehemiah in Nehemiah 8 and 12. Together they give the Old Testament's only account of the story of the Judahite community centered on Jerusalem when it was part of the Persian Empire. It is convenient to divide the books into four sections.

Ezra 1–6 (the time beginning in 539). The story begins with the transition of power in the Middle East from Babylon to Persia in 539. Fifty or sixty years previously, the Babylonians had conquered Jerusalem, devastated the temple there, and transported many Judahites from Jerusalem to Babylon. Ezra 1–6 tells of how the Persians then encourage the Judahites to go back home and how, against opposition from neighboring peoples, the Judahites rebuild the temple. Thus the period that now begins can be referred to as the Second Temple period.

While Ezra is often thought of as the great hero of the return from the exile, actually it was not until the next century that he made the journey from Babylon to Jerusalem (I often get students to repeat after me, "Ezra was nothing to do with the return from exile"). The heroes of the return from the exile are Sheshbazzar and Zerubbabel as governors (in a formal or informal sense); Jeshua (or Joshua) as the priestly leader (a different Joshua from the one in the book of Joshua, seven hundred years previously); and Haggai and Zechariah as prophets. Further, it is easy to get the impression that the Babylonians transported the whole population at the beginning of the sixth century (so that the land of Judah would be unoccupied for this period), and that the whole population then returned toward the end of that century. Actually the Old Testament makes clear that the Babylonians transported only a few thousand people—mostly the elite, such as members of the royal family and the administration, priests, and prophets—and that only some of these people then returned when they were free to do so. After all, by the time half a century had elapsed, most of the Judahite community in Babylon would have been born there, and would have no more interest in "returning" to this land they had never seen than Jews in Los Angeles or New York or London wish to do so today.

Ezra 7–10 (the time beginning in 458). So Ezra's grandfather might have been born at about the time the return from the exile happened, but his family did not join the returners. The reign of several Persian kings followed before Ezra was born in Babylon. In the reign of King Artaxerxes, Ezra 7–10 recounts, Ezra makes the journey to Jerusalem in 458, eighty years after the first return that led to the temple building. He brings with him a copy of the Torah of Moses and finds the Judahite community not living in accordance with the Torah in their willingness to marry people from the neighboring peoples who are not committed to the God of Israel, and he leads them in an act of repentance concerning that practice.

Nehemiah 1–7 (the time beginning in 445). Thirteen years after Ezra's journey, back at the center of the Persian Empire in Susa, another loyal Judahite is serving at the imperial court and hears about the sad bricks-and-mortar state of the community in Judah. Nehemiah determines to do something about the city's broken-down defenses. When he gets to Jerusalem, he also takes action to deal with social and economic problems in the community caused by poor harvests and the demands of imperial taxation.

Nehemiah 8–13. In the last part of the two books, Ezra and Nehemiah appear together in Jerusalem, teaching from the Torah, leading the community in a renewal of its covenant commitment to Yahweh, taking measures to build up the population of Jerusalem, and taking further action in connection with men who have married women from other communities who were not committed to Yahweh.

The books give dates for both Ezra and Nehemiah in terms of the reign of King Artaxerxes, and it is easiest to assume that the dates refer to the same Artaxerxes and that this is Artaxerxes

I. But there were a number of kings with that name, and it is just possible that Ezra lived in the time of Artaxerxes II, not Artaxerxes I.

As is the case with the other narrative books in the Old Testament, we have no idea who wrote Ezra and Nehemiah. The names of the books do not imply that they are the authors; both men are referred to in the third person, though the book of Nehemiah additionally incorporates prayers and other material in which Nehemiah speaks in the first person. The two books also include lists of people from the Second Temple period, such as people who made the journey to Judah from Babylon, and quotations from documents such as imperial decrees concerning the affairs of the community. So it looks as if someone in the period that followed Ezra and Nehemiah has compiled the book by bringing together such materials and composing accounts of incidents that took place during the century or so after 539, so as to provide the community with an account of its renewal over that century.

It was a renewal with many facets. These included rebuilding the temple and restoring its worship, implementing the expectations of the Torah in connection with the community maintaining its distinctive identity as the people of Yahweh over against other ethnic groups, rebuilding the city's defenses and providing it with a proper population, and taking action to see that its people were characterized by mutual support and generosity rather than each family living for itself. Yet the books do not come to a triumphant end or reach closure; in their last chapter, Nehemiah is undertaking further reforms designed to reach the same ends as Ezra had been concerned with when he first arrived in Jerusalem. The books would thus give their readers both reason to praise God for what had been achieved during the century they cover, and reminders of issues to which they might need to continue to give attention.

In the English Bible, Ezra–Nehemiah follows Chronicles and the opening verses actually repeat the closing verses of Chronicles. The concern with the temple in Ezra 1–6 corresponds to the agenda of Chronicles and the lists of members of the community, priests and Levites, and so on. On the other hand, the two books have concerns that are not addressed in

Chronicles, such as the emphasis on keeping the people of God pure in relation to people who acknowledged other deities and the emphasis on mutual support within the community. This suggests that we should not see the books as simply continuing Chronicles. Indeed, in the Hebrew Bible, Ezra–Nehemiah precedes Chronicles, and this supports the idea that Ezra–Nehemiah did not originally follow Chronicles; if anything, they followed 1 and 2 Kings. This would mean that Chronicles was written later, as a new prequel to Ezra–Nehemiah.

Esther

The English Bible then has the book of Esther following Ezra–Nehemiah, again with some logic because it belongs to the same period of time. It concerns a particular incident in the period when the Persians rule the Middle East, when the emperor is a king whom both the book of Ezra and the book of Esther call Ahasuerus. It is usually assumed that Ahasuerus is the king known in English as Xerxes I, who reigned from 486 to 465. The events in Esther thus belong between the events in Ezra 1–6 and those involving Ezra and Nehemiah. One big difference in Esther is that it concerns people who stayed in Susa rather than those who left to join the community in Jerusalem. Consequently, they are not exactly people who are now in exile, because (in theory at least) there is nothing to stop them leaving Susa. They are people living in dispersion rather than in exile, as most of the Jewish community has done ever since. The book thus deals with issues that arise for such people, and specifically deals with the pressure to abandon distinctive Jewish commitments and with the persecution that may come for refusing to do so. It tells of the Jewish community's extraordinary escape from extermination as a result of the boldness of a young girl.

Like Ezra–Nehemiah, Esther appears in a different context in the English Bible from its position in the Jewish Bible. There, it is one of the Five Scrolls. These may seem rather a random collection of books, but they have in common that the Jewish community came to connect each of them with one of its annual festivals, which is the occasion when the book is especially read:

Song of Songs	Pesach or Passover (March/April)
Ruth	Shavuot or Pentecost (May/June)
Lamentations	Tisha B'av, the Anniversary of the Fall of Jerusalem (July/August)
Ecclesiastes	Sukkot or Booths (September/October)
Esther	Purim (February/March)

Esther alone makes explicit its link with a festival. The name Purim (meaning *Lots*) derives from the reference to drawing lots in Esther 9. As is the case with Ezra–Nehemiah, we do not know who wrote the book or when it was written, though the author was evidently well-acquainted with many aspects of life in the Persian Empire.

Whereas the books of Ezra and Nehemiah read like basically historical books, the evidence with Esther is more ambiguous. There are many indications that the story is told larger than life; for instance, the gallows intended for the hanging of Mordecai are the height of a six-story building. Further, there is no reference outside the Old Testament to a queen called Vashti. Such considerations suggest that Esther is a divinely inspired short story. It does seem likely to me that it is based on something that happened rather than simply being made up from scratch. But I can't prove that this is so. The story illustrates some truths about God, about the preservation of the Jewish people, about human sinfulness and stupidity, and about the role of coincidence and bravery, which are true whether or not this is a historical story or more like a short story. The question whether it is more factual or more fictional thus does not affect its message, as is so with Jesus' parables (most of which are short stories rather than historical stories, and are often also larger than life).

EZRA 1:1-4

On Not Settling Down as a Refugee

[1]In the first year of Cyrus, king of Persia, fulfilling Yahweh's word from the mouth of Jeremiah, Yahweh aroused the spirit of Cyrus, king of Persia, so that he issued a proclamation in his entire kingdom, and also in a document: [2]"Cyrus, king of Persia, has said this: 'Yahweh the God of the heavens has given me all the kingdoms of the earth, and he himself has appointed me to build him a house in Jerusalem, in Judah. [3]Anyone among you from all his people: may his God be with him so that he may go up to Jerusalem in Judah and build up the house of Yahweh the God of Israel, the God in Jerusalem. [4]Anyone who remains, from all the places where he is a resident—the people of his place are to provide him with silver, gold, goods, and livestock, along with a voluntary offering for the house of God in Jerusalem.'"

My wife's daughter and her husband have just returned from a visit to camps in eastern Chad occupied by 175,000 Darfuri refugees from western Sudan. They go there to make it possible for the voice of the Darfuri refugees to be heard in the West. They take computers and cameras with which the Darfuris can upload pictures of their life in the camps via satellite, and Darfuri young people can exchange text messages with young people in the United States. But one of the tragedies of the camps is that, year-by-year, they become more like permanent townships, as has happened with "refugee camps" in Palestine. People fled from the threat of genocide to the camps in Chad thinking and hoping that they might be there for just a few months, but years pass and they find themselves still there. Darfuri children and teenagers can no longer remember what it was like in the villages from which they came, and of course the younger children were born in the camps and have no memory of or connection with their family's original home.

The **Judahite** community in **Babylon** went through an analogous experience; hence the strongly expressed commitment in Psalm 137 never to forget Jerusalem, and the self-curse if one should do so. To punish Jerusalem for its rebelliousness against Babylon, in 597 the Babylonian king transported a

number of people from Jerusalem to exile in Babylon—lead
such as the person who was then king, Jehoiachin; member
of his administration; priests; and prophets. The people left
behind in Jerusalem in 597 who escaped this deportation had
good reason (or thought they had good reason) to heave a sigh
of relief, to congratulate themselves on their good fortune, and
to assume that the worst of Babylonian oppression was over.
They had theological reason for making that assumption; they
knew that God was committed to Jerusalem, to its temple, and
to its line of Davidic kings. There was no way God could finally
abandon them. The exiles would surely soon be back home.
The exiles themselves would think the same.

They needed to see that they were wrong. Jeremiah 29 tells
how, sometime after the deportation in 597, the prophet wrote
to the deportees to contradict that idea and to tell them to
settle down. They are not coming home soon. They might as
well build houses to live in, plant gardens and eat their produce, marry and start families, identify with the Babylonian
cities where they were located and pray for them (evidently
these deportees were not in refugee camps), and not believe
prophets who tell them they will soon be going home. Jeremiah
knows that the rebellious state of the Judahites in Babylon
and the Judahites in Jerusalem who escaped the deportation
(not merely rebelliousness against Babylon, but rebelliousness
against God) means that God has not finished with them yet.
Yet the people who believed that God could not finally abandon them were not wrong. Jeremiah goes on to promise that in
seventy years' time God will indeed bring the deportees back
to their homeland. God does ultimately intend the Judahites'
life to go well, not badly. God has plans to give them hope and
a future. Jeremiah 51 then speaks of God "arousing the spirit of
the Median kings" to take redress on Babylon for the temple's
subsequent destruction in 587.

One way God squares the circle of a commitment to faithfulness and a commitment to justice is to let justice have its
way in the short term but to let faithfulness have its way in the
long term. Cyrus's proclamation evidences that Jeremiah was
right. But from 597, it was to be quite a long term. When Jeremiah said that the exile in Babylon would last seventy years,

the point was not that it would last seventy rather than sixty-
nine or seventy-one but that it would last a lifetime. Virtually
no one who left Jerusalem in 597 would be alive to go back. It
would be their children and grandchildren who would be able
to go "back," people who had never seen Jerusalem and who
knew only their life in Babylon; hence, no doubt, the fact that
not so many of them were interested in moving to the back-of-
beyond country that they had never seen. Cyrus's proclamation
that they may now make the move to Jerusalem implicitly recognizes that fact. On one hand, it expresses the wish that God
may aid the people who are willing to make this brave move.
On the other, it lays down the expectation that the people for
whom staying in Babylon is fine, thank you very much, must
offer financial support to the people who are prepared to make
the move.

In 587 there had been another rebellion against Babylon—
that led to the destruction of the temples and the city—and
another deportation. For decades nothing much happened
to change the situation, but then in the 550s things began to
move. **Persia** had been a part of the Median Empire, but the
Persian king Cyrus led a rebellion that reversed this arrangement and made Persia top dog in its region. He set about
extending Medo-Persian authority much more broadly across
western Asia and into Turkey. He then moved south to add to
his empire the ailing Babylonian empire so that the Judahites in
Babylon and in Judah itself came under his sovereignty. Prophecies in Isaiah 40–47 had declared it would happen; **Yahweh**
the God of Israel was behind these political and military events.
They would be the means of Yahweh's restoring Israel itself. You
could say that the declarations in Isaiah 40–47 are dotting the
i's and crossing the t's of Jeremiah's promise in his letter and his
other prophecies.

It is those promises in Jeremiah that the book of Ezra sees
Cyrus fulfilling when he encourages the Judahites to leave
Babylon for their homeland to rebuild the temple that the
Babylonians had destroyed. It was the God of Israel who had
aroused Cyrus's spirit. Now Cyrus's conscious intention in
carving out his empire was hardly to respond to a prompting
from the God of the Judahites. "The God of who?" you can

imagine him asking. He created his empire for the same selfish reasons as Greece or Rome, Britain or the United States. But without Cyrus realizing, there was a divine initiative behind his action. It is always worth asking whether there is a divine initiative behind the actions of political powers, even if they are not aware of it.

Of course Cyrus is prepared to make a politician's somewhat cynical acknowledgment of the deity recognized by his underlings. He says that Yahweh, the God of the heavens, has given him his power over the entire known world and has charged him to build the temple in Jerusalem. He would be glad to be known politically as the emperor who made it possible for the Judahites to make offerings there, even though he was not someone actually committed to Yahweh. In a document called the Cyrus Cylinder (because it is cylindrical in shape) he speaks of himself as a worshiper of Marduk—the Babylonian god—because he claims Marduk's support in his conquering of Babylon. The irony is that Yahweh really is the God of the heavens, the lord of the whole cosmos. It really was Yahweh who gave Cyrus power. Although he did not realize, he really was Yahweh's agent in making it possible for the Judahites to move back to Babylon and rebuild the temple.

Yesterday I had a random e-mail and then a follow-up phone call from a man who wanted to know how I understand some verses in the Old Testament that he thinks refer to the establishment of the State of Israel in 1948. Many Christians have assumed that material in the prophecies of people such as Jeremiah refer to events in our own day. It's not exactly wrong, in the sense that these prophecies do say something about God's eternal purpose, and so they enable us to see something about how God's purpose is being worked out—or is not being worked out—in our day. But (I tried without success to explain to my caller) there is something wrong with the idea that a prophet such as Jeremiah spoke directly about specific events in the twentieth century. That makes the prophet's visions or prophecies of no immediate significance for the people to whom they were given. In Scripture, God speaks to people where they are. Our privilege is then to overhear that speaking in order to see how God may be speaking to us where we are as we ask what may be the implications of the prophet's words for us.

The opening of Ezra presupposes the assumption that prophets speak to people where they are and make it possible for them to see what God is doing with them. Prophets do speak about the future, but it is the future that affects the people to whom the promises and the warnings are given, or that affects their children and grandchildren, and works out how God is thus being faithful to them. Yet maybe the opening of Ezra gives us a basis for praying for the refugees of Darfur and Palestine and other forgotten peoples. God can be involved in world politics, inspiring countries such as Britain and the United States to implement selfish policies that actually serve needy peoples for whom God is concerned.

EZRA 1:5–11

Precious Possessions Unexpectedly Restored

> [5]So the ancestral heads of Judah and Benjamin, and the priests and Levites, everyone whose spirit God aroused, set to in order to go up to build up Yahweh's house in Jerusalem. [6]All their neighbors supported them with silver objects, gold, goods, and livestock, and with choice things solely for every voluntary offering. [7]Cyrus the king of Persia brought out the objects from Yahweh's house that Nebuchadnezzar had brought out from Jerusalem and put in his god's house. [8]When Cyrus the king of Persia brought them out into the control of Mithredath the treasurer, he counted them out to Sheshbazzar, the Judahite leader. [9]This is the count: thirty gold bowls, a thousand silver bowls, twenty-nine knives, [10]thirty gold dishes, four hundred and ten double silver bowls, and a thousand other objects. [11]All the objects of gold and silver came to five thousand four hundred. All these Sheshbazzar took up when the exiles were taken up from Babylon to Jerusalem.

A woman I know once had to flee from a marriage that had become abusive. She was more fearful for her daughter's safety than for her own. After an incident that convinced her it was unsafe to stay a moment longer, she hustled her daughter into the car one afternoon and simply got out of there in the clothes they were wearing and drove in a direction where she could assume her husband would not find her. She was right about the danger and about the action that was needed; but one of the most painful aspects of the hasty flight was that she had to leave behind nearly all the things that reminded her of her own youth and her daughter's childhood. She has virtually no mementoes or photographs of those years.

To judge from the way the Old Testament tells the story, one of the most agonizing aspects of the fall of Jerusalem to the **Babylonians** in 587 was the destruction of many of the precious and holy accoutrements of the temple, and the Babylonian king's appropriation of what he did not destroy. In the account of the city's fall and destruction in 2 Kings 25, you can feel the pain in the lines as it lists the pots and shovels and dishes and censers and bowls that were seized. For people left behind in **Judah**, the temple was an empty, defiled hulk. Paradoxically, the fact that the items that were appropriated and not destroyed did accompany the exiles to Babylon actually made things worse, because Nebuchadnezzar did what victors regularly did with such things. He deposited them in his own god's temple. They became things dedicated to Marduk. They sat there as a taunting reminder of the plausible Babylonian claim that Marduk had defeated **Yahweh**. Of course a prophet such as Jeremiah knew that this was not so and that actually the destruction issued from Yahweh's own action in abandoning the city, the temple, and its accoutrements, because of Judah's rebelliousness; but a Babylonian would laugh at that piece of theological interpretation, and we know from the book of Jeremiah that many Judahites were unconvinced by it.

Unintentionally, however, by putting these objects into his god's temple Nebuchadnezzar had made sure they would be kept safe and would not end up on the Babylonian antiquities market and eventually in the British Museum. Cyrus is in a position to produce them and to get the temple treasurer to give them to the man who will lead the Judahites back to Jerusalem so that they can again enter into Yahweh's service in the temple. Cyrus will again have done this for his own reasons, as part of encouraging the Judahites to stay subservient to him, but we might again see Yahweh's inspiration behind his action. The accoutrements will constitute one of the markers of the fact that the so-called **Second Temple** continues the worship of the First Temple. The people of God in Judah will continue the worship that their ancestors had offered. Their story is one with the story of Solomon and David and Moses.

The man to whom the objects are entrusted, Sheshbazzar, appears only in Ezra 1 and 5, and we know nothing about him except what is said there. His name is Babylonian, but it was quite common for Judahites to have Babylonian names (Daniel and his friends are examples), and he is identified as a Judahite. He is later identified as governor, which would seem to imply that his responsibility involved not merely seeing that the accoutrements did find their way back to the temple rather than mysteriously disappearing on the way to Jerusalem. It would suggest he had some continuing responsibility to the **Persian** authorities for looking after their interests in Judah. Yet he soon disappears from the story, and Ezra 3 will attribute the initiation of the temple restoration work to one Zerubbabel, who is also later described as governor. So whatever Sheshbazzar's precise position, it seems that for one reason or another his work was confined to the beginning of the restoration of the community in Jerusalem.

God's direct involvement in this episode of the story is expressed in the same terms that had been used in the opening verse of the book. As God aroused the spirit of Cyrus, so God aroused the spirit of the Judahites to make them want to make the journey to rebuild the temple. We have noted already that it is not surprising that God needed to do some arousing. The Judahites in Babylon were not like people in a refugee camp who were itching to get back to the land where they were born. They had taken Jeremiah's encouragement to heart and built themselves houses and started families. It is thus not remarkable that many of them had no desire to leave Babylon, and the fact that many of them were willing to do so, like the amazing commission of Cyrus that encourages them to go, makes one think, "God must have been involved in moving their hearts in this direction." On the other hand, the story emphasizes how even the people who did not make the move supported the people who did. The word for *voluntary offering* is the term traditionally translated *freewill offering*. In the **Torah** there are some offerings that Israel is expected to make, such as community sacrifices made each morning and evening, and sacrifices made by individuals in connection with purity or in fulfillment of a vow. There are other offerings made for no reason than to express devotion to God, and references in Ezra 1 to such voluntary offerings presuppose that the rebuilding of the temple is going to need generous voluntary offerings of this kind.

The Old Testament regularly talks about "going up" to Jerusalem, because the city is a thousand meters or three thousand feet above sea level; from almost any direction, you have to go up to get there. The temple objects thus likewise get "taken up" to the city. Even today, Jews say that someone makes *aliyah* (makes a going up) when speaking of making the move to live in Israel; the group Sheshbazzar leads is the first *aliyah*.

It seems to have been not just fellow Judahites who supported the people who made the journey. Cyrus apparently referred simply to an expectation that Judahites who decided to stay in Babylon would support their kinfolk in practical ways. In the event, this support came from the people's neighbors more generally. While referring now to these people as neighbors might mean nothing, this motif recalls the exodus story. The move from Babylon to Judah is a repetition of the exodus, and when the Israelites left Egypt, Yahweh made the Egyptians favorably disposed toward them so that they gave them objects of silver and gold to take with them, which facilitated the making of the dwelling for God in the wilderness. The Judahites' Babylonian neighbors, like Cyrus himself, are likewise making a contribution to the worship of Yahweh.

Life in Judah in the Persian period was often tough and it might have been tempting for people to wonder whether Yahweh really was present and active in the community. The story of the Second Temple community's beginnings emphasizes Yahweh's involvement and points to the way Yahweh is doing again what Yahweh did in bringing Israel out of Egypt into the land in the first place. What Yahweh thus did in bringing people back to Jerusalem to rebuild the temple is not to be underestimated by their descendants.

EZRA 2:1–67

Who We Were

¹These are the people of the province, who went up from among the captives in exile whom Nebuchadnezzar the king of Babylon exiled to Babylon and who returned to Jerusalem and Judah, each to his city, ²who came with Zerubbabel, Jeshua, Nehemiah, Seraiah, Reeliah, Mordecai, Bilshan, Mispar, Bigvai, Rehum, Baanah. The number of the men belonging to the Israelite people: ³the descendants of Parosh 2,172; ⁴the descendants of Shephatiah 372; ⁵the descendants of Arah 775; ⁶the descendants of Pahath-moab (through the descendants of Jeshua and Joab) 2,812; ⁷the descendants of Elam 1,254; ⁸the descendants of Zattu 945; ⁹the descendants of Zaccai 760; ¹⁰the descendants of Bani 642; ¹¹the descendants of Bebai 623; ¹²the descendants of Azgad 1,222; ¹³the descendants of Adonikam 666; ¹⁴the descendants of Bigvai 2,056; ¹⁵the descendants of Adin 454; ¹⁶the descendants of Ater (through Hezekiah) 98; ¹⁷the descendants of Bezai 323; ¹⁸the descendants of Jorah 112; ¹⁹the descendants of Hashum 223; ²⁰the descendants of Gibbar 95; ²¹the descendants of Beth-lehem 123; ²²the people of Netophah 56; ²³the people of Anathoth 128; ²⁴the descendants of Azmaveth 42; ²⁵the descendants of Kiriath-arim (Chephirah and Beeroth) 743; ²⁶the descendants of Ramah and Geba 621; ²⁷the people of Michmas 122; ²⁸the people of Beth-el and Ai 223; ²⁹the descendants of Nebo 52; ³⁰the descendants of Magbish 156; ³¹the descendants of the other Elam 1,254; ³²the descendants of Harim 320; ³³the descendants of Lod, Hadid, and Ono 725; ³⁴the descendants of Jericho 345; ³⁵the descendants of Senaah 3,630.

³⁶The priests: the descendants of Jedaiah (through the household of Jeshua) 973; ³⁷the descendants of Immer 1,052; ³⁸the descendants of Pashhur 1,247; ³⁹the descendants of Harim 1,017. ⁴⁰The Levites: the descendants of Jeshua and Kadmiel (through the descendants of Hodaviah) 74. ⁴¹The singers: the descendants of Asaph 128. ⁴²The descendants of the gatekeepers: the descendants of Shallum, the descendants of Ater, the descendants of Talmon, the descendants of Akkub, the descendants of Hatita, the descendants of Shobai, altogether 139. ⁴³The assistants: the descendants of Ziha, the descendants of Hasupha, the descendants of Tabbaoth, ⁴⁴the descendants of Keros, the descendants of

Siaha, the descendants of Padon, ⁴⁵the descendants of Lebanah, the descendants of Hagabah, the descendants of Akkub, ⁴⁶the descendants of Hagab, the descendants of Salmai, the descendants of Hanan, ⁴⁷the descendants of Giddel, the descendants of Gahar, the descendants of Reaiah, ⁴⁸the descendants of Rezin, the descendants of Nekodah, the descendants of Gazzam, ⁴⁹the descendants of Uzza, the descendants of Paseah, the descendants of Besai, ⁵⁰the descendants of Asnah, the descendants of Meunim, the descendants of Nephusim, ⁵¹the descendants of Babbuk, the descendants of Hakupha, the descendants of Harhur, ⁵²the descendants of Bazluth, the descendants of Mehida, the descendants of Harsha, ⁵³the descendants of Barkos, the descendants of Sisera, the descendants of Temah, ⁵⁴the descendants of Neziah, the descendants of Hatipha. ⁵⁵The descendants of Solomon's servants: the descendants of Sotai, the descendants of Hassophereth, the descendants of Peruda, ⁵⁶the descendants of Jaalah, the descendants of Darkon, the descendants of Giddel, ⁵⁷the descendants of Shephatiah, the descendants of Hattil, the descendants of Pochereth-hazzebaim, the descendants of Ami. ⁵⁸All the assistants and the descendants of Solomon's servants 392.

⁵⁹These are the people who came up from Tel-melah, Tel-harsha, Cherub, Addan, Immer, but who were unable to show their ancestral household and origin, whether they were from Israel: ⁶⁰the descendants of Deliah, the descendants of Tobiah, the descendants of Nekoda 652. ⁶¹Of the descendants of the priests, the descendants of Habaiah, the descendants of Hakkoz, the descendants of Barzillai (who had married a woman from among the daughters of Barzillai the Gileadite and was called by their name)—⁶²these looked for their record among the people enrolled but they could not be found, and they were disqualified from the priesthood. ⁶³So the administrator told them that they should not eat of the most holy things until the emergence of a priest for Urim and Thummim.

⁶⁴The entire assembly altogether was 42,360, ⁶⁵besides their male and female servants; these were 7,337, and they had 200 male and female singers. ⁶⁶Their horses, 736; their mules, 245; ⁶⁷their camels, 435; their donkeys, 6,720.

When we decided we would get married in the December just past, I naively assumed that this implied a honeymoon somewhere tropical such as Bali, but I found myself honeymooning in Scotland at a time when the temperature never rose above freezing. My fiancée knew that her ancestors had come to the Americas from Scotland in the seventeenth century and she was longing to visit the area where they came from. Worry not, we had a great time, and one reason was that it was a delight to see and share her reaction to this opportunity to connect with her past. It enabled me to get a little more understanding of what has always seemed a quaint American preoccupation with tracing one's ancestors and connecting with where they came from. I knew I didn't have the same impetus to put in the kind of effort involved in researching my family history, and I realized that this was because I could take it for granted; I knew where I came from. I was born in the city where my family had lived for generations.

The **Judahites** for whom Ezra–Nehemiah is written are in a position that has parallels both with mine and with my wife's. They are in a position like mine in the sense that they are living in the country where their families have lived for the best part of a millennium. But they are in a position more like my wife's insofar as more recently their families have been thrown out of the country (as my wife's ancestors were thrown out of Scotland for rebelling against the English) and have subsequently had to contest their place in the country with other people.

In this connection, records like the ones in Ezra 2 fulfill several functions. First, they preserve a list of people who came to Judah from **Babylon** in the period beginning in 537. The list will reappear in a different form in Nehemiah 7, and its reappearance there is one indication that it is more than simply a record of people who came in the year 537 itself. We have noted that the move that began then continued over some decades, even centuries. Indeed, names in the list such as Nehemiah, Seraiah, and Mordecai appear elsewhere in Ezra, Nehemiah, and Esther, though this may be coincidence; the names may not refer to the same people. The list is a composite and complicated one; for instance, it moves between listing people by family to listing them by towns, and the total in verse 64 cannot be related to the numbers that come earlier.

We know from elsewhere in the Old Testament that there was understandable tension between people who went into exile and people who had been able to stay in Canaan. Which group really represents the future of the community? To put it in terms of an image that appears in Jeremiah 24, were the exiles the bad figs and were the people who were spared that experience the good figs? One can see how people could look at it that way. Yet Jeremiah turns the image on its head and sees the exiles as the good figs and the people left behind in 597 as the bad figs. When people came back from exile, were they to be seen as real Judahites? This list establishes who has a claim to belong to the community in the sense that they have a proper Judahite family and/or geographical background. God had chosen a people that was marked by its being a family and by its association with a particular country, as well as by its being a people that acknowledged **Yahweh**. This community's association with a family and with a country is evidence that God's faithfulness to that original purpose and promise was still being fulfilled. The exile did not mean that God's promise had failed. The exiles' ability to show that they belong to this family and country shows that they have a share in this purpose and are an embodiment of God's faithfulness.

Another important concern of the community would be that the oversight of the temple was in the hands of the people God had designated, and in this connection the lists relating to priests and other **Levites** would be significant. The musicians, **gatekeepers**, **assistants**, and descendants of Solomon's staff would all count as Levites in a loose sense in that all would have a support role in connection with the temple. Perhaps the very fact that they were preserved through the exile was evidence that God's hand was at work in ensuring that they were available for their necessary ministry after the exile. The assistants and the descendants of Solomon's staff would be people who were not Israelite by birth and thus they witness to the other side of the coin as they were invited into the community despite their ethnicity. The community was not a closed one. It was quite possible for people to be adopted into the family of Israel.

References to priests, Levites, musicians, gatekeepers, and assistants will recur in Ezra and Nehemiah. They remind us what a bustling, active, animated place the temple was. It wasn't like a church, empty and unused except for an hour or two a week. Every day there were the regular sacrifices; through the day people were bringing their own sacrifices and seeking prayer and advice, and in addition there were prophets and other teachers offering people instruction. The temple was a lively community.

EZRA 2:68–3:5

Worship, Scripture, Gospel

[68]Some of the ancestral heads, when they came to Yahweh's house in Jerusalem, gave a voluntary offering for Yahweh's house, to put it in place on its site. [69]In accordance with their resources they gave to the treasury of the work sixty-one thousand drachmas of gold, five thousand minas of silver, and a hundred priests' robes. [70]The priests, the Levites, some of the people, the singers, the gatekeepers, and the assistants settled in their cities, and all Israel in their cities. [3:1]When the seventh month arrived, with the Israelites in their cities, the people gathered as one person in Jerusalem. [2]Jeshua the son of Jozadak and his brother priests, and Zerubbabel the son of Shealtiel and his brothers, set to and built up the altar of the God of Israel to offer burnt offerings on it as it is written in the teaching of Moses the man of God. [3]They set up the altar on its site because they were in fear of the peoples of the countries, and offered burnt offerings on it to Yahweh, the burnt offerings for morning and evening. [4]They made the festival of Sukkot as it is written, and the burnt offering day by day by the [proper] number, the amount for each day in accordance with the rule, [5]and afterward the regular burnt offering and [the ones] for the new moons and for all the occasions set by Yahweh that were made sacred, and for anyone who made a voluntary offering to Yahweh.

I was asked to talk to a group of pastors today about why I think the Old Testament is important, and I gave one of my standard replies. I have the impression that in southern California many of the churches that, in theory, place considerable emphasis on Scripture and the gospel have actually lost touch with both of these and have assimilated to the culture of the world around them. In their concern to reach outsiders, they have assimilated their message to what will ring bells with people, and in their concern to make worship interesting they have given up the reading of Scripture in worship, because it is obviously boring. I think one reason this development has been possible is that fifty years ago U.S. culture was much closer to the framework suggested by Scripture than it is now; but the change has been gradual, and we are like the frog put in a bucket of cold water that is then gradually heated, so that the frog never realizes it is being boiled to death.

The **Judahites** who made the move to Jerusalem from **Babylon** made no such mistake. Perhaps they were subject to less temptation because the culture of Babylon was more obviously alien to the gospel expressed in their Scriptures (many of the people who did not make the move were content to assimilate to life in Babylon). One can see indications of this in their attitude to their worship, to their Scriptures, and to their gospel.

First, they knew that worship was a means whereby we give ourselves to God. The story mentions two kinds of offerings, burnt sacrifices and voluntary offerings. What these have in common is that the offerer gets nothing out of offering them. There are other sacrifices in which the offerer shares, which reminds us that there is nothing wrong with worship being something we enjoy and get something out of. But a burnt sacrifice is what its name implies; with this regular form of sacrifice, the whole animal goes up in smoke to God. Israel makes such offerings at dawn and at dusk every day. You give up the animal in its entirety. Likewise a voluntary offering is simply something you give to God, a one-time gift. On this occasion the voluntary offering is related to the need to provide the resources to rebuild the temple. It is easy for us to think that worship is designed to benefit us and that the criterion for evaluating worship is whether we feel good when we come out of church. In Israel, worship was offered for God's sake, not for the sake of the worshipers.

Second, the forms of worship were determined by what was written in the teaching of Moses. We don't know what form the teaching of Moses, the **Torah**, would have taken at this point in

21

Israel's history. In the next century, Ezra will come from Babylon bringing "the teaching of Moses" with him (see Ezra 7). As far as we can tell, the content of this teaching had developed over the centuries from Moses' day through to Ezra's day (and maybe later). As new situations developed, the Holy Spirit guided people such as prophets and priests and theologians to see what Moses would say if he were here now. They would point to the implications of exodus faith for the changing contexts in which people needed instruction. Whatever form the teaching took in the time of Zerubbabel and Jeshua, they knew they had to encourage people to worship not just in light of how they felt but in light of this guidance.

Third, this need is underscored by the way their worship reminded them of their gospel story, the story of what God had done for them. The biggest worship festival of Israel's year is Sukkot. The word refers to makeshift shelters or bivouacs; it is usually translated "tabernacles" or "booths." The Torah relates how the Israelites had to live in such shelters when they left Egypt. Acting out that experience reminded them of the way God rescued them from Egypt; it reminded them of their gospel story.

These shelters have another significance. Sukkot comes in the autumn, in September or October, and it is Israel's great harvest festival. People live in shelters so that they can keep an eye on their crops as they ripen to make sure that the rogues from the next village don't steal them, and/or so that during the harvest they don't have to spend hours commuting to their fields every day. The shelters thus seem to have started as a practical device for everyday life; the practical device was then harnessed so as to make the shelters a reminder of the gospel, of the journey from Egypt. Israel shows how believing in the gospel doesn't mean abandoning the culture; it does mean tying the culture to the gospel, not assimilating the gospel to the culture. Something similar would be true about the other "occasions set by **Yahweh** that were made sacred," namely, Passover or Flat Bread Festival in the spring and Pentecost in May or June. All these observances related to the agricultural cycle; all came to commemorate aspects of Israel's gospel story.

Zerubbabel and Jeshua embody the joint leadership of the **Second Temple** community. You could say that they stand both for a distinction and for a relationship between church and state, but these are nothing like the distinction or relationship between church and state in Europe or in the United States. As the son of Shealtiel, Zerubbabel is the grandson of King Jehoiachin, the king exiled to Babylon in 597. He is therefore a member of the line of David. If there were now a king in Judah, it could be him. Jeshua likewise belongs to the line of Aaron, so he can function as what would later be called the high priest. It might seem that he was tainted by exile, but God declares the intention to confirm his position as priest (see Zechariah 3). As a Davidic leader, Zerubbabel is more involved with affairs of state while, as an Aaronic priest, Jeshua is more involved with religious affairs, but this is not to imply that those are separate realms. In Israel, affairs of state are affairs in which God is involved and which must be conducted in accordance with the teaching of Moses. Conversely, the reestablishment of worship is a matter in which the Davidic ruler is here involved, as David had once been involved in making arrangements for the temple.

The Babylonians had set fire to the temple in 587, but they had not demolished it as they did the walls of the city. It would have been possible for some forms of worship to continue there during the exile, such as the prayer for God's forgiveness and mercy that is expressed in the book of Lamentations. While the temple therefore needed substantial restoration, the community could build a new altar in it before undertaking the rebuilding. This action would make it possible to restore the regular routine of worship at dawn and at dusk as well as the celebration of Sukkot. The burnt offerings that formed the heart of that regular routine were the embodiment of the community giving itself to God, acknowledging Yahweh as God, seeking God's blessing for a new day, and then thanking God for the day that was past and seeking God's protection for the night. The offerings made at the beginning of each month would have a similar significance as they looked forward to a new month.

The story is more explicit about another kind of protection of which the community felt a need in the context of its fear of "the peoples of the countries," a fear that might have inhibited its restoring the worship of the temple rather than encouraging it. In a number of senses, the arrival of the Judahites from Babylon disturbed the status quo in the region. Given that the actual numbers of people who had been taken into exile was relatively small, somebody has been occupying and farming the land around Jerusalem. Somebody has been praying those prayers in the temple. Politically, the Babylonians and then the **Persians** had a governmental structure for the region, in which Judah was apparently governed from Samaria in the old northern kingdom. Judah was also surrounded by entities such as Ammon and Moab that seem to have been casting an acquisitive eye on Jerusalem. The community was not being paranoid in fearing for its political future. Its need of God's protection provided a practical reason for establishing the proper structure for worship and the means of laying hold on God.

EZRA 3:6-13

Shouts of Joy and the Sound of Weeping

⁶From the first day of the seventh month they began to offer burnt offerings to Yahweh, though Yahweh's palace had not been started. ⁷They gave money to the quarrymen and craftsmen, and food, drink, and oil to the Sidonians and Tyrians, to bring cedar wood from Lebanon by sea to Joppa, in accordance with the authorization to them by Cyrus, the king of Persia. ⁸In the second year of their coming to the house of God in Jerusalem, in the second month, Zerubbabel, son of Shealtiel, and Jeshua, son of Jozadak, and the rest of their family (the priests, the Levites, and all the people who had come from the captivity to Jerusalem) began, and put in place Levites from the age of twenty years and upward to oversee the work on Yahweh's house. ⁹So Jeshua, his sons and his brothers, and Kadmiel and his sons (descendants of Judah) accepted appointment together to oversee the people doing the work on God's house, [with] the sons of Henadad, their sons and their brothers, the Levites. ¹⁰When the builders started Yahweh's palace, the priests in their vestments with trumpets and the Levites, the descendants of Asaph, with cymbals were put in place to praise Yahweh in accordance with the directions of David, king of Israel. ¹¹They sang responsively in praise and thanksgiving to Yahweh,

"Because he is good, because his commitment stands forever for Israel," and all the people raised a great shout in praise of Yahweh, because Yahweh's house had been started. [12]Many of the priests and Levites and ancestral heads, the old men who had seen the first temple, were weeping with a loud voice at the start on this house, while many were raising their voice in a shout in celebration. [13]The people could not distinguish the sound of the celebratory shout from the sound of the people's weeping because the people were raising a great shout. The sound was audible from afar.

To my own great joy, a friend of mine recently got engaged after being on his own for nineteen years. He is overwhelmed by happiness; I have never seen him so joyful. Yet a weird thing about it is that when he talks about it, it also makes him cry, though he has a hard time explaining why that is so. It has something to do with being able to believe that this great thing has happened. Perhaps he's afraid it can't really be true. He half-expects to wake up one morning and find it's a dream, or to find that his fiancée has decided it's all a mistake. I suspect another factor is that he has never really faced the pain associated with his aloneness, and in a strange way the prospect of his loneliness ending has made it possible to own how tough it was.

Beginning work on the temple generated a similar mixed reaction of celebration and weeping in the **Judahite** community. The weepers were people who had seen the first temple in its glory, which means they must have been in their sixties or seventies. We are not told why they were weeping while others were celebrating. Maybe they wept because they alone could recall the awfulness of the temple's destruction (and wondered whether it might happen again?). While they might have been depressed because they couldn't imagine that the temple was going to be as glorious as it had once been, there is no other hint that the community was anything other than thrilled with its restored temple. Maybe they were appalled at the magnitude of the task they had set themselves. My hunch is that their tears were a paradoxical expression of their happiness that the work had begun, an expression of joyful disbelief that this moment had come. Both the shouts and the weeping thus had the same significance.

The basis of the community's praise is that **Yahweh** is good and that his **commitment** lasts forever. People might have wondered whether Yahweh had abandoned any commitment to them. They knew they could not really complain if this was so; they had forfeited any right to expect Yahweh to stay committed to them. But Yahweh is caught by the word *commitment*. The Hebrew word denotes a kind of faithfulness that continues even when the other party does not deserve that it should do so. Despite the people's faithlessness that had led to the exile, Yahweh's commitment could still be their hope. The fact that after half a century they are now able to begin restoring the temple is a sign that their hope was not misplaced. Paradoxically, their praise relates to something they themselves were doing. It is because *they* are initiating work on the temple that they are praising God's goodness and commitment. They know they would not have been able to do it were it not for God's faithfulness. In this context, praise and thanksgiving are both appropriate. Praise strictly suggests recognition of the great permanent truths about God, such as God's goodness and commitment. Thanksgiving relates to some new thing that God has done in the lives of an individual or a community, and this community certainly has something to give thanks for and testify to.

The word *temple* suggests a specifically religious building. The Old Testament has words with that connotation such as a word that means "sanctuary," but this is not the term it regularly uses to refer to the temple. Instead it uses more everyday words that denote a house or a palace, both of which feature in these verses. The temple is Yahweh's house or Yahweh's palace. The first word (*house*) links the term with the dwelling that ordinary people live in; the second (*palace*) reminds readers that this is a dwelling fit for a king. The temple is not a shrine, a place that commemorates something in the past or commemorates a person who is dead and gone. It is a place where someone lives. Of course the Israelites know that God does not really live in the temple; the Psalms make clear their awareness that God really lives in the heavens and that God's real palace is located there. (They also of course know that this statement is itself a metaphorical one; 1 Kings 8 gives Solomon's prayer at the original dedication of the temple, and it makes clear the awareness that God could no more be contained within the universe than within an earthly building. The heavens within the cosmos stand for another realm in which God lives, a realm that existed even before the cosmos existed.) But the earthly temple constitutes an earthly equivalent or embodiment or avatar of God's palace in the heavens. It meant that there is a place on earth where you know you can be in God's presence, in a special sense (the Israelites also know that there is yet another sense in which God is present everywhere, so that you can pray anywhere and know God's protection anywhere). Whether or not you could *feel* God was in the temple, you *knew* that God was indeed there, because God had promised to be present there; such promises had been expressed to David and Solomon (2 Samuel 7; 1 Kings 8). You could bring your offerings and know they were accepted, bring your prayers and know they were heard.

Although the story speaks of the *starting* of work on the temple, we have noted that this did not mean starting building from scratch. Regular worship had been being offered in the shell of Solomon's temple for some months. The main material need for the restoration work was timber, which would be needed to replace the roof and paneling of the building that had been burned in 587 (though setting the temple on fire could have led to the shattering or melting of some of its stone). As had been the case in Solomon's day, the timber comes from Lebanon by the arduous process of floating logs down the Mediterranean, and then carrying them up to Jerusalem. The imperial record of which chapter 6 will speak implies that a subvention from Cyrus to cover the cost of this expensive project backed up his mere permission to undertake the work.

The chapter has already noted that the arrangements for worship followed the teaching of Moses. It now adds that they also followed the directions of David. There are two reasons for this second emphasis. Like the reference to Moses' teaching, it establishes the continuity of the worship of the **Second Temple** with that of the First Temple. The people know that God is involved with Israel for the long haul; its entire story is part of God's story. In making sure they operate in light of

David's directions as well as those in Moses' teaching, they are playing their part in making sure they are part of that story. The other reason is that some of the people around them also claim to be part of this story, but it's not clear whether they really are. Specifically, the people in the province of Samaria are, or claim to be, the descendants of the old kingdom of **Ephraim**, but the old kingdom of Ephraim had turned its back on David. If they return to David, they can be part of the story; if they do not do so, they are on their own. Judah needs to make sure it meets the criterion of faithfulness to David's directions as well as criterion of faithfulness to Moses' teaching.

EZRA 4:1–6

Discouragement

[1]The adversaries of Judah and Benjamin heard that the exiles were building a palace for Yahweh, the God of Israel. [2]They approached Zerubbabel and the ancestral heads and said to them, "We will build with you because we look to your God like you do, and we have been sacrificing to him since the days of Esarhaddon the king of Assyria, who brought us up here." [3]Zerubbabel, Jeshua, and the rest of the ancestral heads of Israel said to them, "It is not for you and us to build a house for our God, because we alone will build it for Yahweh the God of Israel, as King Cyrus, the king of Persia, commanded us." [4]Then the people of the country were weakening the efforts of the people of Judah and making them afraid to build. [5]They were bribing decision makers in order to frustrate [the Judahites'] decision all the days of Cyrus, king of Persia, and until the reign of Darius, king of Persia. [6]And in the reign of Xerxes, at the beginning of his reign, they wrote an accusation against the inhabitants of Judah and Jerusalem.

Over Christmas I was able to visit the seminary where I studied for the ministry. It had been founded in the 1930s as a result of a split off from another Church of England seminary a mile or so away, over whether or not faculty should be required to affirm a particular basis of faith; there was no great disagreement between the two institutions about the substance of the

Christian faith, only disagreement over what people had to sign. The buildings are also only a short distance from a Baptist seminary and a Methodist seminary. In my student years we shared some lectures with the other Church of England seminary, though we had nothing to do with those other institutions. More recently the two Church of England institutions merged, and the resultant entity also shares courses with the Baptist and Methodist ones. How careful do institutions and denominations need to be in cooperating with each other? When do they have to split and when can they work together?

The people who approach the **Judahite** leadership about joining with them in building the temple claim to be one with them in faith, but their origin makes them suspicious. We have noted that the province of Samaria lies in the region of the former kingdom of **Ephraim**, which had split off from Jerusalem and the line of David after Solomon's son Rehoboam mishandled relationships with them. The split off was understandable. It was also a fulfillment of God's intention to bring about some punishment of David's line for Solomon's religious policy; as a byproduct of marrying wives from other countries in order to encourage diplomatic relations, Solomon had introduced the worship of other deities into Jerusalem. But then as a result of the split, Ephraim developed its own religious system, also containing elements that were alien to proper Israelite faith. Second Kings 17 relates how Ephraim eventually paid for its innovation when **Yahweh** let it fall to the superpower of the day, the **Assyrians**.

The Assyrians then transported many of its people and replaced them with people from other parts of its empire. The Samarians here refer to a transportation in the time of an Assyrian emperor called Esarhaddon who lived a few decades later than the events related in 2 Kings 17. That chapter confirms their claim that the Assyrians made arrangements for immigrants to learn how to worship Yahweh, but it refers to their also continuing to worship the gods they brought with them, and this is a plausible pattern. One might compare the common pattern whereby people who have been converted to faith in Christ also continue to keep the practices of their traditional faith.

Such considerations would give the Judahites a basis for hesitating to accept too readily the Samarians' offer of help; though a less suspicious response would be to see their approach as a fulfillment of God's longing for the people of Ephraim to return to adherence to Jerusalem and to the line of David. Perhaps political and economic considerations also played a part both for the Judahites and for the Samarians. The Judahites would want to be independent and not take action that would eventually lead to their subordination to the Samarians; the Samarians would be interested in encouraging that development. The Judahites might also want to be able to look back on the rebuilding as something they had achieved on their own. And they are able to claim that they are obeying Cyrus to the letter. It is useful to be able to claim that you are being obedient to a higher authority.

Developments over the next few centuries cast an ironic light on this exchange. Not long after these events, the Samarians built a temple of their own on Mount Gerizim, overlooking Shechem; they argue that this rather than Jerusalem was the place of Yahweh's designation referred to in Deuteronomy. What we know of the Samarians' religion suggests that it was, if anything, more conservative rather than more syncretistic than that of the Jews; like the Sadducees, the Samarians accepted only the **Torah** and not the later books in the Old Testament. Over the centuries tension between Jews and Samarians continued as the New Testament indicates, though it was the Jews who became the political force in the region (under Rome, eventually).

In the meantime, taking a hard line became a costly move for the Judahites. It was presumably as a result of their rebuff that the Samarians became their adversaries and worked against the Judahites' attempts to build up *their* community, not least by attempting to get the imperial authorities on their side over the next half-century, in the reigns of Cyrus (559–529), Cambyses (529–522), Smerdis (522), Darius the Great (521–486), and Xerxes or Ahasuerus (485–465). But the reference to the activity of "the people of the country" could naturally point not only to the Samarians but to other people living in Judah who had not been taken into exile. We have already been told that the temple-builders were afraid of them.

One way or another, it seems that the work of God generally meets with adversaries. Sometimes it's our fault, sometimes it's not. Sometimes people just want to oppose something because it's good; it is as if there is something willfully perverse about their desires. The story reminds its readers not to be surprised when this is so, and not to be too discouraged because (the continuation of the story will show) opposition may not have the last word.

EZRA 4:7–23

Rulers Are Not a Threat to People Who Do Right

[7]Then in the days of Artaxerxes, Bishlam, Mithredath, Tabeel, and the rest of his associates wrote to Artaxerxes king of Persia. The writing of the letter was in Aramaic and translated.

Aramaic: [8]Rehum the administrator and Shimshai the secretary wrote a letter about Jerusalem to King Artaxerxes as follows. [9]"Rehum the administrator, Shimsai the secretary, and the rest of their associates, the authorities and officials, of Tarpel, Persia, Uruk, Babylon, Susa (that is, the Elamites), [10]and the rest of the peoples that the great and glorious Ashurbanipal exiled and settled in the city of Samaria and the rest of Beyond-the-River (so now [11]this is a copy of the letter they sent him) to King Artaxerxes. Your servants, men of Beyond-the-River: so now [12]be it known to the king that the Judahites who came up from you to us have come to Jerusalem. They are building up the rebellious and wicked city. They have completed the walls and repaired the foundations. [13]Now be it known to the king that if this city is built up and its walls are completed, they will not render tribute, taxes, or tolls, so the kings' interests will suffer harm. [14]Now since we share the salt of the palace and it is not right for us to see the king's dishonor, therefore we have sent and made it known to the king [15]so that you may search in your predecessors' record of events and know that this city is a rebellious city, harmful to kings and provinces. People have been making mutiny in it from of old. Because of that this city was destroyed. [16]We make it known to the king that if this city is built up and its walls are completed, as a result of that you will not have any share in Beyond-the-River."

[17]The king sent word: "To Rehum the administrator, Shimshai the secretary, the rest of their associates who live in Samaria, and the rest of Beyond-the-River, greetings. So now [18]the letter you sent to me has been explained and read before me. [19]An order was made by me, and they searched and found that this city from of old has arisen against kings. Rebellion and mutiny have been made in it. [20]There have been powerful kings over Jerusalem and they have exercised authority over the whole of Beyond-the-River. Tribute, taxes, and tolls were rendered to them. [21]Now make an order to stop these men. That city will not be built up until the order is made by me. [22]Be careful about acting negligently in this matter. Why should damage grow so as to harm kings?" When the copy of the letter of King Artaxerxes was read before Rehum, Shimshai the secretary, and their associates, they went with speed to Jerusalem to the Judahites and stopped them with compelling force.

I write in the midst of a referendum in Sudan that may result in the country splitting into two. Like most other African states, Sudan is (commentators have pointed out) an artificial construct deriving from the involvement of European powers in Africa, though it is the only one of these artificial constructs that is near to dissolving into entities that correspond more to the ethnic and religious makeup of their peoples. A couple of decades ago it did not occur to me as a Brit to feel guilty about my country's imperial past, but now it does so, as it is now easy for people in the United States to feel guilty about their country's current quasi-imperial relationship with much of the third world. At the same time, people in the United States can rightly feel proud about the way their country's politics and economics remains the object of the world's envy and aspiration, while many aspects of Britain's imperial involvement in Africa and Asia brought benefits as well as soaked up resources.

Relations between the **Persians** and the different parts of their empire would have some similar ambiguity about them. From a **Judahite** perspective the Persians could be benefactors (as Cyrus was) or constraints on the community's renewal (as Artaxerxes is here, but not elsewhere). While Artaxerxes' rule cost the region in taxes, we do not read about wars in the Persian period as we do in earlier centuries; tensions between the peoples around Judah continue through the reigns of the kings we noted in the comment on Ezra 4:1–6 and into the reign of Artaxerxes (465–424), but at least they get referred to the imperial authorities for resolution.

The book of Ezra abandons chronological order for a while in chapter 4 in surveying the way these tensions expressed themselves between the reigns of Cyrus and Artaxerxes. In other words, if you wanted to read the story in Ezra–Nehemiah in chronological order, you would read verses 5–6 after Ezra 6 and read verses 7–23 after Ezra 10. Verses 7–23 make no reference to the rebuilding of the temple (which is otherwise the focus in Ezra 1–6); it is ancient history by the time of the events they refer to.

First there is the letter from Bishlam and company (verse 7), whose contents we are not told; nor do we know anything about the people who wrote it beyond what we are told here. Aramaic was the international diplomatic language in the **Second Temple** period; it also became the everyday language of the Jewish people. It is a sister language of Hebrew and someone who knew one language could more or less understand the other.

In introducing the second initiative (verses 8–23), the second occurrence of word *Aramaic* signifies that at this point the book of Ezra itself is written in Aramaic. Most of the Old Testament is written in Hebrew; in this book, Hebrew resumes at Ezra 6:19, but there is another stretch of Aramaic in chapter 7. Daniel is the other Old Testament book that mixes the two languages in this way. As is the case in Daniel, the transition comes at a logical point, when the book is reporting the words of people who would not speak Hebrew, though as in Daniel, there is no such logic about the way Aramaic continues even when those people are no longer speaking.

Once more, we know nothing of the people who are mentioned in connection with the letter, people who were involved in the administration of the Persian Empire in the province of Beyond-the-River, that is, the area west of the Euphrates (beyond the River Euphrates if you live in Persia). Their task is to safeguard the king's interests in the western region of his empire to make sure that taxes get paid to him, and to make sure that order is maintained. They describe themselves as sharing (literally *salting*) the salt of the palace, a figure of speech that seems to suggest mutual commitment, though we do not know why it has this connotation (the Old Testament similarly refers elsewhere to a salt covenant). It does mean that Rehum and company are solemnly bound in loyalty to the Persian king.

The further reference to Samaria tightens the link with the earlier part of the chapter. The reason for collecting these accounts of the way people cause trouble for the Judahites is that the stories have in common that the people who are causing the problems are the people of Samaria. The Judahites are closer to the Samarians than to people such as the Ammonites or Moabites, but, in a strange way, sometimes our relationship with the people closer to us can be more fraught than our relationship with people farther away. That certainly applies in the realm of faith. Anglicans may well be sharper with other Anglicans than with Presbyterians; Presbyterians may be sharper with other Presbyterians than with Baptists; Baptists may be sharper with other Baptists than with Anglicans. So it is with the tension between the Judahites and their neighbors the Samarians, who say that they worship the same God as the Judahites but whose commitment to that God seems to the Judahites to be questionable. We have noted that for both sides (as is the case with disputes among Christians), questions about independence, power, and economics interweave with questions about faith.

At first sight the letter from Rehum and company looks somewhat self-contradictory in declaring that the Judahites have completed the city wall and laid the foundations for other rebuilding, then in speaking as if the completing of the walls and of the city's rebuilding is incomplete. If they exaggerate in describing the walls as already built, then their letter must predate the time of Nehemiah and belong sometime in the first half of Artaxerxes' reign. Artaxerxes' commission to Nehemiah, which came in 445, will then constitute the further "order by me" that countermands his reply to Rehum and company. But maybe Rehum and company mean that the danger to Artaxerxes lies in the Judahites' completing the rebuilding of

the city *as well as* the walls; in which case, the letter must post-
date Nehemiah's work.

The letter may be a straight transcript of the one they sent,
but there are some ironies in it that may suggest it has been
adapted to fit the context in Ezra. Either way, the writers are
of course right to stress Jerusalem's rebelliousness, which had
been the cause of its siege by the **Babylonians** in 597 and 587,
while Artaxerxes is rather generous in his comments on Jerusalem's past power. Some irony lies in the way the sins of the
parents are once again visited on the children; Jerusalem's past
rebellions provide the emperor with a reason not to give them
too much freedom in the present. The Judahites might resent
the action of Rehum and company and regret Artaxerxes' decision, but in a sense they cannot complain. On the other hand,
it will transpire that in the end they do manage to build up the
walls and the city. While God does let the sins of the parents be
visited on the children, this is not the end of the story.

EZRA 4:24–5:5

New Inspiration

[24]So work stopped on God's house in Jerusalem. It stopped until
the second year of the reign of Darius king of Persia, [5:1]when the
prophet Haggai and Zechariah son of Iddo, the prophets, prophesied to the Judahites in Judah and Jerusalem in the name of the
God of Israel, which was over them. [2]Then Zerubbabel son of
Shealtiel and Jeshua son of Jozadak set to and began to build
God's house in Jerusalem, and God's prophets were with them,
supporting them. [3]At that time Tattenai the governor of Beyond-
the-River, Shethar-bozenai, and their associates came to them
and said to them, "Who made you an order to build this house
and complete this furnishing?" [4]Then they said to them, "What
are the names of the men who are constructing this building?"
[5]But God's eye was on the Judahite elders, and they did not stop
them while an account could go to Darius and then a letter could
come back about this.

I would not be writing the Old Testament for Everyone series
were it not for a political development in Britain after the

Second World War. In the city where I was born, the socialist-controlled city council decided to work for equal opportunities for kids from working class backgrounds by buying places for them at the premier private school in the city, which sent scores of people to Oxford and Cambridge each year. I was given one of those places. No one in my family had ever stayed at school beyond the age of fourteen, let alone attended college. So that's how I came to learn Latin, Greek, and then Hebrew at university. If I had been born a few years earlier or a few years later (when another change of government terminated the program) this would never have happened. (Or, you might speculate, God would have had to turn me into a theologian some other way.) Of course I had to take the opportunity that I was given.

The **Judahites** in **Babylon** had the opportunity to move to their homeland to rebuild the temple in Jerusalem because of a political development that God brought about in fulfillment of a prophecy in Jeremiah: the ascendancy of the **Persians** in the Middle East. But the Judahites had to take advantage of the opportunity. They gave up work on the temple because of a political development—the opposition of other peoples in their region—though they were responsible for giving in to these pressures. Fifteen years later the accession of Darius the Great to the Persian throne provides a friendlier context for their taking up the work again.

The way chapters 4 and 5 of Ezra are divided is inclined to confuse the book's logic at this point. The main part of chapter 4 has reviewed the ups and downs of relationships between Judah and Samaria over half a century or so and the way this affected attempts to rebuild the city of Jerusalem as well as the temple. The last verse of chapter 4 then picks up the story of the building of the temple itself. It was still the time of Cyrus when the work was begun and abandoned. Cyrus was succeeded by his son Cambyses, who died after seven years in mysterious circumstances. The identity of his successor, Smerdis, is also mysterious, but it is clear enough that he was assassinated and succeeded by one of the assassins, who became Darius the Great. It was thus a period of disorder in the Persian Empire that gave people such as the Judahites scope to do what they wanted in the knowledge that as long as they did not behave too outrageously the Persians would probably be too preoccupied to worry.

So the political situation gave the Judahites their opportunity, but there would have been no resumption of the work on the temple unless they had seized their opportunity. Key to their doing so was the urging of two prophets whose actual words appear elsewhere in the Old Testament, in the books named after them. There is an interesting complementary aspect to their messages. Haggai is more stick; Zechariah is more carrot. There is a nice ambiguity about the statement that the two prophets prophesied *to* the Judahites, because that word often means "against," and it is the regular task of prophets to confront their people (even when they are bringing good news, because they usually do so when people believe there can be no good news). The two prophets preach both *to* and *against*. The people have to decide how to hear what they say. And both the carrot and the stick were means of the prophets supporting the people in the work on the temple.

The book of Haggai reveals that there is more than politics lying behind the neglect of the work on the temple. The economic situation is tough. People have been able to restore their own houses, but they have kept postponing doing something about God's house, and that suggests something wrong with their priorities. Once, a prophet had to tell David that God was unenthusiastic about his wanting to build a temple; now, a prophet has to tell the people that they are in trouble with God for not wanting to do so. On the other hand, to judge from the space occupied by Zechariah's visions in his book, maybe it is also significant that God spends a lot more time encouraging the Judahites about the temple-building project than to beating them about the head by means of Haggai's exhortations. "You can do it" is God's message through Zechariah—not because they have the natural ability but "by my spirit" (Zechariah 4:6). The book of Ezra makes a similar point in another way: "the **name** of the God of Israel was over them." It's not clear whether that applies just to the two prophets or to the people as a whole, but the effect is the same. The name of God being over you means you belong to God. That places an obligation on you; it

37

also implies that you are assured of protection and provision. When Tattenai and company are asking about the names of the builders, it reflects how, as far as they are concerned, the building is a human project. The author of this book knows that what counts is the fact that the name of God is over the work. It is a divine project.

Yet once again nothing is straightforward. Once again it is not clear that politics are going to work the community's way. A Babylonian record mentions Tattenai as governor of Beyond-the-River province in Darius's day. (In Ezra 6, Tattenai himself will also refer to someone else—presumably Zerubbabel—as governor of the Judahites, but that denotes a lower level of authority; the governor in Jerusalem will be subordinate to a governor with wider authority such as Tattenai, as indeed Tattenai was subordinate to a higher authority.) That means Tattenai is not a local figure like Rehum, and he does not represent Samarian interests over and against those of Judah. His inquiry about what the Judahites are doing is open to discovering that there is nothing problematic about it. So God's providence continues to make the politics work the Judahites' way as they are able to continue the building work while the inquiry takes place.

Not only was God's name over them; God's eye was on them (v. 5). Zechariah 4:10 speaks of God's eyes ranging over the whole earth. God keeps an eye on things, as we say, not in a threatening sense but in a reassuring and comforting sense. Tattenai and company are responsible to the emperor for keeping an eye on events in Judah and they are fulfilling their responsibility. But there is Someone else keeping an eye on Judah.

EZRA 5:6–17

The Whole Story

⁶A copy of the letter Tattenai, governor of Beyond-the-River, and Shethar-bozenai and his associates, the officials of Beyond-the-River, sent to King Darius. ⁷They sent a message to him, and in it was written as follows: "To King Darius, all good wishes. ⁸Be it known to the king that we went to the province of Judah to the house of the great God. It is being built up of

dressed stone, and timber is being set in the walls. This work is being done thoroughly and is progressing in their hands. [9]Thereupon we asked of these elders as follows. We said to them, 'Who made you an order to build this house and complete this furnishing?' [10]We also asked for their names to make them known to you, so that we could write down the name of the men who were at their head. [11]They gave back word to us in this way: 'We are the servants of the God of the heavens and the earth. We are building up the house that was built many years before this, when a great king of Israel built it and completed it. [12]Yet because our ancestors angered the God of the heavens, he gave them into the hand of Nebuchadnezzar the Chaldean, king of Babylon. He destroyed this house and exiled the people to Babylon. [13]However, in the first year of Cyrus, king of Babylon, King Cyrus made an order to build up this house of God. [14]The utensils of the house of God, gold and silver, which Nebuchadnezzar took out of the palace in Jerusalem and brought to the palace in Babylon, King Cyrus also took out of the palace in Babylon and gave to someone named Shezhbazzar whom he appointed governor. [15]He said to him, "Take these utensils, go off, deposit them in the palace in Jerusalem. The house of God is to be built up on its site." [16]This Sheshbazzar then came. He made a start on the house of God in Jerusalem, and from then until now it has been being built, but it is not finished.' [17]Now, if it pleases the king, there should be a search in the king's treasury there in Babylon, if it is the case that an order was made by King Cyrus for building up this house of God in Jerusalem. And may the king send us his decision concerning this."

A friend of mine who had been widowed met and fell in love with a woman who had been on her own for many years. I know from my own experience that there are tricky aspects to romance when you are middle-aged or older (for instance, instead of having to get your parents' approval of the match, you have to get your children's approval). He told me that for the two of them, the trickiest aspect of the development of their relationship was that both of them knew they needed to tell the other person the whole story of their lives. The problem was that for each of them there were aspects of their lives about which they felt deeply guilty. My friend had had an affair, about which he thinks his wife never knew, but there were people who did know about it, and he could never be sure that the truth would not come out one day, and he knew that this new relationship needed to be based on truth and openness. His new love had been mixed up with drugs years ago, and had done things of which she was now deeply ashamed, and she was not sure whether my friend would still be interested in her when he learned her whole story. But she too knew she had to tell it. (It was all okay in the end.)

In Ezra and Nehemiah, the **Judahites** are brave about telling their whole story to one another, to God, to us who read the book, and, in this case, to the **Persian** authorities. Admittedly it again makes sense to assume that verses 7–17 are not actually the transcript of a letter that the provincial authorities sent to the emperor. The theological teaching in the letter as well as the account of Judahite history doesn't look like the kind of thing that would appear in a letter from a provincial governor to his boss. The letter expresses the kind of thing that Judahites needed to acknowledge for themselves at the time and the kind of thing the Judahite readers of the book would need to acknowledge. But that makes no difference to the significance of the letter; indeed, it gives more point to its statements of faith and its willingness to tell the whole story.

The shameful bit of the story is that the need to rebuild the temple resulted from the way the Judahites had angered God. It forms a pair with the declaration put on the lips of Rehum and company in Ezra 4—that Jerusalem was a rebellious and wicked city. The book of Ezra never lets its readers escape the facts about their own history. They know they could not complain if God cast them off or if the Persian authorities stopped them from doing what they wanted to do for God's glory. They have offended both God and the imperial authorities. They are without excuse. If they are able to achieve anything, it is by the grace of God and the grace of the authorities. Telling the whole story requires a strange kind of confidence in God, a confidence that God already knows the whole story so that there is neither the need nor the possibility of hiding it from God; and if God knows it, what harm can there be in other people knowing it?

40

As well as indicating that they told the whole story about themselves, the letter to Darius indicates that they told the whole story about God, "the great God," "the God of the heavens and the earth." The second phrase explains the first. The books of Ezra and Nehemiah are more reticent about using the **name** of God, **Yahweh,** than earlier books, at least when talking to foreigners or describing the way foreigners talk. They are more inclined to use descriptions of God such as the one that appear here that show that their God is not merely a tin-pot, little provincial deity who could not be compared with a big deity like the god of **Babylon** or Persia. The Judahites presuppose the outrageous claim that the God of this little provincial people actually is the great God, the God of the heavens and the earth, the God whose will is done in the heavens (there are no other gods who rival God's authority there) and whose will is therefore also done on the earth (there are no human emperors who can frustrate God's will there). They are bold enough to put such statements on the lips of their provincial overlords and to have them reported to the emperor himself.

The story implies that one indication of the greatness of Yahweh as the God of the heavens and the earth is the extraordinary fact that the great Cyrus issued this decree and looked into where the temple utensils were. The hand of God can work in ways we could not have imagined.

EZRA 6:1–15

Sometimes You Are Dumbfounded

[1]Then an order was made by King Darius and they searched in the documents building where treasures were kept in Babylon, [2]but a scroll was found in the fortress at Ecbatana in Media province. In it was written as follows: "Memorandum. [3]In King Cyrus's first year, King Cyrus made an order: 'The house of God in Jerusalem. The house is to be built up, a place where people will offer sacrifices, with its foundations buttressed, its height sixty cubits [thirty yards or meters], its width sixty cubits, [4]three courses of dressed stone and a course of new timber. The expense will be paid by the king's house. [5]Also the utensils of the house of God, gold and silver, which Nebuchadnezzar took

41

out of the palace in Jerusalem and brought to Babylon are to be returned, and [each] is to go to the palace in Jerusalem to its place. You are to deposit [it] in God's house.'"

⁶"Now Tattenai, governor of Beyond-the-River; Shethar-bozenai; and their associates, officials of Beyond-the-River province, stay away from there. ⁷Leave the work on this house of God alone. The governor of the Judahites and the elders of the Judahites are to build up this house of God on its site, ⁸and an order is made by me about what you are to do with these elders of the Judahites to build up this house of God. The expense is to be paid scrupulously to these men out of the assets of the king, out of the tribute from Beyond-the-River, so as not to make [them] stop. ⁹Whatever the needs—young bulls, rams, and lambs for burnt offerings to the God of the heavens, wheat, salt, wine, and oil in accordance with the word of the priests in Jerusalem—it is to be given them day by day without fail, ¹⁰so that they may present pleasing sacrifices to the God of the heavens and pray for the life of the king and his sons. ¹¹And an order is made by me that anyone who defies this message, a piece of timber will be removed from his house and he will be lifted up and beaten upon it, and his house will be made forfeit, because of this. ¹²And may the God who establishes his name there overthrow any king or people who puts out his hand to defy [this] to damage this house of God in Jerusalem. I, Darius, have made the decree. It is to be put into effect scrupulously."

¹³Then, in keeping with what King Darius sent, Tattenai, governor of Beyond-the-River; Shethar-bozenai; and their associates accordingly put it into effect scrupulously. ¹⁴The elders of the Judahites built and made progress through the prophesying of Haggai the prophet and Zechariah son of Iddo. So they built and finished by the order of the God of Israel and by the order of Cyrus, Darius, and Artaxerxes, king of Persia. ¹⁵This house was completed on the third day of the month of Adar; it was in the sixth year of the reign of King Darius.

If you are a Christian in Lebanon or Iraq or Israel or Egypt or Iran, you may well fear for your future. You know that you are a second-class citizen; a number of people in some of those countries have lost their lives simply because they are Christians. If you are a Christian in Jordan, you are likely to be more relaxed. While the Christian population of the country is a smaller proportion than it was fifty years ago, the Christian community remains an accepted part of the national community. Apparently the key figure in encouraging the continuation of this state of affairs is the King of Jordan, Abdullah II. While Christians live under Islamic law in the same way as anyone else, this law is administered in Jordan in a way that Christians can live with. There is a kind of complement to the idea that we render to Caesar what belongs to Caesar and to God what belongs to God. It is also Caesar's job to render to God what belongs to God. When rulers prove themselves people who are not a threat to people who do right but who act forcefully against people who do wrong, they are fulfilling their duty to God, whether they realize it or not, and even if they are acting out of their own interests. They are fulfilling their vocation. And when the New Testament urges congregations to make intercession for kings and people in authority so that we may be able to live peaceful and holy lives, it is urging that we pray that they may fulfill their vocation.

Darius does so, and so do Tattenai and his colleagues. **Judah** is in effect a **Persian** colony, and other parts of Ezra–Nehemiah make clear that the Judahites, like any colonial people, would like to have their freedom rather than be ruled by the Persians. Yet Paul's comment in Romans 13 about the beneficent possibilities of imperial rule proves its truth for the Judahites. In Jerusalem and elsewhere, as is the case in the West, Christian communities often do not get on with each other, and there is an equivalent in the story in Ezra 1–6 in the tension between the communities that acknowledge **Yahweh** in Jerusalem and Samaria. Yet there is no real tension between the Jerusalem community and the Persian authorities. Tattenai as governor of Beyond-the-River province as a whole is doing his job in investigating what is going on in Jerusalem and in reporting to Darius; he did not attempt to stop the work while he sent his report. It would not be surprising if this made the Judahites redouble their efforts to get on with it.

In turn, Darius establishes the truth of the Judahites' claim concerning Cyrus's authorization and support of the work on the temple (again, the word *palace* each time refers to God's royal earthly dwelling) and not only confirms these but increases the level of the imperial support for the work. The Judahites must have rubbed their eyes in disbelief when they read his letter. Far from stopping the work, the emperor will pay the building costs. There was no reference to Cyrus paying the building costs in the account of his edict at the beginning of Ezra; is this itself news to the Judahite community, who thought they had to raise the cost themselves (the critique of their procrastination in Haggai 1 might cohere with that possibility)? After all, we have to be realistic, don't we? Did the colonial administrators conveniently forget this element in Cyrus's edict? It is all very well for the administration to pass a bill mandating some new policy, but what does the Ways and Means Committee say about where the money is coming from? Darius knows there needs to be an answer to that question, and provides it. Tattenai would normally be expected to make sure that taxes from the colonies reached the imperial administration; far from stopping the work, he is now told to recycle provincial taxes for the building work. Yes, the Judahites must be rubbing their eyes. How could they have imagined that God would bring about something so stupendous? Nobody likes paying taxes, but what about when you can see them coming back to you in such a way?

Darius's further innovation is that additional imperial subvention will cover the cost of animals and other requirements for the offerings in the temple. Judahite eyes open yet wider. The rationale for Darius's action in fact helps us to infer at least part of the rationale for Cyrus's original edict. Sacrifices are, among other things, the accompaniment to prayer, and Darius knows he needs all the prayer he can get. It is worth his while to support people who will pray for him. Perhaps there is less wisdom in the threats he makes concerning people who try to frustrate his intentions, or maybe we today think in that way because we are wimps and/or are in denial about the way we are protected by the threat of violence on the part of our protectors such as the police. When you are a person in authority such as a president or a king, you have to live in the real world.

So the work on the temple is completed by the order of God and by the order of the imperial authorities. The Judahites' story illustrates how there need not be conflict between these two orders. Now Ezra 4 has already told us another story about a later time when things did not work out in this way. There, an imperial order stopped building work on the city. In later such contexts there would be people in Judah who needed a vision for the possibility that God's order and imperial order could work together rather than be in conflict, a vision to give them hope and inform their prayer, a faith that goes beyond human imagination. Christian communities in many countries around the world need the same vision to give them hope and inform their prayer, and their fellow-Christians need that vision as they pray on their behalf for that which we *know* is impossible.

EZRA 6:16–22

Joyful Celebration

[16]The Israelites, the priests and the Levites and the rest of the exiles, performed the dedication of this house of God with celebration. [17]For the dedication of this house of God they presented one hundred bulls, two hundred rams, four hundred lambs, and twelve goats as a purification offering for all Israel, according to the number of the clans of Israel. [18]They set up the priests in their divisions and the Levites in their groups for the service of God in Jerusalem, in accordance with what is written in the book of Moses. [19]The exiles made Passover on the fourteenth day of the first month, [20]because the priests had purified themselves and the Levites altogether were pure, all of them. They slaughtered the Passover [offering] for all the exiles, for their brother priests, and for themselves. [21]The Israelites who had returned from the exile, and everyone who had separated himself from the defilement of the nation in the land to join them in inquiring of Yahweh the God of Israel, ate. [22]They made the Flat Bread Festival for seven days with celebration, because Yahweh had made them celebrate when he inclined the mind of the king of Assyria to them so as to support them in the work on the house of God, the God of Israel.

The couple I referred to in connection with Ezra 5:6–17 often say that they cannot believe the wonderful thing that has happened to them. The man never expected to find this new love

45

a couple of years after his wife died. The woman expresses her astonishment with more feeling because she had been on her own for years, and she knew that statistically it was unlikely she would find someone else. At least as significant was the fact that she went out with men from time to time but could never imagine making a commitment to one of them. And then . . . whoosh, when she wasn't looking, she met this guy with whom she soon knew she wanted to spend the rest of her life, and miraculously he felt the same about her. God's accomplishment of the impossible demonstrated that what she had settled for as a life that was good enough (particularly in light of the mistakes of her past life) was sadly inadequate compared to God's vision for her. The celebration in their hearts and the celebration in their friends' and family's hearts was a delight to share.

The temple dedication aroused feelings of this kind in the **Judahite** community. Psalm 90 may help us share them. The people have been consumed by God's anger, it says, the anger that Tattenai's letter in Ezra 5 shows they recognized. They know they deserved that anger, and they have been living under God's wrath and thus with trouble and sorrow for seventy years. Maybe it will become eighty years, the psalm speculates.

The returned exiles now know that the exile has not done so. They have come back. The time of wrath is over. Psalm 30 in turn makes that point. The psalm's heading suggests it was used for the temple's dedication, even though it expresses itself as if the speaker is an individual who once felt secure as the recipient of God's favor, then saw his life collapse and seemed to have descended to the depths of the realm of death. But God did not leave him there. He has proved that God's anger lasts only a moment but his favor lasts a lifetime (it doesn't feel like that when you are on the receiving end of God's anger, but the experience of God's deliverance puts the experience of trouble into perspective). Weeping may last the night, but celebration comes with the morning. God did not let the psalmist's enemies rejoice over him. God has turned his wailing into dancing, taken off the gloomy garb he was wearing and clothed him in party clothes.

Such would be the testimony of the community that has returned from exile and is once more dumbfounded at the wonder of what God has done in making it possible for the temple to be rebuilt. There was celebration all right, even if this new act of dedication was less splendid than the original one described in 1 Kings 8. The number of sacrificial animals may seem to be a lot, but that earlier story speaks of 22,000 cattle and 120,000 sheep; furthermore, there is no account here of a cloud that represents God's splendor filling the house, as it did in the earlier story. Yet there is no hint that the community is disappointed by the event it celebrates or feels it is less significant than that dedication. It is indeed dumbfounded at the grace of God. Although people saw no cloud, the story implies that they knew God was present to be worshiped and inquired of by them. Cyrus is heir to the old **Assyrian** Empire that was once the agent of God's wrath, so it is as if God has now made the same Assyrians the means of exercising mercy.

Another distinctive feature of this dedication festival is that it involves a purification offering, which was unmentioned in connection with that first dedication. The people celebrating are defiled. They are defiled because they or their ancestors had been involved in worship of other deities, which was one reason they were taken into exile. They are defiled because they had been living cheek-by-jowl with foreigners who worshiped other deities. They are defiled because no doubt some of them had been involved in that worship themselves. By coming to the sanctuary, this community would risk defiling it and making it impossible for God to be there. So the community needs purifying. The possibility of making offerings to effect that purification is another indication of the grace and mercy of the God who wishes once again to come to live among the people. Such cleansing requires the grace and mercy of God who provides for the means of cleansing; it also requires the responsiveness and submission of the people, who actually make the offering.

The whole community joined in the celebration, and the story emphasizes that in some sense this meant the whole of Israel. For its purification twelve goats are offered, the number that corresponds to the number of the Israelite clans (I prefer the word *clans* to *tribes* because *clans* reflects the fact that they all belong to one family). It is a particularly concrete expression of the conviction and the claim that this community represents the whole of Israel. Ezra 4 has more realistically described the people involved in building the temple as "Judah and Benjamin," the clans that belonged to the old southern kingdom. But there are among them some people from the northern clans who have moved south for various reasons, so it is not quite fiction to regard the Judahite community as representing all twelve clans, and it is theologically important. The community around the temple really does represent God's faithfulness to Israel in its entirety. The issue continues to be significant for the Jewish community in the twenty-first century, whose physical descent largely goes back to the community of people who lived in Judah after the exile, or to people who constituted the original dispersion.

The building work had been completed early in the month of Adar, the last month of the year. Conveniently, this meant that the temple dedication led directly into the celebration of Passover, a few weeks later; Passover comes at the beginning of the year according to this way of counting, followed by the Flat Bread Festival. Both these festivals celebrate the exodus from Egypt; Flat Bread (bread made without yeast) also marks the beginning of the barley harvest. The people who joined in the celebration of the two festivals included all the people who had "separated themselves from the defilement of the nation in the land," as well as the people who had returned from exile.

Who are these people? They will include people who are not Israelite by birth—people who would later be called proselytes. The **Torah** is explicit that foreigners can join in Passover if they are willing to join Israel, which would involve the males being circumcised. These foreigners will include people such as the resident aliens who had come to live in Judah because of some crisis in their homeland that had driven them to move abroad in this way. They will include people living in the territory of **Ephraim**, Samarians who profess to worship **Yahweh** (who are now accepted to join in the temple worship in a way they were not when they wanted to join in the temple building), and resident aliens of Israelite stock who originally came from that area. Most tantalizingly, the comment offers another hint at recognition of the presence of a significant body of Judahites who had not gone into exile.

So far the book has indicated that the temple-builders were afraid of "the peoples of the countries" and that "the people of the country" were weakening the efforts of the temple-builders, not least by bribing the authorities to stop their work. It has also hinted that the temple-builders may have made a rod for their own back by their tough stance in relation to these other Judahites. The theological principle lying behind their stance is that it is crucial to avoid defiling the temple, and they are concerned at the risk that these other Judahites will do so, just as foreigners would. But this account of the temple building indicates that they recognized the need to walk a tightrope in their relationship with these people as they considered the possibility of other Judahites as well as foreigners and northerners joining in the festival celebrations. The key question is whether they will make sure people do not bring defilement on the sanctuary, because that would mean disaster.

The community's openness to these other Judahites deconstructs any sharp antithesis over who constitute the real people of God. Whether you are exiles or people who had never gone into exile, the question is whether you have opened yourselves to purification. You could come from what you thought was the right group, but it would do you no good if you were in a state of defilement. Conversely, other people could come from what you thought was the wrong group, but they would become acceptable to God if they submitted themselves to God's cleansing. The people who ate the Passover could include exiles, people who had not gone into exile, Samarians, or foreigners; the only question was, are they people who are committed to making Yahweh the one they "inquire of"—the one to whom they turn for guidance and for the answers to their prayers—and have they submitted themselves to purification for whatever defilement has affected them?

EZRA 7:1-10

Enter the Priest-Theologian

¹After these things, in the reign of Artaxerxes king of Persia, Ezra son of Seraiah, son of Azariah, son of Hilkiah, ²son of

Shallum, son of Zadok, son of Ahitub, [3]son of Amariah, son of Azariah, son of Meraioth, [4]son of Zerahiah, son of Uzzi, son of Bukki, [5]son of Abishua, son of Phinehas, son of Eleazar, son of Aaron the head priest—[6]that Ezra went up from Babylon. He was an expert scholar in the teaching of Moses, which Yahweh the God of Israel had given. The king had given him every request of his, in accordance with the hand of Yahweh his God upon him. [7]So some Israelites, some priests, Levites, singers, gatekeepers, and assistants went up to Jerusalem in King Artaxerxes' seventh year.

[8]He came to Jerusalem in the fifth month (this was the king's seventh year), [9]because the start of the journey from Babylon was on the first day of the first month and he came to Jerusalem on the first day of the fifth month in accordance with the good hand of his God upon him, [10]because Ezra had given his mind to studying the teaching of Yahweh and to observing and teaching statute and ruling in Israel.

Yesterday I was talking with an architect about the design of a church building and discussing one of the basic issues about designing church buildings. Two of the central activities in a church are the celebration of the Lord's Supper or Holy Communion and baptism, and the reading of Scripture and the exposition of Scripture in preaching. Both celebration and exposition are central, but it's hard to give expression to both of them in the design of a space for worship. It's an important issue because the design of the space both expresses a particular faith understanding and encourages a particular faith understanding in the congregation. Many older churches are long and thin and focus on the position of the ministers and choir, and that expresses a faith understanding concerning the nature of church and worship, while many modern churches are rather like auditoria where concerts happen, and that's a telling indication of a faith understanding concerning the nature of church and worship.

One of Ezra's strengths is that he is both a priest and a teacher. The story of the rebuilding of the temple has emphasized the activity of priests in leading its worship; priests had a key role in the offering of sacrifices and, in the ongoing description of Ezra's role, that aspect of worship will have an important place.

The opening of his story emphasizes his priestly credentials. He belongs to a line that goes back to Aaron via a series of senior priests. That may be significant in light of the way he presumably has to negotiate or win his way with the senior priest and the other priests who are already fulfilling their ministry in the temple. But priests also had a role in teaching the **Torah**, and Ezra is a scholar or theologian, too; he is an expert in the Torah. He is a successor to Moses as well as a successor to Aaron.

The Apocrypha or Deutero-canonical writings contain several other works that bear the name of Ezra (actually Esdras, the Greek and Latin version of the name). One of them, really written after the time of Christ, tells a story about a vision Esdras has. In the vision, the Torah has been burnt, presumably in the course of the destruction of Jerusalem in 70 AD, but God dictates the Torah and the rest of the Scriptures (plus seventy other books) to Ezra, who gets five scribes to write them down. It's "just a story," but the idea is plausible that back in his own day Ezra was associated with the process whereby the Torah in its final form came into existence and that his mission to Jerusalem is the means whereby this final version of the Torah came to be implemented there.

Whatever the process whereby it came into existence, the Torah is neatly described both as the teaching of Moses and the teaching of **Yahweh**. On one side, it is teaching given through a human agent, written in a human language. Historically, it developed over centuries, from the time of Moses through the history of **Ephraim** and **Judah** and via the exile where we may imagine people such as priests carefully making sure that their exile in **Babylon** did not mean that their people's traditions got lost but that neither did they remain fossilized. The exile had happened because Judah played fast and loose with the teaching of Moses. They willfully forgot its key requirements; they did not worship Yahweh alone, they did not forswear worship by means of images, they did not avoid attaching Yahweh's **name** to things to which it did not belong.

People like Ezra knew that there could be no future unless they made a commitment to living by Moses' teaching. While they could not take for granted that Yahweh would ever want to have anything to do with them again, they could take for granted that there could be no such hope that this might be so unless they did make such a commitment. All they could do was cast themselves on God's mercy. Their commitment to living by Moses' teaching in the future was a sign that they really were throwing themselves on God's mercy. It meant reaffirming their traditions, but it also meant working out how their traditions needed to be reformulated so as to have some purchase in a new situation. In that much later vision that pictures the Torah having been burnt and lost, Esdras prays for God to send the Holy Spirit into him so that he can be the means of the Torah being restored to Israel. In Babylon the Holy Spirit has been active in inspiring the Judahites both to preserve the Torah and to perceive how it needs reformulating for the future.

In other words, as well as being the teaching of Moses (and of Ezra and of other people whose names we don't know) the Torah that Ezra brings is the teaching of Yahweh, the gracious gift whereby God endows the community with the means to show that it really is committed to God this time. And that is indeed how it turned out. After the time of Ezra, the Judahites became a people who did worship Yahweh alone, who did abjure the making of images, who were careful about the way they used Yahweh's name, and who kept the Sabbath; in the New Testament, you never read of Jews failing to keep these basic expectations of Moses' teaching. Ezra has been described as the father of Judaism, and this is one connection in which that is an appropriate designation.

One of the neatest compliments that could be paid him is that he had given himself to studying, observing, and teaching the Torah. He wasn't just a person who studied because he liked studying; his studying motivated him to teach. But neither was he someone who simply studied and taught but who could roll up his scroll at the end of the working day and forget about its teaching. He was a person who lived by what he read and taught. He observed the Torah.

The story of Ezra's mission begins by telling us that it took place "after these things"; it followed on the rebuilding of the temple. You could easily get the impression that it took place a year or two later than those events. Along with the fact that Ezra comes from Babylon, this assumption might contribute to the impression that Ezra has something to do with the return of the Judahites from exile. This is not so. The temple building was finished in 516, but Artaxerxes came to the throne of **Persia** in 465, so the date of Ezra's mission is 458 (indeed, it has sometimes been suggested that the Artaxerxes in whose time Ezra lived was Artaxerxes II, which makes Ezra's date 398, another half-century later). "After these things," the harmless-looking introduction to the chapter, obscures the fact that with chapter 7 we move on half a century. There's continuity in the story; Ezra 1–6 concerns the restoration of the temple, Ezra 7–10 the restoration of the community. But Ezra lived well over a century after the fall of Jerusalem and the time the Judahites were taken off to Babylon. The mere rebuilding of the temple has not meant the rebuilding of the community. Of course community building is never finished; each generation and each century has to face new issues, as we will discover in Ezra's story. It's also possible to wonder why Ezra's family had not responded to earlier opportunities to make the move to Jerusalem. They did not live in exile; they lived in dispersion. Ezra himself became someone who was not satisfied with that life. He evidently became passionate about the Torah and passionate about seeing it properly implemented in Jerusalem. But (repeat after me) "Ezra was nothing to do with the return from the exile."

EZRA 7:11–28

What We Owe and What We Give Because We Want To

[11]This is a copy of the letter King Artaxerxes gave Ezra the priest-scholar, scholar in matters concerning Yahweh's commands and statutes for Israel: [12]"Artaxerxes, king of kings, to Ezra the priest-scholar in the law of the God of the heavens (and so on). Now. [13]An order has been made by me that anyone in my kingdom from the people of Israel and its priests and Levites who voluntarily offers to go to Jerusalem with you, may go. [14]Because you are sent by the king and his seven counselors to inquire about Judah and Jerusalem in terms of the law of your God, which is in your hand, [15]and to take silver and gold that the king and his counselors have made as a voluntary offering to the God of Israel whose dwelling is in Jerusalem,

¹⁶and any silver and gold that you find in all Babylon province, with the voluntary offering of the people and the priests that they offer voluntarily for the house of their God in Jerusalem. ¹⁷Therefore with this money acquire scrupulously bulls, rams, and lambs, and their grain offerings and drink offerings, and present them on the altar in the house of your God in Jerusalem. ¹⁸And what seems good to you and your brothers to do with the rest of the silver and gold, in accordance with the will of your God, you may do. ¹⁹The utensils given to you for the service of your God's house, deliver in full to God in Jerusalem. ²⁰The rest of the needs of your God's house that it falls to you to give, you may give from the king's treasury. ²¹I, King Artaxerxes—by me an order is made to all the treasurers in Beyond-the-River, that anything Ezra the priest-scholar in the law of the God of the heavens asks of you is scrupulously to be done, ²²up to a hundred talents of silver, a hundred measures of wheat, a hundred measures of wine, a hundred measures of oil, and salt without prescribed limit. ²³Anything that is by the order of the God of the heavens is to be done scrupulously for the house of the God of the heavens, so that wrath does not come on the realm of the king and his sons. ²⁴And to you we make it known that all priests, Levites, musicians, gatekeepers, assistants, and workers in this house of God—it is not permitted to impose tribute, taxes, and tolls on them. ²⁵And you, Ezra, in accordance with your God's wisdom, which you possess, appoint authorities and judges who will give judgment for all the people in Beyond-the-River, for all who acknowledge the laws of your God, and make them known to anyone who does not acknowledge them. ²⁶Anyone who does not observe the law of your God and the law of the king, judgment will be done to him scrupulously, whether by death, banishment, confiscation of property, or imprisonment." ²⁷Yahweh the God of our ancestors be worshiped, who put into the king's mind in this way to glorify Yahweh's house in Jerusalem ²⁸and extended commitment to me before the king and his counselors and all the king's powerful officials. I myself took courage in accordance with the hand of Yahweh my God upon me and gathered leaders from Israel to go up with me.

It's January as I write, and I need to get around to working on my income taxes. One result of doing so will be that I will know how much I gave away last year, and I will thus know whether I "owe" some giving. My year-by-year assumption is that I should give a tithe—a tenth—of what I earn to my church and to other Christian and philanthropic causes. That's simply what I am bound to do by God's expectations of me. That's what I "owe." Only when I go beyond that tenth do I enter the realm where I am *choosing* to give. That's the difference between obligations and what translations traditionally refer to as "freewill offerings."

It's a difference we have come across already in Ezra 1, and it reappears here in the letter expressing Artaxerxes' commission to Ezra (it's another passage in Aramaic, like part of chapter 4, as is appropriate given that this is the language the emperor might naturally be expected to use). Artaxerxes recognizes that there are offerings **Yahweh** prescribes for the temple in Jerusalem, but in addition, he makes contributions beyond the ones that are required. These will include the utensils he goes on to refer to, which must be not ones that were taken from the temple in the previous century (which Cyrus returned) but new ones. He anticipates that the **Judahites** in his empire will also want to make offerings that they are under no obligation to make.

The voluntary principle receives expression in people's lives as well as in their offerings. There was no obligation for people to make the move to Jerusalem. It is possible to be loyal to Yahweh in **Babylon** or Susa, in London or Los Angeles. Anyone who does make the move is making a voluntary offering of their whole lives, their whole future. Such people would know what we know from reading Ezra and Nehemiah, that conditions in Judah were tough in a variety of ways. In our own day, many Jewish people who have "gone up" to their ancient homeland over the past century or so have known that fact. Ezra and his contemporaries find themselves filled with a passion for the temple, for the flourishing of the community around it, and for the embodying of the **Torah** in its life.

Like Cyrus and Darius, Artaxerxes knows he needs all the prayers and divine help he can get as emperor, and he wants to make sure he does what it takes in order to open himself to it. No doubt he took a similar stance to the deities of other subject peoples as he took to the God of **Israel**, and as with Cyrus it is tempting to suspect that he was cynical in his attitude and/ or that his fear of God's wrath reflects an ill-informed faith. While this may be so, the problem may lie in our assumptions. We have no way of knowing how cynical his attitude was. His practice raises the question whether we give as he did.

The terms of his letter hint more clearly than other documents have done that his policy was to try to ensure the stability and order of his empire by encouraging the implementation in a colony such as Judah of a set of laws that the Judahites could own as their own. In looking into the history of Christian-Muslim relations in Jordan, to which I referred in connection with Ezra 6, I came across an interesting and slightly disturbing fact. Whereas King Abdullah II, as well as encouraging good relations between the religious communities in his country, has been able to use his power as king to implement considerable social, educational, political, and economic developments, Western powers have been pressing him to introduce more democracy in the sense of giving more power to an elected government. The trouble is that he would thus have less power to encourage such positive developments. Subsequently, the news media have reported the deposing of the president of Tunisia and have asked whether the problem in the Arab world is that whereas once it had dynamic leaders who were autocratic and might have been brutal but who did give their people hope, now it lacks these. They suggest that the solution might not be Western-style democracy (which also lacks dynamism and currently fails to give its people hope) but better autocracy. The Middle East in Old Testament times was autocratic; sometimes it was also enlightened.

If Artaxerxes is as concerned with the stability of his empire and with furthering his own interests as he is with honoring God, then that fact adds to the dumbfounding nature of the way God is at work through him. The point is reflected in Ezra's words of praise that are appended to the letter. These refer again to the hand of God being on Ezra; the expression came twice in the introduction to his mission at the beginning of chapter 7. The mission involves an extraordinary coming together of the furthering of the imperial purpose and the furthering of God's purpose. The introduction to the mission spoke of Artaxerxes granting every request of Ezra's, so either the idea for the mission came from Ezra and the king agreed, or the idea came from Artaxerxes and Ezra said "Yes, but I will need the following. . . ." Either way, the hand of God was involved in Artaxerxes' agreeing to the nature of the mission. As is often the case, it seemed impossible to explain the astounding events involved in Artaxerxes' commission without seeing it as an expression of God's **commitment** to Ezra.

In this chapter and in subsequent chapters in Ezra there is some interweaving between words put on Ezra's lips and words that speak of Ezra in the third person, which suggests that the author of the book as a whole is someone who has incorporated memoir material from Ezra and other material and integrated it into the book.

EZRA 8:1–23

Another Exodus

¹These are the ancestral heads and the enrolling of the people who went up with me from Babylon in the reign of King Artaxerxes. ²Of the descendants of Phinehas, Gershom. Of the descendants of Ithamar, Daniel. Of the descendants of David, Hattush, ³of the descendants of Shecaniah. Of the descendants of Parosh, Zechariah, and with him were enrolled males, one hundred and fifty. ⁴Of the descendants of Pahath-moab, Elihoenai son of Zerahiah, and with him two hundred males. ⁵Of the descendants of Shecaniah, the son of Jahaziel, and with him three hundred males. ⁶And of the descendants of Adin, Ebed son of Jonathan, and with him fifty males. ⁷And of the descendants of Elam, Jeshaiah son of Athaliah, and with him seventy males. ⁸And of the descendants of Shephatiah, Zebadiah son of Michael, and with him eighty males. ⁹Of the descendants of Joab, Obadiah son of Jehiel, and with him two hundred and eighteen males. ¹⁰And of the descendants of Shelomith, the son of Josiphiah, and with him one hundred and sixty males. ¹¹And of the descendants of Bebai, Zechariah son of Bebai, and with him twenty-eight males. ¹²And of the descendants of Azgad, Johanan son of Hakkatan, and with him one hundred and ten

males. [13]And of the descendants of Adonikam, the last, these are their names: Eliphelet, Jeiel, and Shemaiah, and with them sixty males. [14]And of the descendants of Bigvai, Uthai and Zaccur, and with them seventy males.

[15]So I gathered them at the river that comes to Ahava and camped there for three days. I looked at the people and the priests, but did not find any Levites there. [16]So I sent for Eliezer, Ariel, Shemaiah, Elnathan, Jarib, Elnathan, Nathan, Zechariah, and Meshullam as heads, and for Joiarib and Elnathan as teachers, [17]and sent them off to Iddo, the head, at Casiphaia the [worship] place, and put words in their mouth to speak to Iddo and his brother, the attendants at Casiphaia, the [worship] place, to bring us ministers for the house of our God. [18]In accordance with the good hand of our God upon us they brought us a man of insight from the descendants of Mahli son of Levi son of Israel, Sherebiah, and his sons and relatives, twenty people, [19]and Hashabiah and with him Jeshaiah of the descendants of Merari, his relatives and their sons, twenty people, [20]and of the assistants that David and the officials had given for the service of the Levites, two hundred and twenty servants; all of them were recorded by name.

[21]I called a fast there at the River Ahava to afflict ourselves before our God in order to seek from him a straightforward journey for us and our little ones and all our possessions, [22]because I was embarrassed to ask the king for a force and cavalry to help us against enemies on the journey, because we had said to the king, "The hand of our God is upon all who inquire of him, for good, but his strength and anger are upon all who abandon him." [23]So we fasted and inquired of God about this and he let himself be interceded by us.

Yesterday in church the sermon took the form of a congregational discussion of the Gospel for the day, the story of Jesus calling his first disciples. Karen made the opening comment about how speedily the fishermen responded. Kathleen talked about the way we need to mend our nets if we are to catch anything, and Anthony commented on the significance he could see in this for his own life. Later in the service when we shared items for prayer and praise, Julian told us about the way the Holy Spirit had guided him step-by-step about what to do when he awoke some weeks ago aware that there was something wrong with his heart, and Gail asked us to pray for her husband who had to have a surgical procedure this week, and we prayed for Jamie who was troubled by sciatica. Then in the announcements we heard that a cross made by Eardley had proved just right for a new retreat center opening a short distance from our church. When this volume is published, one or two of the congregation will likely read it, and now on this page they will find their names and the names of their sisters and brothers.

I imagine something similar happening as people in **Judah** read Ezra's list of names. "That's me! That's my father! That's my grandfather!" Further, the list draws attention to the extended family reunions that would take place in Jerusalem, because the list of **ancestral heads** is (not surprisingly) very similar to the list in Ezra 2. That chapter comprised a list of people who moved to Judah over a century or so; the present list with its much lower numbers offers a snapshot of the people who made that move with Ezra. Even if you were not related to any of these people, the list vividly conveys the fact that Ezra's mission involves real people. (It mentions only males, because in that social context it was normally males who were the heads of families.) Given that this occasion by no means meant that all Judahites had now made the move, Ezra's mission involved these people in leaving members of their extended family in **Babylon**. But it also meant their joining members of their extended family in Judah.

One reason for needing some **Levites** in the party is that the **Torah** portrays it as the job of Levites to carry sacred objects such as the utensils for use in worship that Artaxerxes has donated. But that points to another significance in the Levites' presence. A century previous, before the **Persian** conquest of Babylon made it possible for the first group of exiles to make the move from Babylon to Judah, God's promises to them in Isaiah 40–55 envisaged their coming exodus from Babylon as resembling a repetition of Israel's original exodus from Egypt to the promised land. The journey of the first people who made that move from Babylon, described at the beginning of Ezra, was thus indeed a kind of repetition of the exodus (which you could see as coming to a conclusion with the building of the temple in Solomon's day). Now Ezra's own journey nearly a century later is another repetition of the exodus, again designed to lead to offerings in the temple. One implication of this understanding is that the new exodus did not happen once and only once, so that if you missed it, this was too bad. Each generation has the opportunity to decide that although their parents and grandparents and great-grandparents were happy to stay in Babylon, they themselves will make the move.

But a proper reenactment of the exodus needs to be one involving Israel as a whole, and that means it needs some Levites, because they have a prominent place in the story of the original exodus. We don't know why no Levites originally volunteered to join Ezra's party. One reason may simply be that not many of the nonpriestly Levites (the Levites who did not belong to Aaron's line) had been exiled; they were not as important as priests. And/or perhaps the fact that there were few of them meant that they had quite satisfactory jobs to do at Casiphaia, if that was indeed a worship place as I assumed in the translation above (we don't know where it was). For them, there would then have been more sacrifice involved in moving to Judah.

It looks as if the gathering by the River Ahava had both a religious and a practical function. The "river" will have been one of the canals that spread the waters of the River Euphrates around Babylon, the "waters of Babylon" where Judahites had been accustomed to gather and grieve over their exile (Psalm 137). In the context of the different attitude of the Persian administration they have a much more encouraging reason for gathering. Religiously, they need to seek God's protection and help for their journey. They back up their prayer with "self-affliction," which meant fasting. The point of fasting is not self-discipline; it is designed to reinforce their prayer for protection and help, to show God that they mean business. Old and New Testaments seem quite relaxed about the idea of underscoring prayer in this way in order to get God's attention. Going without food shows how serious we are in calling on God.

Amusingly, Ezra is all the more motivated to call on God because of another testimony he has given to his trust in God and his commitment to not "abandoning" God. He now realizes his boldness may have been over-hasty or reckless or dumb or presumptuous in claiming what God was going to do for him (especially publically in front of a king) and then being left vulnerable to enemies when the king could have provided some protection, particularly if the king was directed by God to do so. We will discover in the book of Nehemiah that this is not the kind of mistake Nehemiah makes. He is a more systematically practical guy. But it looks as if Ezra's embarrassed strategy and his fasting are effective. God "lets himself be interceded," assures the people that their prayer has been heard. Now they just have to wait to see how things actually work out in fulfillment of God's reassurance, wait to see whether they really complete the journey safely.

EZRA 8:24–36

The Hand of God

[24]I separated twelve of the priestly officials, Sherebiah and Hashabiah and with them ten of their brothers, [25]and weighed out to them the silver and gold and the utensils, the contribution for our God's house that the king, his counselors, his officials, and all Israel who were present, had raised. [26]I weighed out into their hand the silver, six hundred and fifty talents; the silver utensils, a hundred talents; the gold, one hundred talents; [27]the gold bowls, twenty, worth a thousand darics; and two utensils of good, shining bronze, as precious as gold. [28]I said to them, "You are sacred to Yahweh, and the utensils are sacred, and the silver and gold are a voluntary offering to Yahweh the God of your ancestors. [29]Be diligent and look after them until you weigh them out before the officials of the priests and Levites and the ancestral officials of Israel in Jerusalem in the chambers of Yahweh's house." [30]So the priests and Levites received the weighed out silver and gold and the utensils to bring to Jerusalem to our God's house. [31]We set off from the River Ahava on the twelfth of the first month to go to Jerusalem. The hand of our God was upon us and he saved us from the hand of enemies and ambush on the journey. [32]We came to Jerusalem, stayed there three days, [33]and on the fourth day the silver and gold and the utensils were weighed out in our God's house into the hand of Meremoth son of Uriah the priest and with him Eleazar son of Phinehas, and with them the Levites

61

Jozabad son of Jeshua and Noadiah son of Binnui , [34]by number or by weight with regard to everything. The entire weight was recorded at that time. [35]The exiles who came from the captivity presented burnt offerings to the God of Israel, twelve bulls for all Israel, ninety-six rams, seventy-seven lambs, and twelve goats as a purification offering. The whole was a burnt offering to Yahweh. [36]They gave the king's edicts to the king's satraps and the governors of Beyond-the-River, and they supported the people and the house of God.

There's one other aspect of the way Ezra talks that reminds me of the couple I spoke of in connection with chapters 5 and 6— the ones who had fallen in love unexpectedly when neither of them was as young as they once were. They can't believe that what feels to them as this extraordinary thing that has happened to them is just something that happened. They talk about it as a miracle. They could easily have missed each other. There was no visible miracle—no thunderbolts in the sky. But it seems too wonderful to understand as simply a chance occurrence. They don't speak of it as something brought about by the hand of God, but they could do so.

That is Ezra's expression. Variants on it have come six times. It was the hand of God that made the king agree to everything Ezra asked for. It was the hand of God that Ezra spoke of when he expressed to Artaxerxes his conviction that the party would get to Jerusalem safely. It was the hand of God that provided some **Levites** to complete the makeup of Ezra's party. It was the hand of God that did protect them on the journey. It was the hand of God that did bring the journey to Jerusalem to a successful conclusion. The use of this particular expression implies a paradox. When someone's hand is upon you, you feel it. There's no mistaking it or missing it. Yet the way Ezra uses the expression, it refers to something that is not perceptible or visible in that quasi-physical way. There is a kind of religious intuition that feels and sees the hand of God, yet it is not mere feelings or blind faith, because (Ezra might say) if you believe in the reality of God at all, the most rational explanation of what happened is to attribute it to God's invisible hand.

Ezra speaks thus as a man of faith, and he was perhaps impractical in the way he made it impossible to ask for imperial protection on the journey, but he is also practical in the way he makes sure that the party's very valuable cargo reaches its destination. It would not be surprising if all that gold and silver disappeared on the eight-hundred mile journey, and it might even be unscrupulous members of his party who give in to the temptation to disappear with it; hence the reminder that the cargo is sacred, as are priests to whom it is entrusted. Stealing it would be an act of sacrilege. People will be well-advised to regard stealing it as too risky.

One can imagine that the party's safe arrival would lead to the making of offerings in the temple, and not only because this was what Artaxerxes had commissioned. The offerings are mostly multiples of twelve, which again suggests the idea that they represent the whole of Israel with its twelve clans. The burnt offerings, given wholly to God, are an expression of praise. The purification offerings are recognition that people who have always lived away from Jerusalem will have accumulated defilement. Living in **Babylon** they could not have gained cleansing from the defilement of their community's involvement with alien gods, one of the reasons why their families were exiled. They will have accumulated the regular defilement that issues from contact with death and other experiences they could not avoid. They must not bring that defilement into the sanctuary. It would have been a huge relief to know that it could be dealt with and that they could join in the temple's regular worship.

EZRA 9:1–4

The Importance of Separation

[1]When these things were finished, the officials approached me to say, "The people of Israel and the priests and Levites have not separated themselves from the peoples of the countries, [but acted] in accordance with the abhorrent practices of the Canaanites, Hittites, Perizzites, Jebusites, Ammonites, Moabites, Egyptians, and Amorites, [2]because they have taken

some of their daughters for themselves and for their sons, and the sacred seed has mixed with the peoples of the countries, and the hand of the officials and overseers has been first in this trespass." [3]When I heard this thing, I tore my garment and my coat, pulled hair from my head and my beard, and sat shocked. [4]Anyone who was in awe of the words of Israel's God was gathering to me because of the exiles' trespass. I was sitting shocked until the evening offering.

I shocked our Bible Study a few weeks ago by saying that I couldn't see how Christians could visit Las Vegas, and I then shocked them a little later by making a similar observation about one of them who intended to celebrate his thirtieth birthday by following the whiskey trail in Kentucky. It's partly a cultural thing; people in the United States seem able to accept Las Vegas for what it is and not trouble too much about whether it is (among other things) exploitative and self-indulgent, and this extends to many Christians. Of course, I come from a culture in Britain that is exploitative and self-indulgent in its own ways and where Christians may also not question things. Few of us are affected by anything that could be called Puritan narrowness.

Israel was called to be different from the cultures around it, but Israel, too, rarely managed to live up to its calling, though the ministry of Ezra and Nehemiah perhaps brought a turning point in this matter. When Deuteronomy talks about the abhorrent practices of Israel's neighbors, it refers to practices such as making idols, worshiping other gods, sacrificing a son or a daughter, practicing divination, and consulting the dead; and the story that follows Deuteronomy in Kings and Chronicles notes from time to time that these are the practices that were indulged in by Israel's leaders and its people and that led to their being thrown out of the country in the same way as their predecessors had been. Ezra gives a fairly standard list of these peoples—the Canaanites, Hittites, Perizzites, Jebusites, and Amorites. The process whereby these people disappeared was actually a gradual one, and for centuries they continued to constitute a temptation to the Israelites to worship their way. But by Ezra's day there are no Canaanites, Hittites, Perizzites,

Jebusites, or Amorites in **Judah**. That may be one reason that the passage includes reference to the Ammonites, Moabites, and Egyptians, who appear elsewhere in Deuteronomy and are also around in Ezra's day; Ammon and Moab are provinces of the **Persian** Empire, like Judah. But the more general point about mentioning these peoples is the assumption that the **Torah** laid down a principle about relationships with other peoples, a principle that can be reapplied to relationships with the peoples who are in existence in Ezra and Nehemiah's time.

The books of Ezra and Nehemiah never explain why Judahites have married people from other communities. The background may be analogous to that which has applied to the Jewish community in our own day, as well as to other ethnic groups in the West. The exile meant the departure of most of the leadership and wealthy people from Jerusalem and Judah and subsequent decades likely meant the arrival into this vacuum of many people with initiative and resources from the surrounding area who would then become the people with prestige and power in Judah. For Judahites, marrying into such families would be a step up in life and might also buttress their security. These dynamics would affect both ordinary Judahites not taken into exile, and people who eventually made the move from **Babylon** to Judah.

The Torah does not ban marriage to all non-Israelites, and famous figures such as Joseph and Moses marry outside the community. While the story of Ruth emphasizes her Moabite identity, it does not suggest there is anything controversial about her marriage to either of her Israelite husbands. The basis for unease about intermarriage is not ethnic. Ezra 9 makes clear that it is not intermarriage itself that is the problem but the religious adherence of the couples involved. It is here that Ruth sets the standard; she has come to acknowledge **Yahweh**. In contrast, the marriages that are reported to Ezra are ones that involve a compromise over religious commitment. While the husband may continue to acknowledge Yahweh, the wife will continue to practice her own religion. Although the Torah associates the "abhorrent practices" listed above with the Canaanites and their contemporaries, they are also known among other peoples; they are common features of traditional religion in the Middle East and elsewhere. So it would not be surprising for these practices still to appear in Ezra's day, whatever the precise ethnic identity of the people involved.

The problem about the sacred seed mixing with the people of the countries in this way is that the family is a single unit. If one of the married couple worships other gods or practices divination (or wants to sacrifice one of their children), that affects the whole household. Even if one spouse is loyal to Yahweh and to the requirements of the Torah, such practices bring defilement on the whole household. They cannot avoid compromising the family's Israelite identity. They involve a **trespass**, a failure to respect Yahweh's rights over Israel. They involve ignoring the words Yahweh had laid down in the Torah.

It is for this reason that the action over mixed marriages is the first feature of Ezra's activity that the book reports, and indeed the issue on which the rest of the book focuses. The beginning of Ezra's story in chapter 7 began with an "after these things" that did not hint that sixty years had elapsed, and something similar may be true about the "When these things were finished" with which this story opens. Maybe we are not to assume that we are told the story in Ezra and Nehemiah in chronological order. Sometimes the Bible story tells us things in order of importance rather than in chronological order. It is only in Nehemiah 8 that we will read of Ezra the teacher doing some teaching, but it would not be surprising if the report in Ezra 9 formed a response to teaching activity that he had already engaged in. The people involved are described as Israel, including the priests and **Levites**, which implies that they are not limited to any particular group within the community. Ezra later refers to the people as the exiles. If some time has elapsed since Ezra's party arrived, they might include some of the people who came with him as well as people who had made the journey from Babylon over the previous century, though it would not be surprising if they also included people among the descendants of Judahites who had never gone into exile but had come to identify with the community in which people who returned from exile had gained the leadership. Such people might themselves have been used to getting on with their neighbors in too relaxed a fashion, and to intermarrying with them.

So the focus on this action immediately after the report of Ezra's arrival reflects its importance. It is a life and death issue for the community. God's purpose for Israel to be a light to the world, to bring about the world's blessing through Israel, depends on Israel continuing to exist with its distinctive testimony to who the real God is and how people may relate to this God. If it goes out of existence, the intention fails. There is good reason for Ezra to collapse in a state of shock. His physical expressions of his horror at what he hears are the actions of one who is mourning and grieving like someone who has been bereaved.

EZRA 9:5–15

How to Make Your People's Confession

⁵At the evening offering I got up from my self-affliction and in my torn garment and robe got down on my knees and spread my hands to Yahweh my God ⁶and said, "My God, I am embarrassed and ashamed to lift up my face to you, my God, because our wayward acts have increased to above our head, and our offense is great and extends to the heavens. ⁷From the days of our ancestors until this day we have been in great offense, and in our wayward acts we, our kings, our priests, have been given into the hand of the kings of the countries, with sword, captivity, pillage, and shame of face, this very day. ⁸But now for a little while there has been grace from Yahweh our God, who has left us a group of survivors and given us a stake in his holy place. Our God has brightened our eyes and given us a little life in our servitude. ⁹Because we are serfs, but in our serfdom our God has not abandoned us but has extended commitment to us before the kings of Persia. He has given us life and raised up our God's house and put in place its ruins and given us a fence in Judah and Jerusalem. ¹⁰But now what can we say, our God, after this? Because we have abandoned your commands ¹¹that you issued by the hand of your servants the prophets, saying, 'The country that you are entering to take possession of it is a country polluted by the pollution of the peoples of the countries through their abhorrent practices with which they have filled it from one end to the other in their defilement. ¹²So now do not give your daughters to their sons or take their daughters for

your sons, and do not inquire after their well-being or benefit, ever, so that you may be strong and eat the good of the country and enable your children to possess it forever.' [13]After all that has come upon us because of our wicked deeds and our great trespasses, when you, our God, have held back [from punishing], below our waywardness, and given us a group of survivors like this, [14]shall we again break your commands and intermarry with the peoples characterized by these abhorrent practices? Will you not be angry with us so as to finish us off so that there is no one left, no group of survivors? [15]Yahweh, God of Israel, you are in the right, because we are left as a group of survivors this very day. Here are we before you with our offenses, because we cannot stand before you on account of these."

One August day when I was a seminary student, I was driving home with a friend after having lunch with the rector of a parish in London. "He's a great guy," I observed, "it's a shame he's so brusque," and commented on an exchange between him and his housekeeper before we left. "But you're just like that," my friend said. "I'm not," I protested. "O yes you are," he replied, pointing out a recent exchange I had been involved in (significantly, I can't remember what that was). I had been unwittingly illustrating the way we see our own faults in other people. So when we do see a fault in someone else, we are wise to ask whether we see it because it is also ours. It was said of a Jewish teacher in the Ukraine called Zusya that he felt the sins of the people he met as his own, and blamed himself for them. Maybe he had learned that lesson; or maybe rather his feeling the sins of other people as his own meant he identified with them whether or not they were also his own.

When Ezra prays, he seeks God's mercy for "our wayward acts." Perhaps he is aware that he could be tempted to the same action as some of his fellow **Judahites**, but more likely he is identifying with the people who have undertaken these marriages. One indication is that he is not merely personally identifying with their waywardness but identifying the community as a whole with it. The action of a minority affects the whole people. A week ago, a young man who was mentally disturbed went on a shooting spree at a political event and killed nine people. The event has generated national shame and heart searching, causing people to ask, "What is wrong with us?" It has also generated shame on the part of the young man's family. We know we cannot simply say "It wasn't us, it was just a crazy individual." We are bound up with each other as families, communities, and nations. The stain and the guilt of the event spread from the individual to the family, the community, the nation.

Ezra knows that the stain and guilt of the marriages affect Judah as a whole, and prays in light of that fact. The time of the evening offering is the natural time to pray; prayer goes with sacrifice and sacrifice goes with prayer, so that word and action go together. Each day, the priests offer sacrifices at dawn and at dusk. The morning is the time when the people can dedicate the new day to God and seek God's blessing on it; the evening is the time when they can look back on the day in thanksgiving and contrition. On this particular day, there is something serious to give focus to their contrition. Recalling our history as the people of God regularly builds up our awareness of who we are. Ezra's prayer reminds us that one slant on the history is the way that it illustrates how we have often gone wrong, and that is the slant the people need at this moment when they come to pray their evening prayers.

The usual stance for prayer in Scripture is to stand before God as one stands before a king, with one's hands extended in appeal, though before God or king one might also go down on one's knees as a sign of self-humbling in order to underline one's status and need in making the request. Ezra has been in a position of simple self-abasement before God through the day. He now stays on his knees but adopts that second position for prayer, extending his hands to God. As happens when the community offers sacrifice, prayer is thus not merely a matter of feelings and words; it involves the whole person.

The solemn thing about the community defilement is that it is consistent with the people's lives over centuries. Admittedly, the story of Israel over preceding centuries does not suggest that ordinary people have been much involved in intermarriage, as kings such as Solomon were, for diplomatic reasons. But the people of God are always good at finding new ways to get in a moral mess, and this is the one that emerges in Ezra's context. So at this moment, intermarriage was its particular expression of *waywardness* (turning out of the right way, the way that will lead to the destination) and its form of *offense* (of failing to give God his due). The people have failed to learn from what has happened over their history. Their ancestors' waywardness and offenses led to the exile, and the people's own subjection to imperial subjugation continues to "this very day."

Ezra's comment on the continuing of such subjection indicates that his willingness to work with the possibilities offered by the **Persian** emperor's flexibility does not mean he simply accepts Judah's colonial status. Yet he recognizes that things are not as bad as they were a century ago. The people have been on the receiving end of God's grace. God's making it possible for Judahites to return from **Babylon** was not something they deserved. The prophecies in Isaiah 40–55 make explicit that the exiles had not learned anything from the fall of Jerusalem or the exile. Their freedom to return and rebuild the temple simply issued from God's grace. That was why the Judahites did not disappear from history the way other peoples did (remember the Perizzites, the Hittites, the Jebusites . . .).

That was why they found themselves still having a stake in Jerusalem. Paradoxically, the life of a tent-dweller provides them with a metaphor for picturing their being able to resettle in the city. They are like people who have been able to drive their tent pegs securely into the ground and thereby ensure that their tent remains stable. To move to another metaphor, God's grace is why they are like people who were weakened by lack of food and water but have been refreshed, so that their eyes are now brightened. That is why they have life in them, even though their political status is still that of serfs of the Persian Empire, people without political rights or independence. That is why Jerusalem and Judah are surrounded by a metaphorical fence, like a vineyard (a common image for the people of Israel), which will ensure that they are protected from wild animals—that is, from the attacks of their neighbors.

It is all this expression of God's grace that makes the community's waywardness scandalous and inexplicable. They knew that one basis for God's giving them the country was the waywardness of its inhabitants; God did not throw the Canaanites out simply because they were in the way. Yet now the Judahites are bringing into the heart of the community the very same waywardness. What were they thinking? The obligation that rested on them included that they should not be seeking the well-being or benefit of the Canaanites. There are contexts in which the people of God must radically dissociate themselves from wrongdoers, like the Corinthian church having nothing to do with the believers who were sexually immoral and giving them up to Satan (1 Corinthians 5).

Ezra associates the instructions about this matter with prophets, which is slightly odd as they actually come not from the Prophets but from the **Torah**, from passages such as Deuteronomy 7. But this reminds us that there is a sense in which the instructions in Deuteronomy are prophetic. They come from Moses, who is called a prophet. They parallel the challenges of prophets such as Hosea, and historically there was interplay between the Torah in general and Deuteronomy in particular and the emphases of such prophets. The Torah influenced them and they influenced the formulations that appear in the Torah.

The prayer closes with a paradox. Ezra prays as the representative of a people standing before God with its offenses, yet he acknowledges that it cannot stand before God because of them. His prayer thus involves boldness and reticence. He knows that God is in the right, he has no basis on which to appeal to God for mercy, and he does not do so. He just kneels there and lets his appeal be unspoken.

EZRA 10:1–5

Where There Is Commitment There Is Hope

[1]While Ezra was pleading and making confession, weeping and falling down before God's house, a very great congregation from Israel—men, women, and children—gathered to him because the people were weeping profusely. [2]Shecaniah, son of Jehiel of the descendants of Elam responded to Ezra, "We have trespassed against our God and let foreign women from the peoples of the country come to live with us. But now there is hope for Israel despite this, [3]so now let us seal a covenant to our

71

God to send away all the women and those born to them, by the decision of my lord and of those who are in awe of our God's command. It should be done in accordance with the teaching. ⁴Set to it, because the matter rests on you, and we are with you. Take courage and act." ⁵Ezra set to and swore the officials of the priests, the Levites, and all Israel to act in accordance with these words, and they swore.

Two student friends of mine fell in love while they were in seminary. It is a common enough occurrence, though never one that becomes something one fails to rejoice in. The trouble is that in this instance they were the same sex. That meant that their love had to be a secret from the seminary, whose "community standards" require a commitment to confining sexual activity to heterosexual marriage. While the couple wanted to get married, at the time same-sex marriage had not become a reality, but they made a covenant commitment to each other and wore rings (not on the usual finger) that symbolized this commitment. Their relationship also raised questions about their vocation, because one of them had sensed God's call to the ministry, but like the seminary her denomination required a commitment to confining sexual activity to heterosexual marriage. So for a while they had a sexual relationship, but they eventually felt that the secretive nature of their bond made for a lack of integrity in relation to their denomination, as well as for trouble if the nature of their relationship became known, so at some personal cost they pulled back from any sexual expression of their relationship and it became a celibate one.

There are some overlaps between the issues raised by same-sex relationships in our culture and those raised by the marriages to foreign women in the **Judahite** community in Ezra's day. The story of my two friends' relationship will arouse strong feelings for different people, in at least two directions. Some people will be outraged by the fact that this love relationship had to be frustrated by the rules of the seminary and the denomination (a church near where I live displays a poster declaring "We believe in marriage equality"). Other people will be outraged by the couple's continuing deceit, behaving as if they affirm the denomination's position when they do not do so and when they secretly undermine it. (In case you wonder, I am sympathetic to the position that the couple eventually adopted. I recognize that Scripture does not point to the acceptance of same-sex marriage, but I am sympathetic to the position of people who are attracted to people of the same sex and have to wrestle with the issue for themselves.)

Likewise, strong feelings are aroused by the marriages Ezra 9 describes and by the action proposed by Shecaniah and accepted by Ezra. In a Western cultural context we may be scandalized by Shecaniah's proposal, so we need to see the logic that lies behind it, suggested by chapter 9. Accepting these marriages imperils the very existence of Israel, already reduced to a small remnant. Further, in a Western context *the* point of marriage is the love relationship between two people, but that is an oddity of our Western context. In most cultural contexts, marriage is about a number of other things (such as cementing relationships between communities or providing a context in which children may grow or ensuring that women are provided for); the predominant emphasis on a personal relationship is a cultural distinctiveness of ours. Yes, I like it, too; but it is still a cultural oddity of ours. There is no particular reason to think that these Judahites and their Ammonite or Moabite wives made their marriages on the basis of having fallen in love as opposed to encouraging relationships between the communities or making it possible for single men to find a wife in order to start a family that would help look after the family land.

One hint of the fact that these would not be primarily love matches is the mention in Ezra's prayer of "giving your daughters to their sons or taking their daughters for your sons." Marriage is a family and a community business, not something that comes about simply because two people meet and fall in love. The implication is not that young people marry against their will; Old Testament stories about marriage typically portray a process in which the couple has their say one way or another. But the dynamics of the process are very different from Western ones. Further, Ezra's strange reference to not being concerned for the well-being or benefit of their foreign neighbors is suggestively juxtaposed to this description of the process whereby marriages come about. The marriages are designed to bring about well-being and prosperity for one side or the other or both. In other words, they have an economic rationale. Ah, now we are on ground that Western people can recognize, because economic development can be considered our supreme good! The Judahites are forbidden to look at life in that fashion.

The way the strong feelings work in the other direction in Judah also means that the story says nothing about what happens to the wives who get divorced and to their children. This omission does not imply that they simply get cast out into the wilderness to survive on their own (to judge from the story of Naomi, Ruth, and Orpah, they would go back to their birth families). It simply reflects the fact that what happens to them is not the issue the story needs to focus on. Admittedly, even if the basis for the marriages was often the practical considerations just noted, the marriages may well have become loving and devoted ones, as arranged marriages often do, and in at least some cases breaking them up would cause hurt to the members of these families. That fact reminds us that doing the wrong thing can cause long-term hurt even if we repent of the action. Indeed, it is putting things right that causes trouble. The fact that David repented of his action with Bathsheba and Uriah (2 Samuel 12) did not mean his life went back to where it was before. His son died and his story suggests that his relationship with God and his family life were never the same again. There is often a price to be paid for wrongdoing, and frequently it is people other than the wrongdoers who pay it.

We are perhaps to assume that people not only noticed that Ezra was praying and making confession the way he was, but that they also noticed the content of what he said. Certainly the people hearing this book read aloud in later decades and centuries were expected to learn from the content of his prayer, as we are expected to learn from the content of the prayers that Paul tells his congregations about in his letters when he relates to them that he is praying for them. We have noted that Ezra did not make any requests to God to forgive the people for their action. His prayer illustrates something about the nature of "making confession." While confession of sin in Scripture is an expression of sorrow, it does not involve going on to God about how sorry we are to the extent that it may for modern Christians; similarly, confession of faith does not involve going on to God about how grateful we are to the extent that it does for us. Confession involves giving a factual account of the wrong we have done or of the great things God has done.

But then (the prayer may imply) we cannot go on to plead with God to forgive the community for its actions when it has done nothing about the wrongdoing. It might be possible to ask God by implication not to let wrath fall on the community as it deserves, and thereby finish it off. But postponement would be the only thing that could be asked for until the community does something about the situation. It is Shecaniah's proposal that opens up the possibility of God's action being preempted and not merely postponed, or the possibility of a prayer like Ezra's going to ask for pardon (there are several men named Shecaniah in Ezra–Nehemiah, and we are not sure whether this Shecaniah can be identified with one of the others). Shecaniah knows that with God it's never over until it's over. "There is hope for Israel despite this," if the community does take action. The community needs to make a new commitment to God, to seal a specific **covenant** to God about this matter, a kind of codicil to the people's well-known covenant with God, reaffirming an aspect of that covenant. The **Torah** itself does not deal with the question of what people should do if they ignore its expectation that Israelites do not intermarry with people who worship other gods, so the proposal that the men terminate these marriages does not directly emerge from the Torah, but it is in keeping with the Torah in the sense that it seeks to restore the status quo that the Torah envisages.

EZRA 10:6–44

The Tough Action

⁶Ezra rose up from his place before God's house and went into the chamber of Jehohanan son of Eliashib. When he went there, he did not eat food and he did not drink water, because he was mourning over the trespass of the exiles. ⁷They issued a proclamation in Judah and Jerusalem to all the people from

the exile: that they should gather in Jerusalem. ⁸Anyone who should not come in three days, according to the decision of the officials and elders, all his property would be devoted and he would be separated from the congregation of the exiles. ⁹So all the men of Judah and Benjamin gathered in Jerusalem in three days; it was the ninth month, the twentieth day. All the people sat in the square at God's house, trembling about the matter and because of the rains. ¹⁰Ezra the priest rose up and said to them, "You have trespassed. You have brought foreign women home, adding to Israel's offenses. ¹¹But now, make confession to Yahweh, your ancestors' God, and do his will. Separate yourselves from the peoples of the country and from foreign women." ¹²The entire congregation responded with a loud voice, "Yes, [it is incumbent] upon us to act in accordance with your word. ¹³Nevertheless the company is large and the time is the rains. We do not have the stamina to stand outside, and the work is not for one day or two because we have become many in rebelling with regard to this matter. ¹⁴Our officials should stand to represent the entire congregation, and anyone in our cities who has brought foreign women home should come at set times, and with them the elders of each city and its authorities, until we turn away the angry burning of our God from us on account of this matter." ¹⁵Only Jonathan son of Asahel and Jahzeiah son of Tikvah stood against this; Meshullam and Shabbatai the Levites supported them. ¹⁶So the people from the exile acted in this way; Ezra the priest [and] the men who were the ancestral heads, for each ancestral family, and all of them by name, separated themselves and sat on the first day of the tenth month to inquire into the matter. ¹⁷They finished with all the men who had brought foreign women home by the first day of the first month.

¹⁸There were found among the sons of the priests who brought foreign women home Jeshua son of Jozadak and his brothers Maaseiah, Eliezer, Jarib, and Gedaliah. ¹⁹They set their hand [in pledge] to send away their wives and they offered a restitution offering, a ram from the flock, for their offense. ²⁰Of the sons of Immer, Hanani and Zebadiah. ²¹Of the sons of Harim, Maaseiah, Elijah, Shemaiah, Jehiel, and Uzziah. ²²Of the sons of Pashhur, Elionai, Maaseiah, Ishmael, Nethanel, Jozabad, and Elasah. ²³Of the Levites, Jozabad, Shinei, Kelaiah (that is, Kelitah), Pethahiah, Judah, and Eliezer. ²⁴Of the singers, Eliashib.

Of the gatekeepers, Shallum, Telem, and Uri. [25]Of the Israelites: of the sons of Parosh, Ramiah, Izziah, Malchijah, Mijamin, Eleazar, Malchijah, and Benaiah. [26]Of the sons of Elam, Mattaniah, Zechariah, Jehiel, Abdi, Jeremoth, and Elijah. [27]Of the sons of Zattu, Elioenai, Eliashib, Mattaniah, Jeremoth, Zabad, and Aziza. [28]Of the sons of Bebai, Jehohanan, Hananiah, Zabbai, and Athlai. [29]Of the sons of Bani, Meshullam, Malluch, Adaiah, Jashub, Sheal, and Ramoth. [30]Of the sons of Pathahmoab, Adna, Chelal, Benaiah, Maaseiah, Mattaniah, Bezalel, Binnui, and Manasseh. [31]Of the sons of Harim, Eliezer, Isshijah, Malchijah, Shemaiah, and Shimeon, [32]Benjamin, Malluch, and Shemariah. [33]Of the sons of Hashum, Mattenai, Mattattah, Zabad, Eliphelet, Jeremai, Manasseh, and Shimei. [34]Of the sons of Bani, Maadai, Amram, and Uel, [35]Benaiah, Bedeiah, Cheluhu, [36]Vaniah, Meremoth, Eliashib, [37]Mattaniah, Mattenai, Jaasai, [38]Bani, Binnui, Shimei, [39]Shelemiah, Nathan, Adaiah, [40]Machnadebai, Shashai, Sharai, [41]Azarel, Shelemiah, Shemariah, [42]Shallum, Amariah, Joseph. [43]Of the sons of Nebo, Jeiel, Mattithiah, Zabad, Zebina, Jaddai and Joel, Benaiah. [44]All these had taken foreign wives, and there were some of them who were women who had borne children.

One holiday weekend when I was a boy, we went for a family vacation to stay with an aunt who lived by the ocean. As we were nearing our destination my father got frustrated at the way we had been forced to drive for some distance behind a slow truck and decided to overtake it when the road seemed clear, despite the fact that there was a "no overtaking" double line down the center of the road. He was not breaking the law, because at that time such a double line was only advisory, but the line was there for a good reason. The road was about to go down a dip and my father could not see that actually it was not clear, and we crashed into a car coming the other way. No one was hurt, but my father was taken to court and fined and his driver's license was endorsed. Now after a certain period of time one can have such an endorsement removed from one's license, and some years later I asked my father why he had not asked for this to happen. His reply was that he wanted to leave the reminder of the mistake he had made, maybe partly as a reminder for me.

I wonder why Ezra includes the list of men who had undertaken foreign marriages? In the immediate aftermath of the event, publicizing the list would surely underline a sense of shame among the men who appear on it, though they might eventually be able to look at it the way my father did his endorsement. Being among the offenders but keeping it a secret and worrying whether people would ever discover it, or having it be something that people knew about but that no one ever talked about, might be a greater burden than the sense of shame that one had at least done something about. Confession before other people as well as before God brings a kind of relief.

So the fact that the chapter lists men who did the right thing might give them a sort of sense of honor. They did the wrong thing, but they put it right. The reason for including the list in the book is perhaps to make a more general statement of that kind before God. It constitutes a claim to have taken really seriously the question of marrying people who would compromise commitment to Yahweh. The amusing note about having a hard time because of the rain underlines the point. Late in the ninth month, when the year starts with Passover would imply December, the time for the early winter rains.

Ezra apparently goes to the chamber of Jehohanan, son of Eliashib, to draw up the proclamation that follows. In Nehemiah's day there was a senior priest called Jehohanan who was a grandson of someone called Eliashib, but if Ezra's mission dates to the time of Artaxerxes I, this probably is a different Jehohanan. "Devoting" someone's property would mean it was forfeited to God and would become part of the assets of the temple. The final sanction mentioned in the proclamation means that a man who has married someone from one of the other communities has to make a choice about who he belongs to. He can be an Ammonite or a Moabite if he wishes, and serve Ammonite or Moabite deities, or he can be a Judahite and serve Yahweh. He cannot try to combine allegiances. He has to choose whom he serves.

Ezra's response to the assembly makes explicit the point that emerges from his prayer and from Shecaniah's proposal. When things go wrong, the repentance required needs to involve confession (Ezra's contribution) and a return to doing God's will (the action that issues from Shecaniah's proposal). But there is a third element in the response. In addition, the priests offer a restitution offering. Maybe the story assumes that they offered it on behalf of all the men involved, or maybe their priestly status made them especially guilty. Either way, the nature of a restitution offering is to offer something that symbolically makes up for the wrong one has done. It gives further expression to the fact that people are changing their allegiance.

Ezra 9–10 shares a feature of many other biblical stories: that it does not comment on the right and wrong of what it relates. It does not say that Ezra did the right thing, though its general attitude to Ezra strongly implies that the priest-scholar did do so. Yet its omitting to make the point leaves a loophole to readers. Often the Bible tells of people doing things that it would not approve of, yet it does not make this point explicit. So we might wonder whether the book leaves open to us the possibility of asking whether Ezra's action fits the rest of Scripture. Perhaps there was no ideal action for Ezra to take; breaking up the marriages was a horrific action but simply accepting the practice of intermarriage really would imperil the future of the community. It could mean the Jewish community disappearing like the Ammonites and Moabites and the Christian church never coming into being. We would be wise to think twice before assuming that as Western readers we are likely to see right and wrong more clearly than Ezra did.

NEHEMIAH 1:1–4

A Group of Survivors, Troubled and Disgraced

[1]The acts of Nehemiah son of Hacaliah. In the month of Kislev in the twentieth year, when I was in the fortress of Susa, [2]Hanani, one of my brothers, came, he and some men from Judah, and I asked them about the Judahites, the group of survivors that was left from the exile, and about Jerusalem. [3]They said to me, "The people who are left, who are left from the exile, are in great trouble and disgrace there in the province. Jerusalem's wall is broken down and its gates set on fire." [4]When I heard these things I sat and wept and grieved for days. I was fasting and pleading before the God of the heavens.

It was a week after we moved to California that Princess Diana was killed in a car crash, and over the weeks that followed I was perplexed by accounts in the media of the national reaction to this event in Britain. On a smaller scale this sense of puzzlement recurs from time to time as I watch or read of events in Britain and of what British people are (allegedly) thinking. It has recurred this week as I have watched the movie *The King's Speech* and read newspaper accounts of responses to it in Britain. People often ask me about some aspect of British life, and I have to remind myself and them that fourteen years have passed since I lived in Britain and that I now may have little more clue about Britain than anyone else who lives in the United States and relies on the media for an understanding of what is happening across the Atlantic. With some shame I realize that I now pray regularly for the United States and the church here and not for Britain and the British church (I will change that tomorrow).

Nehemiah apparently knew nothing about how things were back in **Judah**. Susa was one of the most important capitals of the **Persian** Empire; it lies to the west of Persia proper, and thus not so far from **Babylon**. The obvious way to read this story is to assume that the king is still Artaxerxes I, and that the year is the twentieth of his reign (445). The date is thus a century after the time when Cyrus first encouraged Judahites to move from Babylon to rebuild the temple, and half-way through the lifetime of the Persian Empire, which Alexander brought to an end in the 330s. Thirteen years have passed since Ezra's mission, but it has been maintained that one or both actually belong later, in the reign of Artaxerxes II. We will discover from chapter 8 that Ezra is still in Jerusalem, though we will also discover from chapter 13 that Nehemiah made at least one trip back to Susa, and perhaps Ezra did something similar.

The way news arrives from Nehemiah's brothers and some other Judahites indicates the possibility of movement between Jerusalem and the Persian capital, though it may imply that (like Ezra and Nehemiah) Hanani and company were involved in the imperial administration and its oversight of Judah; they had not just gone to Judah on a family visit or on vacation. The description of the community as "the group of survivors that was left from the exile" could recognize that it included both people who had returned from exile in Babylon and people who had not been in Babylon but had survived the exile in Judah itself and identified with the community headed up by people who had moved from Babylon over the previous century. But the expression indicates that the community was still in a weak and reduced state. It is only a group of survivors. The point is underscored by the further description of it as in great trouble and disgrace. We already know from Ezra of tensions between Judah and the other local communities (the neighboring Persian sub-provinces are Samaria, Ashdod, Edom, Moab, and Ammon), and one can imagine that the trickiness of these relations would underline the Judahite sense of shame that they were in a bad state.

The problem would be more serious than a sense of embarrassment, at which people might just need to shrug their shoulders. A city has walls and gates for its protection; even Susa is a fortress city. In the twenty-first century, Jerusalem's impressive walls and gates are simply an impressive tourist attraction, but in the fifth century they would potentially be a matter of life and death. And they are broken down and burned. While it is possible that Hanani is simply reporting that the city is still in the state it has been since its destruction by the Babylonians, the devastating effect of the news on Nehemiah rather suggests that some other disaster has happened more recently and that this is when news of it reaches Susa; Hanani is referring not merely to the long-lasting trouble and disgrace. We have no other record of such an event, but it would again fit with the account of troubled relations in the region, and it wouldn't be surprising if the Judahites were better at building a temple and sorting out intermarriage problems than at fighting off a siege.

NEHEMIAH 1:5–11a

Boldness as God's Servant

⁵I said, "Oh! Yahweh, God of the heavens, great and awe-inspiring God, keeping covenant and commitment to people who dedicate themselves to him and keep his commands!

⁶Please may your ear become attentive and your eyes opened to listen to the plea of your servant that I am making before you today, day and night, for your servants the Israelites, making confession concerning the failings of the Israelites of which we have been guilty in relation to you. I and my ancestors have failed. ⁷We have acted very damagingly in relation to you. We have not kept the commands, the statutes, and the rulings that you commanded your servant Moses. ⁸Will you be mindful of the word you commanded your servant Moses, 'Should you people offend, I for my part will scatter you among the peoples, ⁹but should you turn to me and keep my commands and do them, if your dispersed people are at the end of the heavens, from there I will gather them and bring them to the place where I chose to have my name dwell.' ¹⁰And they are your servants and your people that you redeemed by your great strength and your strong hand. ¹¹Oh! My Lord! Please may your ear become attentive to your servant's plea and to the plea of your servants who want to revere your name. Will you enable your servant to succeed today and give him compassion before this man."

In church yesterday we were discussing Jesus' "Beatitudes" or Blessings in the Sermon on the Mount and we got into a friendly fight over what we have to do as Jesus' disciples, or rather about the implications of the way the Blessings don't focus on what we have to do; they are addressed to people who can't do much, who are poor in spirit or mourning or meek or hungry or persecuted. Someone commented on the way women in Sudan who have been raped still rejoice in God, and someone else recalled how many people in Haiti after the earthquake there were still rejoicing in God. Afterward a member of the congregation said that the discussion had made it possible for her to turn a corner in her relationship with God. She is someone passionately committed to working for justice and passionately angry with God for not doing more to bring about justice in the world; she had seen that she needed not to assume too much of the burden herself and not to miss what God was doing.

Nehemiah's prayer raises some related issues. He prays as someone who is himself committed to what he prays about and he prays urgently to get God to take the action that only God can take; further he recognizes the failure of the people on whose behalf he prays. His reaction to the news from Jerusalem reminds us of Ezra's reaction to the news about the marriages, though it is expressed in different terms. Nehemiah sits (in shock like Ezra?) and weeps and mourns like a person grieving over someone's death. Psalm 137 expresses the commitment of **Judahites** in **Babylon** never to forget Jerusalem; this Judahite in Susa accepts the same commitment, and reacts to the news from Jerusalem like someone whose beloved has died. On the other hand his fasting compares with Ezra's action as his company was preparing for their journey to Jerusalem and they needed to seek God's protection for their journey, and his pleading does compare with Ezra's action when he hears about the marriages.

Nehemiah's prayer begins with the two forms of confession that we noted in connection with Ezra's prayer. First there is confession of who God is; that is a common feature of prayer in the Bible. It is the foundation for all that follows. We pray because God is the God who has invited us to call him by **name**, the name **Yahweh**, but the God who is not merely someone in a personal relationship with us but is the all-powerful Lord (the God of the heavens). To put the same two points the other way around, this God is great and awe-inspiring, yet also one who keeps **covenant** and **commitment**, one who can be relied on to be faithful to words and undertakings. The sting in the tail that Nehemiah knows he needs to recognize is that you can only appeal to these qualities if you are people who dedicate themselves to God (the verb is the one conventionally translated "love," but it signifies a self-giving loyalty, not merely an emotion) and who keep God's commands. Like a human being, it is possible that God may keep a covenant and commitment even though the other party in the relationship does not do so. But we would be unwise to presume this, like a husband who is unfaithful to his wife who assumes that everything will be okay if he expresses regret.

The sting in the tail is a serious qualifier for Nehemiah. He knows that his people have not been faithful to their side of the relationship. Again, like Ezra in his prayer, he knows he has to acknowledge the wayward history of Israel over the centuries. If the destruction of Jerusalem's walls and gates is a recent one, then it is a kind of aftershock of events in 587, and thus of the chastisement that those events embodied. In other words, while the actions of the present generation may have led to their present troubles, there is no presupposition or indication that this is so. As he knows he has to identify with his people's waywardness in order to make confession of it, he knows that the present generation of his people has to identify with their forebears' waywardness and make confession of it. There is no pretending that the sins of one generation are not visited on the next generation.

So Nehemiah knows he has to acknowledge his people's failings; it is the word usually translated "sins," but "failings" is its background meaning. Nehemiah takes this failure seriously; he uses the word three times, making confession "concerning the failings of the Israelites with which we have failed in relation to you; I and my ancestors have failed." You might still say it is a cliché, but if so, his subsequent reference to "damage" is much less so. This word is also repeated to underscore the point—more literally, "with damage we acted damagingly." It is the word used in Ezra to refer to damaging the temple. It is as if people were seeking to damage God or damage God's interests when they failed to do what God said, as if they were seeking to attack God.

Yet Nehemiah also knows that the same **Torah** that warned of the consequences of willful failure also promised that chastisement need not be the end. In a way God is indeed like a wife whose husband can have good hope that she will welcome him back, if there is real change in his life. Further, like Moses, Nehemiah can appeal to the fact that it is not really in God's interests to abandon Israel because this means wasting the effort God put into redeeming Israel from Egypt in the first place.

There is one further basis for his prayer, though it involves a paradox. Like Ezra, Nehemiah identifies with his people in their wrongdoing. He knows we cannot say that our nation's or our church's failure belongs to them and not to us. We are part of our nation and church and are implicated in their failure. Yet Nehemiah goes on to appeal to the fact that he is God's servant. He has applied the term "God's servants" to his people, the people who failed and did damage, but evidently that was a kind of honorary description. They had not been behaving like servants. But when he calls himself God's servant, he means he really is committed to his master. The point is made explicit by his going on to refer to servants who revere God's name—in other words, people who know who God is and who behave accordingly. Revering God implies doing what God says. Alongside the fact of long-lasting failure on the part of God's servants, Nehemiah wants God to note the commitment of servants like himself and Hanani, and even to take more account of the latter than the former. On their behalf he is prepared to say, "I am willing to do whatever you ask to make up for the offense we caused you—tell me what that is." He thereby puts himself in the position of being the unconditional servant of the master.

In his particular circumstances, he knows that the first thing he needs is for the king to feel some compassion for him. It is not a regular kingly virtue, though there is a possibility that his particular relationship with the king means Artaxerxes will care about something that Nehemiah cares about, when he might not care about the sorry state of an obscure city on the edge of his empire for its own sake.

Nehemiah knows how to go about appealing to God to do what Nehemiah himself passionately desires for his people.

NEHEMIAH 1:11b–2:10

Boldness (and Discretion) as a King's Servant

1:11bNow I myself was the king's butler.

2:1So in the month of Nisan in King Artaxerxes' twentieth year, when wine was before him, I took the wine and gave it to the king. I had not been troubled in front of him, 2so the king said to me, "Why is your face troubled? You are not ill. This can only be trouble of mind." I became very much afraid, 3but I said to the king, "Long live the king! Why should my face not be troubled when the city that is my ancestors' burial place is devastated and its gates have been consumed by fire?" 4The king said to me, "What are you requesting?" I pleaded with the God of the heavens 5and said to the king, "If it is pleasing to the king and if your servant seems pleasing before you, that you send me to Judah to the city that is my ancestors' burial place so that I may build it up." ⁶The king said to me, with the consort sitting at his side, "How long will your journey be? When will you come back?" It seemed pleasing before the king, he sent me, and I gave him a date. ⁷I said to the king, "If it is pleasing to the king, may they give me letters to the governors of Beyond-the-River so that they may let me pass on until I come to Judah, ⁸and a letter to Asaph the keeper of the king's park so that he may give me timber for roofing the gates of the fortress that belongs to the house, for the city wall, and for the house to which I shall come." The king gave them to me in accordance with the good hand of my God upon me. ⁹I came to the governors of Beyond-the-River and gave them the king's letters; the king sent with me army officers and cavalry. ¹⁰But when Sanballat the Horonite and Tobiah the Ammonite servant heard, it was very displeasing to them that someone had come to inquire after the good fortune of the Israelites.

I have friends who pray "arrow prayers" for things such as a convenient parking place. In origin, that phrase refers to a prayer like the Jesus Prayer—"Lord Jesus Christ, Son of God, have mercy on me, a sinner"—the kind of prayer one might pray at any time of the day as part of "praying without ceasing," but it can also denote a more specific brief prayer one utters in the midst of some practical need. I quite often thank God for a convenient parking place and for other such trivial blessings, though I have a hard time providing the theological rationale for doing so; did God intervene to make that woman pull out of that spot, or was her move written into God's plan for the world from the beginning? I do sometimes say to God, "It would be nice if . . . (e.g., we found a parking place quickly as I am late for this meeting)." But I lack the conviction or the theological rationale to actually ask for something that is really just a matter of convenience.

I'm not sure whether Nehemiah would think me a man of unfaith. He is a practical, down-to-earth, bricks-and-mortar guy, and part of his reaction to the news from Jerusalem is evidently to commit himself to trying to do something about it. But interwoven with this aspect of its portrayal of him, the story shows him as a man who prays. I wouldn't be surprised if he prayed facing Jerusalem at the times of the morning and evening sacrifice, like Daniel (and Ezra, I suspect). We know that praying was his first reaction to the bad news from Jerusalem.

The close of that prayer indicated that he knows he has to seek to become the means of doing something about his concern for Jerusalem. We should not infer that we are always the people who have to become the means of resolving issues we pray about. It is easy for prayer to become merely an indirect means of our exhorting ourselves to take responsibility for something. While it is possible to be guilty of using prayer as a way of evading action, in Western culture we are at least as likely to assume that everything depends on us, and our prayer is mere formality. The word for prayer that Nehemiah uses is the word *plead*. It is a word that belongs in the courtroom, the word one would use of a person begging for justice or mercy in a situation that we can do nothing about.

It is in following up the plea with which he initially responds to the news from Jerusalem that he prays an arrow prayer in the course of his conversation with the king. Nehemiah lived in Susa as an important member of the king's staff. As butler he would be in charge of the wine cellar; he would also have the responsibility of tasting the king's wine to make sure it wasn't poisoned. The office could mean he was close to the king as companion and confidante, and the way events unfold indicates that he was indeed in a position to make use of his status. He is not in need of a parking place; rather, he knows this is the moment when he can take action in connection with his commitment to try to do something about the news from Jerusalem. He knows he can hardly walk out of his job as the king's right-hand man in domestic affairs. He knows that in any case he needs imperial authorization and support if he is to take any action about that situation in Jerusalem. But he also knows that as the butler he is asking for something way beyond his pay grade. You could say he is asking for some role reversal. Instead of his doing what the king asks, he wants the king to do what he asks. The granting of his request will require something of a miracle.

Maybe his earlier prayer for compassion relates to the fear he now expresses. It is usually assumed that his fear relates to a requirement of etiquette that expects a king's staff to look cheerful; when you go to work, you leave your personal issues at the door. The stories in Daniel and Esther show how volatile kings can be.

The king's response to the dejected look on his face might suggest compassion rather than affront, but Nehemiah also knows he probably has only one shot at getting the king's approval for the plan he has been forming in his mind. Once again he shows that he is a man of action as well as a man of prayer. He comes straight out with the reason for his dejected look, and his phrasing it in terms of Jerusalem's being the city where his ancestors were buried would be calculated to appeal to the king in the context of a culture where one's family burial place would be a place deserving of great respect. At this stage Nehemiah makes no mention of the city walls.

It is when Artaxerxes responds positively to his explanation that he utters his arrow prayer. "Okay, what do you want me to do?" Artaxerxes says, or perhaps "What do you want to do?" It means something that he refrains from punishing Nehemiah for looking gloomy, but will the king's regard for Nehemiah and his compassion extend to authorizing him to go to Jerusalem to do something about the situation there? Will his compassion extend from Nehemiah to the city? That is the subject of his arrow prayer. It's not clear why the presence of the king's consort is mentioned. Maybe the fact that the two men have company makes it harder for the king to grant Nehemiah's request, lest he look weak in front of her; or maybe it provides part of the explanation why Artaxerxes was in a good mood at what was apparently a private dinner rather than a state occasion where a woman would not have been present. If so, it was one of the incidental factors that contributed to Nehemiah's prayer receiving a favorable answer.

Nehemiah goes on to other practicalities. He needs resources. As was the case with the temple rebuilding, he will be able to reuse the stone from the demolished wall, but he will need timber for its towers, gates, and for the temple fortress, the stronghold north of the temple mount that guarded the approach to it. The reference to Nehemiah's own house suggests his family abode, which will need rebuilding in the same way as much of the city. The Jewish name of the imperial overseer of the king's forestry park suggests that it was in the area of **Judah**, and it would make sense for Nehemiah to use local timber rather than haul it from Susa (the word for "garden" is the **Persian** word *pardes* from which we derive the word Paradise—though the word is not used with this sense in the Old Testament).

Nehemiah also needs to be able to establish his authorization to do the work when he meets Artaxerxes' staff, who are responsible for oversight in the province. The wisdom of that request soon emerges in the reference to the displeasure of Sanballat the Horonite and Tobiah the Ammonite, of whom we shall hear much more. The description of Sanballat as a Horonite is puzzling, though it may suggest that he was actually by origin a Judahite from Beth-horon, west of Jerusalem. More significant is the fact that a Jewish document from Egypt mentions him as a governor of Samaria, which fits with comments later in Nehemiah. The designation of Tobiah the Ammonite as a servant may suggest that he was one of Sanballat's subordinates, perhaps with responsibility for Jerusalem if Jerusalem was governed from Samaria. If that was the position of the two men, it would explain why they were not pleased that Nehemiah was interfering in affairs in Jerusalem.

NEHEMIAH 2:11–3:14

No Gifts Required

[11]When I came to Jerusalem and had been there for three days, [12]I set to by night, I and a few men with me. I did not tell anyone what my God had put into my mind to do for Jerusalem, and there was no animal with me except the animal I was riding on. [13]I went out through the Canyon Gate by night, toward the Jackals Spring and the Trash Gate. I examined the walls of Jerusalem that had been breached and its gates that had been consumed by fire. [14]I passed on to the Spring Gate and the King's Pool, but there was no room for the animal under me to pass. [15]So I went up through the wash by night and examined the wall, then returned and came in through the Canyon Gate. Thus I returned, [16]and the overseers did not know where I had gone or what I was doing; I had not yet told the Judahites, the

priests, the heads, the overseers, and the rest of those responsible for the work.

[17]Then I said to them, "You see the trouble we are in, that Jerusalem is devastated and its gates have been consumed by fire. Come, let's build up the wall of Jerusalem and no longer be in disgrace." [18]I told them of my God's hand, that it was good upon me, and also of the king's words that he had said to me, and they said, "Let's set to and build." So they strengthened their hands for the good work. [19]But when Sanballat the Horonite, Tobiah the Ammonite servant, and Geshem the Arab heard, they mocked at us and abused us. They said, "What is this thing that you are doing? Are you rebelling against the king?" [20]I returned a message to them and said to them, "The God of the heavens—he will enable us to succeed. We, his servants, will set to and build. For you there will be no share or rights or honor in Jerusalem."

[3:1]So Eliashib the senior priest and his brother priests set to and built up the Sheep Gate. They consecrated it and put in place its doors, and as far as the Hundred Tower they consecrated it, as far as Hananel's Tower. [2]Next to him the men of Jericho built. Next to him Zaccur son of Imri built. [3]The sons of Hassenaah built up the Fish Gate, roofed it, and put in place its doors, bolts, and bars. [4]Next to them Meremoth son of Uriah son of Hakkoz repaired. Next to them Meshullam son of Berechiah son of Meshezabel repaired. Next to them Zadok son of Baana repaired. [5]Next to them the Tekoites repaired, but their nobles did not bend their neck to the work of their lord. [6]The Jeshanah Gate Joiada son of Paseah and Meshullam son of Besodeiah repaired; they roofed it and put in place its doors, bolts, and bars. [7]Next to them Melatiah the Gibeonite and Jadon the Meronothite repaired (men of Gibeon and Mizpah under the rule of the governor of Beyond-the-River). [8]Next to him Uzziel son of Harhaiah (goldsmiths) repaired. Next to him Hananiah of the perfumers repaired, but they left out Jerusalem as far as the broad wall. [9]Next to them Rephaiah son of Hur, official over half the district of Jerusalem, repaired. [10]Next to them Jedaiah son of Harumaph repaired in front of his house. Next to him Hattush son of Hashabneiah repaired. [11]A second section Malchijah son of Harim and Hasshub son of Pahath-moab repaired, and the Ovens Tower. [12]Next to him Shallum son of Hallohesh, official over half the district of Jerusalem, repaired, he and his daughters. [13]The Canyon Gate Hanun and the inhabitants of Zanoah repaired. They built it up and put in place its doors, bolts, and bars, and a thousand cubits of the wall as far as the Trash Gate. [14]The Trash Gate Malchijah son of Rechab, official over the district of Beth-haccerem, repaired; he built it up and put in place its doors, bolts, and bars.

A cartoon in this week's *New Yorker* pictures a sole cowboy whose horse carries bumper stickers on its rear, proclaiming (for instance) "How's my riding?" and providing a number to call to give your answer; "I brake for cacti"; and "My daughter is an honors student at a dude ranch." While the cartoon made me picture Nehemiah on his horse, the last sticker set me thinking. It reminded me of the conviction that every child is special. It seems a counter-intuitive idea; it robs the word *special* of meaning, even though one affirms its concern to declare that every child matters. In turn that made me think of Paul's declaration in 1 Corinthians 12 about the different gifts in the body of Christ, from which people sometimes infer that everyone has his or her gift. I think that inference devalues the meaning of the idea of gifts. You don't have to have a special gift to be an important member of the body.

In the rebuilding of Jerusalem's walls, no one has a special gift. Or rather, many people had special gifts, but their gifts were irrelevant to the project (in the terms of 1 Corinthians, it is more important that people are living lives of dedication to each other's needs than that they are exercising gifts). There were goldsmiths and a perfumer involved, but their gifts were totally irrelevant. There were priests, but their regular work in God's service was also irrelevant to this project and they didn't make this work a reason for not being involved in the building project. There were administrators or overseers, but they didn't make this work an excuse to avoid getting their trowels out. There were people from Jericho and Tekoa, who didn't make their not being Jerusalemites an excuse (though apparently some of the important people in Tekoa found more important things to do) and people from Gibeon and Mizpah (who didn't appeal to their not living in this province and thus being under the authority of the governor of Samaria, or to its being indiscrete for them to be associated with the work because of this fact). There were women as well as men, even though one might have thought of this laborious work as men's work.

We do not know enough of the extent and shape of Jerusalem nor of the location of its different gates to be sure of the route of Nehemiah's ride or of the course of the building works, though it is clear enough that the places are listed in counterclockwise order around the city. Nehemiah undertakes his survey by night presumably because he knows Sanballat will have aides in the city and because he wants to establish the dimensions of the project before he starts getting people involved in undertaking it. He leaves by the Canyon Gate on the west and proceeds south to the Trash Gate, then turns north to go up the city's east side and back to the Canyon Gate. On that side of the city the slopes are especially steep and this may explain the fact that Nehemiah cannot ride his donkey all the way and has to proceed on foot. Likewise the general trickiness of the southern part of the wall may explain why it is the only area Nehemiah actually investigates; the northern part would provide fewer problems.

When the building work starts, the priests naturally enough accept responsibility for the section near the temple; the Sheep Gate is to the northeast corner, and its name likely derives from its being the way sheep came into the city for sacrifice in the temple. While in due course the whole wall will be dedicated, it would be natural for the priests to want to consecrate their section immediately, with its importance for the sanctuary, or for there to be extra reference to the fact that they consecrated this part of the wall. The towers are perhaps part of the fortress that belonged to the temple, which Nehemiah mentioned to Artaxerxes. The account of the work moves westward and then south to the western gate where Nehemiah started, and on the Trash Gate to the far south. It covers a much broader area than Nehemiah surveyed, but the reference to abandoning part of the city suggests that Nehemiah's wall encloses a smaller area than Jerusalem covered before the exile.

I guess you could say that Nehemiah himself has a special gift as the leader of the project, though the Bible hardly speaks of leadership as a spiritual gift. Further, the Bible talks in terms of servants of God, rather than leaders of people. Indeed, "servant of God" was Nehemiah's own word for himself in chapter 1. His profession also involved him in acting as servant of the king, and he will now need to serve his project and the people involved in it. But crucial to serving the project are qualities we might associate with leadership, exercising initiative in getting to Jerusalem, acquiring resources, surveying the wall, establishing the nature of the work that needs doing, and inspiring the city's leadership to take on the project.

Not for the last time the story implies that Nehemiah is not put off by opposition any more than by the magnitude of a task. It seems to happen over and over that as soon as people make a start on God's work, adversaries arise against them; the pattern runs through Ezra–Nehemiah. Along with Sanballat and Tobiah from the area north of Jerusalem there is now reference to Geshem the Arab, who is also mentioned outside the Old Testament and seems to have been a ruler from the south of **Judah**. Maybe his involvement explains the reluctance of the leadership in Tekoa (in the far south of Judah) to get involved in Nehemiah's project.

Nehemiah's closing retort expresses the greatness of his confidence in the context of their scorn. His opponents are right that his work threatens their interest in having control of Judah. He declares that they will have no share or rights or honor in Jerusalem. Share, rights, and honor in Jerusalem belong to God, who has claimed them by putting his **name** there, a sign of asserting ownership. Nehemiah is affirming that his opponents will be disappointed. They will have no authority there. Judah may stay under **Persian** control, but it will be independent of the other sub-provinces in the region.

NEHEMIAH 3:15–4:6

May Their Mockery Rebound on Them

[15]The Spring Gate, Shallun son of Col-hozeh the official over the district of Mizpah repaired; he built it up, covered it, and

put in place its doors, bolts, and bars, and [repaired] the wall of the Pool of Siloam belonging to the King's Garden, as far as the steps that go down from David's City. ¹⁶After him Nehemiah the son of Azbuk, official over half the district of Beth-zur, repaired as far as David's graves and the artificial pool and the Warriors House. ¹⁷After him the Levites repaired: Rehum son of Bani. Next to him Hashabiah, official over half the district of Keilah, repaired for his district. ¹⁸After him their brothers repaired: Bavvai son of Henedad, official over half the district of Keilah. ¹⁹Next to him Ezer son of Jeshua, official over Mizpah, repaired a second section, from opposite the ascent to the armory at the buttress. ²⁰After him Baruch son of Zaccai burned with zeal; he repaired a second section, from the buttress to the entrance of the house of Eliashib the senior priest. ²¹After him Meremoth son of Uriah son of Hakkoz repaired a second section, from the entrance of Eliashib's house to the end of Eliashib's house. ²²After him the priests, the men of the area around, repaired. ²³After him Benjamin and Hasshub repaired opposite their house. After him Azariah son of Maaseiah son of Ananiah repaired next to his house. ²⁴After him Binnui son of Henadad repaired a second section, from the house of Azariah to the buttress and the corner. ²⁵Palal son of Uzzai: from opposite the buttress and the tower that goes out from the king's house, the upper tower that belongs to the court of the guard. After him Pedaiah son of Parosh ²⁶(the assistants were living on the Ophel as far as opposite the Water Gate to the east and the tower that goes out). ²⁷After him the Tekoites repaired a second section from opposite the big tower that goes out to the wall of the Ophel. ²⁸Above the Horse Gate, the priests repaired, each one opposite his house. ²⁹After him Zadok son of Immer repaired opposite his house. After him Shemaiah son of Shechaniah, keeper of the East Gate, repaired. ³⁰After him Hananiah son of Shelemiah and Hanun sixth son of Zalaph repaired a second section. After him Meshullam son of Berechiah repaired opposite his chamber. ³¹After him Malchijah of the goldsmiths repaired as far as the house of the assistants and the merchants, opposite the Muster Gate and as far as the upper room at the corner. ³²Between the upper room at the corner to the Sheep Gate the goldsmiths and the merchants repaired.

⁴:¹When Sanballat heard that we were building the wall, it incensed him. He became very vexed, but mocked the Juda-

hites [2]and said in front of his brothers and the Samarian army, "What are the feeble Judahites doing? Will they leave it to themselves? Will they sacrifice? Will they finish today? Will they bring to life the stones from the heaps of rubble, when they are burnt?" [3]Tobiah the Ammonite was by his side, and he said, "Whatever they are building, if a fox went up, he would breach their stone wall."

[4]"Listen, our God, because we have become an object of abuse. May their disgrace turn back on their own heads. Make them into spoil in a land of captivity. [5]Do not cover their waywardness or offenses from before you. It should not be blotted out because they have been offensive in front of the builders." [6]And we built the wall, and the entire wall joined up until it was half done. The mind of the people was on doing it.

We were going to a concert at UCLA once and my friend pointed to a building and said, "I built that" (when he was an engineering student). We were looking in a coffee table book at a picture of an art museum and my wife said, "I built that" (when she was a project manager). My father brought a book home one day when I was a boy and said, "I printed this" (he was a printing machine minder). One of my sons recently became an engineer; I hope one day to have him point to a flood management program and say, "I built that." My brother-in-law is a carpet fitter; at their house, I look at the carpet and think, "John (he is also John) laid that." When someone admires a sweater of mine, I can say, "My mother-in-law knitted it." When I had my kitchen remodeled, I like to say, "Joe did that." When I sit on my other son's patio, I think "Steven laid that." When my step-daughter got married near some apartments overlooking the beach, it was because "My grandfather built them."

The list of the people involved in rebuilding Jerusalem's wall resembles the other lists in Ezra–Nehemiah, but I suspect it would have a further significance for its readers and their children and grandchildren. It would be reason for pride in what father, mother, grandmother, or grandfather did. Later generations would know that their security and their pride in their city owed so much to the people named here. The list continues to move around the city counterclockwise and up the east side, with its tough slopes. It takes up the story near the Gihon Spring and Hezekiah's tunnel, which conducts the spring water into the Pool of Siloam. It works its way past the palace and its environs back to the northeast corner and the temple area, where it started. The amount of detail about its route may suggest that this is a new wall not following the course of the one that was destroyed, and there is archeological evidence that it followed a course higher up the steep slope and easier than its predecessor as part of Nehemiah's being satisfied with a wall encircling a smaller area than the city had once been. Once again major administrators from outside Jerusalem get involved in the work. Once again a number of workers take on a second section as well as their first.

The list seems to summarize the final results of the work; the comment about Sanballat then takes us back to an earlier stage in the process, when Sanballat is both annoyed at what is going on and scornful of it. The annoyance reflects his awareness that the success of the work will indeed mean the city's greater security and independence, and a heightening of the morale of its people and of the **Judahites** in general who are involved in the work. His scorn is immediately meant to offer reassurance to his own people, but Nehemiah's prayer indicates that the builders knew about it, and it will also reflect Sanballat's desire to make the work cease; laughing at people's efforts can have that effect. He raises questions about whether the Judahites are capable of completing this demanding project on their own ("leaving it to themselves"). How long is it going to take them? More than a day or two! Is it really possible to turn this rubble back into a wall? Burnt stone cannot simply be reassembled. Are the Judahites ever going to reach the point when they can offer a thanksgiving or dedication sacrifice because the work is done? If that is the point about the question concerning sacrifice, then we already know the answer, because at the very beginning of the list of workers there was reference to the dedication of the first section of the restored wall. Or perhaps Sanballat's question refers to sacrifices that accompany prayers and he is asking whether the builders are going to see a response to their prayers. If that is so, it is a dangerous question because it constitutes a challenge to God to show that prayers do get answered.

The prayer for God's judgment that constitutes a response to Sanballat and Tobiah parallels prayers in the Psalms and in the New Testament. No doubt it was from the Psalms that Nehemiah learned how to pray. Modern Jews and Christians would feel more comfortable if people in the Bible did not pray this way, but the Bible indicates that it is OK to do so. We who question whether it is OK tend to be people who are not living through the kind of crisis that Nehemiah and his community were experiencing. One significance of such prayers is that they appear on the lips of people who are thus praying for their enemies' judgment rather than taking action against these enemies. No assassination squads make their way from Jerusalem to Samaria to take Sanballat out. The prayers are an expression of trust in God to bring about judgment and a desire for God's honor thereby to be vindicated.

While the report of the prayer raises questions for modern readers, another question is why the report of the prayer appears in the book. Maybe one point about the prayer is to counteract the danger that Sanballat and Tobiah's words will have exactly the result they intend, of destroying morale among the builders. The prayer will then have been designed in part to embolden the builders, reminding them that people such as Sanballat and Tobiah do not have the same basis for hope. Including the report of the prayer in the book could function in a similar way for its readers. But whereas Revelation 6 records God's acceptance of a prayer like this one, Nehemiah 4 does not say what God thought of it, though the presence of this story in the Bible means that Sanballat does end up dishonored while Nehemiah and his people end up honored.

If the prayer like the mockery was designed to be overheard by the builders as well as heard by God, but unlike the mockery was designed to embolden them, it apparently succeeded. Further, the offspring of these builders who read this book will be witnesses to the facts: "My father and mother, my grandfather and grandmother, my great grandfather and great grandmother, my ancestors built this wall. I am the evidence that God's word and God's claim to this place live on."

NEHEMIAH 4:7–23
Sword and Trowel, Faith and Hope

[7]When Sanballat, Tobiah, the Arabs, the Ammonites, and the Ashdodites heard that restoration had come to the walls of Jerusalem in that the breached parts had begun to be closed up, it incensed them, [8]and all of them plotted together to come to fight against Jerusalem and cause confusion in it. [9]We pleaded with our God and put in place a watch over [the workers] day and night because of them. [10]But Judah said,

> "The strength of the carrier has failed, and there is so
>   much rubbish.
> We ourselves are not able to build up the wall."

[11]And our adversaries said, "Before they know or see, we will come in among them and kill them, and stop the work." [12]When the Judahites who lived near them came, they said to us ten times from all the places, "Come back to us." [13]So I stationed them at the lowest parts of the place behind the wall at the exposed points—I stationed the people by families with their swords, lances, and bows. [14]I looked, and stood up and said to the heads, the overseers, and the rest of the people, "Don't be afraid of them. Be mindful of the Lord, the one who is great and awe-inspiring, and fight for your brothers, your sons and daughters, your wives and homes." [15]When our enemies heard that it had become known to us and that God had frustrated their decision, we went back to the wall, all of us, each to his work. [16]But from that day, half my boys were doing the work and half were holding lances, shields, bows, and armor, with the officials behind the entire house of Judah [17]who were building the wall. The basket-carriers transporting things: each was doing the work with one hand and with the other was holding the weapon. [18]The builders were girded each with his sword on his side, but building. The person who sounded the horn was next to me. [19]I said to the heads, the overseers, and the rest of the people, "There is much work and it is spread out, and we are divided on the wall, distant one from another. [20]At the place where you hear the sound of the horn, gather there to us. Our God—he will fight for us." [21]So we were doing the work with half holding lances, from the arrival of dawn until the stars came out. [22]Further, at that time I said to the people, "each man

98

and his boy should lodge within Jerusalem and they will be a guard for us at night and labor by day." ²³I, my brothers, my boys, and the men in the guard behind me did not take off our clothes. Each person—his weapon stayed in his hand.

When my students are reading the part of the Old Testament that includes Nehemiah, they often want to write papers on leadership. Come to think of it, whatever parts of the Old Testament they are studying, they want to write papers on leadership. My heart sinks when they ask if they can do so, though I don't ever expect them to understand why it does. Our culture is deeply preoccupied with leadership, and so people assume that the Bible must be preoccupied with leadership, because we expect the Bible to focus on the questions that concern us. Part of the reason the Bible itself is not very interested in the question is that it is more interested in what God has done to put the world right. If you like, it is interested in God's leadership not ours. There is no doubt that Nehemiah, like Ezra, is a great leader; the point I try to get home to my students is that there is no indication that his story is in Scripture because he is supposed to be a model of leadership for (say) pastors. His story is part of God's story. It's not that we are wrong to look for models of leadership in his story. It's that we are focusing on making Scripture answer our questions rather than looking for its agenda.

But yes, he is a great leader, and he is a great leader by being a great servant of God and then of God's project and of God's people, the builders. He deals with a situation in which his own people are in danger of giving up and his opponents look likely to succeed in frustrating his plans. The challenge he has set himself and his people is a monumental one. Sanballat was not exaggerating much when he drew attention to the dimensions of the task of turning heaps of burnt rubble back into a wall. The **Judahites** agree about the quantity of rubbish, and they are tired of carting it around. They want to give up. Their words are prosaic but they express them as lines of poetry, structured the way you would often structure a prayer of lament and protest with three words in the first part of each line but only two words in the second half; the line brings you up short in the way that life itself is bringing you up short. The plea to come back to us looks like the plea of people who live some way from Jerusalem nearer the territory of those other peoples. We have noted in the list of people involved in the building that many came from outside Jerusalem, from places such as Jericho, Tekoa, Keilah, and Beth-zur, all of which were nearer to the border with those hostile neighbors than to Jerusalem itself. Their people were scared at the fact that their menfolk had abandoned them in this dangerous situation.

Further, Nehemiah's opponents are not above dirty tricks to make sure that the task cannot be completed. If they arrived with weapons in their hands, would it just be bluff? Did they really intend to fight, or simply to frighten the Judahites into giving up? Was it Sanballat and/or his colleagues who had been responsible for the destruction of the walls that had been reported to Nehemiah in Susa? The way the story is told, the people opposing the project keep increasing in number. First it was just Sanballat and his sidekick, Tobiah. Then Geshem the mysterious Arab showed up. Now there are the Ammonites and Ashdodites. The political situation makes their involvement not surprising. Within **Persia**'s Beyond-the-River province in the area west of the Euphrates, the sub-province of Judah is surrounded by the sub-provinces of Samaria to the north, Ashdod to the west, Edom or Idumea to the south (the area where Geshem exercised his influence), and Ammon to the northeast (Moab is due east, but the Dead Sea lies in between Judah and Moab, so Judah and Moab have no common border). Thus all Judah's neighbors are now involved in putting pressure on Judah; all have an interest in Judah not getting too confident and self-sufficient or too much Artaxerxes' favorite.

So Nehemiah does three things, apart from not give up. First he prays. This is not surprising; it was his first reaction when the news reached him in Susa. Prayer is his instinctive reaction to a crisis.

Second, he sets a watch, and he equips the workers with weapons as well as tools. Either some people kept guard while others continued the building work, or individuals did the building work with their weapons on hand. Nehemiah keeps close to him a man who can blow the horn to warn people of any impending attack and get them to gather so as to undertake a collective defense rather than be picked off in small groups, spread along the route of the wall as they are.

Third, he does something about the people's morale. He assembles the people as a whole by their families in an open space—maybe the reference to its being an exposed place signifies a show of strength and coolness for the benefit of any representatives of the hostile neighbors who are in the city. The people gather with their weapons and Nehemiah addresses them in the way someone like Joshua or Gideon might have done. He urges them not to be afraid, not because they are well-armed or because they have overestimated the enemy but because of who their God is.

"Our God—he will fight for us." Yet this does not mean that they will necessarily stand and watch. The presence of their weapons indicates that Nehemiah sees no conflict between trust and action, between faith and fighting. On the other hand, he still does not offer any hint of aggressive action toward the allies. There will be no preemptive strike. He is simply giving notice that the Judahites will not lie down and be trampled on. They will not attack, but they will defend themselves. The demonstration of commitment to the task notwithstanding the threats is enough to make the enemies withdraw and to get the Judahites back to work and complete it, so that their names are recorded and live on in this text, a witness to their faith that lives on for us today.

NEHEMIAH 5:1-5

The Community's Moral Challenge

[1]There was a great outcry by the people and their wives toward their Judahite brothers. [2]There were some saying, "With our sons and daughters—we are many. We must get grain in order to eat and live." [3]There were some saying, "Our fields, our vineyards, our homes—we are pawning them in order to get grain during the famine." [4]And there were some saying, "We have borrowed money on our fields and vineyards for the king's tax. [5]Now, we are the same flesh as our brothers, our children are like theirs, but there—we are subjecting our sons and daughters

to servitude. Some of our daughters have been subjected. There is no power in our hand while our fields and vineyards belong to other people."

Two or three weeks ago we bought a new sofa, and we got a ten percent discount because we were willing to sign up for the store's credit card and charge it to that card. This week the credit card bill came with the usual invitation just to make the minimum payment but with the now-mandatory information about how much we would pay over two years if we do simply make the minimum payment. The answer is, more or less 20 percent extra. That's how credit cards work. Now, if you happen to have bought earlier volumes of the Old Testament for Everyone series you will have made it possible for me to pay off the entire amount and I shall do so unless I forget (excuse me for a moment while I take action). On the other hand, I have a friend who lost her job and had to rely on a credit card to buy food. She had no alternative but to pay more or less 20 percent interest on the money for her meals. In Western culture, lending money is a way to make money, and the people who pay the price are the people who cannot afford to do so.

In the Old Testament, lending is a way to show compassion to the needy, not a way to make money. The **Torah** bans charging interest on loans to individuals. Usury does not imply making loans on the basis of particularly unfair terms; it means any charging of interest on a loan. The Torah does safeguard the position of someone who takes the risk of making a loan by presupposing the practice of temporary indebted servitude— that is, a person who gets into economic difficulties and cannot provide for his family can accept a loan of supplies from someone, and commit members of the family or himself to work for that person for up to six years in order to pay back the loan by this work. (It would be in everyone's interests for the children to be the first people who work in this way, so that the head of the family is able to work toward the family farm regaining viability; but *children* need not mean very young people—it just as easily denotes teenagers and young adults.) The Torah's concern is to make sure that the practice of servitude is regulated in a proper way. Translations often refer to people who are working in this fashion as *slaves*, but the English word is misleading—*servants* is a better translation. Such people are not the property of the person they work for and their master cannot ill-treat them. Like our rules about credit, the rules in the Torah are designed to protect the needy, though they do so more generously than the laws of modern Christian nations.

The sequence of events in Nehemiah suggests that the economic difficulties that affect people in **Judah** relate to the wall-building program. Ironically, it seems that some of the wives and children of men who did not have to divorce their wives were having at least as hard a time as may have been the case for the wives and children of the men who did so. Obviously men who are building the wall cannot be working in other ways, but the fact that the protesters are the wives as well as the husbands reflects some assumptions about the basis on which Israelite life worked, at least in theory. Every family was allocated a stretch of land to farm, and this was a joint operation in which the role of husbands and wives was complementary in making sure that the family was able to function. But human selfishness regularly manifests monumental ingenuity in getting around whatever safeguards are put in place to restrain greed and protect the needy, as we stray from the implementation of our own rules about credit and about other economic matters. Indeed, there are said to be tens of thousands of girls brought into the United States each year on the basis that they will get an education in return for working as servants and who end up as something more like slaves. Likewise the Prophets make clear how the kind of system put forward in the Torah was not working centuries before Nehemiah's day. People who did well had been able to maneuver less fortunate or astute or skillful or hardworking farmers out of their land, so that they had ended up as laborers on other people's farms or had ended up moving to the city. If they had a trade there, they might do well, but they would always be vulnerable to economic and other ups and downs.

The first group of protestors seems likely to be such people, Jerusalemites who need to be able to feed their families but are prevented from doing so because they are working on the wall—its workforce had included people such as perfumers, goldsmiths, and merchants. So they cannot earn money to buy grain and bake bread, a staple for them. They are the first people whose *outcry* the chapter refers to. The very word is a grievous one. It is the word for the cry Abel's blood utters from the ground when his brother has killed him, and the word used to describe the Israelites' cry when they are oppressed in Egypt. That is the way Jerusalemites are treating one another.

The second group comprises people who still own their land, perhaps in the immediate environs of Jerusalem or perhaps in one of the areas further away that the list of workers mentions, such as Tekoa and Gibeon. They would have had to abandon their work on the farm to join in the work on the wall. They bring in an extra consideration: that there have in fact been poor harvests and therefore famine. Famine as a natural disaster has not been mentioned in Ezra–Nehemiah, though there is enough mention of poor harvests in Haggai, Malachi, and Joel to suggest that it is a frequent enough occurrence. But the people's point may again be that having to abandon their work on the farm means that the harvest was nothing like what it should be and not enough to feed the families as well as provide for sowing for the next year. So they have to borrow from families that have enough, and they are in danger of going through the same experience as the one to which the prophets refer, of losing their land permanently if they can't pay their debts.

The third group points to a different burden. Globalization is a burden on ordinary people. Being part of the **Persian** Empire may bring benefits to this group, though they can't see what the benefits are, and they do know that it means paying imperial taxes. This obligation, too, puts a pressure on their livelihood. So once again, if they are living at subsistence level and can only just produce enough food for themselves, having to surrender 20 percent to the imperial coffers to keep the emperor and his staff in the style of life to which they are accustomed tips them over the edge into debt. Their lament then is not that they have to lease their farms to another family but that they have to sell the labor of members of their family to other families. In Western culture we take for granted the sale of our labor—work means employment by someone. But the Old Testament's ideal is that people work for themselves in the context of the family. It's weird to sell your labor, the Old

Testament thinks, even for a few years to pay off the family's debt; it breaks up the family.

The protesters point to the fact that they belong to the same wider family as the people to whom they have to surrender their children for a while. These people are, in that wider sense, "our brothers." The vision the Torah sets before Israel is that Israel is the family writ large. You don't charge interest on loans within the family, do you? The protesters also refer to these people as "the same flesh" and observe that "our children are like theirs." The implication is that beneath the family link is a human link. You could say that humanity as a whole is the family writ large. How could human beings charge one another interest when people are in need? (In other words, the Old Testament's argument may not rule out what we might call commercial loans, including the one the store offered my wife and me; it does rule out making someone else's misfortune or self-sacrifice a means of making money.)

A big project such as building the temple or the city wall affects the economy of the entire country by necessarily drawing resources to it. To put it theologically, it requires sacrifice on the part of the community. Yet it can happen that while some people are prepared to make the sacrifice for God's sake and the community's sake, other people are rather inclined to see the project as a means of making a profit for themselves rather than making a sacrifice.

NEHEMIAH 5:6–19

Putting Your Money Where Your Mouth Is

[6]It incensed me very much when I heard their outcry and these words. [7]When my thinking had counseled me, I contended with the heads and the overseers and said to them, "Are you lending with usury, each one against his brother?" and I raised a great assembly about them. [8]I said to them, "We have got hold of our Judahite brothers who were sold to the Gentiles, as far as it lay in us. Will you indeed sell your brothers so that they may be sold to us?" They were silent. They could not find a word. [9]I said, "The thing that you are doing is not good. Will you not walk in reverence for God to avoid disgrace before the Gentiles,

NEHEMIAH 5:6–19 Putting Your Money Where Your Mouth Is

our enemies? [10]Indeed, I, my brothers, and my boys are lending them silver and grain. Do let us abandon this usury. [11]Do give them back their fields, vineyards, olives, and homes, and the percentage on the silver, the grain, the wine, and the oil that you are lending them." [12]They said, "We will give back, and we will not seek anything from them. We will act thus, as you are saying." So I summoned the priests and swore [the people] to act in accordance with this word. [13]I also shook out my pocket and said, "May God shake out like this any man who does not fulfill this word, from his house and property. May he become shaken out like this and empty." The entire assembly said "Amen," and praised Yahweh, and the people acted in accordance with this word. [14]Further, from the day I was commissioned to be governor in the country of Judah, from the twentieth year through to the thirty-second year of King Artaxerxes, twelve years, I with my brothers did not eat the governor's food. [15]The previous governors who were before me placed a burden on the people, and for food and wine for one [day] took from them forty shekels of silver. Further, their boys domineered over the people. I did not do so, out of reverence for God. [16]And further, I supported the work on this wall; we did not acquire land, and all my boys were gathered there at the work. [17]The Judahites and overseers, one hundred and fifty in all, and the people who came to us from the nations that were around us, were at my table. [18]What was prepared for each day: one ox, six choice sheep, and birds were prepared for me, and at an interval of ten days, all kinds of wine in quantities. But with this I did not seek the governor's food, because the service was heavy on this people. [19]Be mindful of all I have done for this people, my God, for good, for me.

I recently read a story about a teenager in Atlanta who saw a black Mercedes coupe on one side of a street and a homeless man begging for food on the other. She commented to her father that if the one man had a cheaper car, the other man could have a meal. "What do you want to do then," her mom later asked, "Sell our house?" Eventually they did exactly that, spent half the proceeds on a smaller house, and gave the other half to support a project that sponsors health, micro-financing, food, and other programs for forty villages in Ghana. Their story goes on to speak of the blessing this brought them as a family. There was a real sense in which they were better off as a family in a smaller house—the opposite of the assumption that the girl's parents had made. They were together more as the smaller house was more family-friendly, though this benefit was not the motivation that drove them to take the action that they did.

We don't know how much sacrifice Nehemiah made. The implication of his claim is that he was sufficiently well-off to be able to work without financial reward or support. In giving, as much importance attaches to what you have left as to what you give; many people can give substantially yet still be left with more than enough. Nehemiah's point is that there is not going to be any opportunity for anyone to suggest he did his work for what he could get out of it. Many people in Christian leadership can say that they would have earned more if they had been working in a secular job, and I guess I am one of them, though they and I would also have to grant that we get more satisfaction out of the Christian work that we do, so the question of motivation is not solved by looking merely at people's bank balance or material assets.

Nehemiah does not imply that he undertook his work in order to benefit himself; indeed, his story so far has implied the opposite. Yet this fact doesn't mean he objects to benefiting from it; indeed, he asks God that he may do so. As was the case with his prayer for judgment on his attackers, he doesn't assume that we need to censor our prayers. Not feeling the need to do so again has the effect of freeing him from needing to take action on his own behalf. He prays for his enemies' judgment and thus does not seek to take judgment on them himself; he would know and his enemies would know that leaving the punishment to God can carry way more threat than if judgment lies with Nehemiah or the rest of the human community. He also prays to do well out of his commitment to the community, and therefore does not seek to take action to ensure that he prospers. He is free to use up his resources for other people's benefit because he is free to pray this way. God is his real employer.

The more specific point about this aspect of Nehemiah's story is its significance in relation to the stance of other people who are well-off. As usual, Nehemiah gets steamed up at what he hears. He is regularly a guy whose emotions run high and who shows how that can be fruitful in generating action. There is something wrong with you if you don't get distraught when you hear bad news about the people of God and if you don't find yourself compelled to pray and to do something about it. There is something wrong with you if you don't take affront when enemies threaten more trouble for your brothers and sisters and if you don't find yourself challenging God to do something about them, as well as taking action to make sure that they can defend themselves. There is something wrong with you if you don't become incensed when the people of God behave the way they are in this chapter and if you don't find yourself confronting them aggressively. Like Saul, Nehemiah is an example of the way anger can be a fruit of the Spirit, a capacity that God uses in order to get the right thing done. Admittedly, it is also worth noting that on this occasion he thinks before he speaks. He lets his thinking offer him advice (to take up his slightly strange but suggestive formulation). After he hears the protests and has felt the anger arising within him, you can almost hear him saying, "Stay cool, Nehemiah, think the issue through a little before you open your big mouth." Then he confronts them and calls a community meeting. It is, after all, a community issue.

The people who are using the economic pressures on people as a means of getting better off are "the heads and the overseers." The two groups will overlap. The former comprises the heads of families, who are using the situation to make their families better off at the expense of other families by means of the conditions they attach to loans that they make. The latter comprises people who have some sort of administrative responsibility in the city, and who are therefore in a position to do the same thing by the way they make the law work. As we know in our own world, the haves and the people with power are always in a position to take advantage of their status in relation to the have-nots and the powerless; so the gap between rich and poor increases each decade. And we can be blind to the way we are doing so. The heads and overseers were involved in the community building project. They had apparently not noticed that they were undermining the community in this other aspect of their life.

Nehemiah needs to be in a position to show that he is not using in this way either his membership in a well-off family or his being a person with authority. He and his associates are lending people grain and silver (that is, money), and—he implies—are not charging interest; other people need to do the same. (Or perhaps he implies that he and his associates *are* charging interest—though presumably not with the more egregious results described in the protests, otherwise more would need to be said—but that they, too, will stop doing so.) The diners' presence at Nehemiah's table models how the community's pulling together can make it possible to meet the great sacrifice involved in rebuilding, while not starving the community into servitude. The community's adversaries then have less vulnerability to work with.

In one of the **Torah**'s sets of rules for coping with poverty and indebted servitude, Leviticus 25 refers to the possibility of Israelites borrowing from foreigners and ending up in servitude to them, and lays down the expectation that members of their wider family might redeem them from their servitude. Nehemiah points out that the community has been doing so when necessary. It is then not consistent with the community's practice for one **Judahite** to be putting another into servitude, and it makes the community look stupid in the eyes of the people from whom they have bought people back. The reference to "the Gentiles, our enemies" will hardly imply that all Gentiles are to be viewed as enemies, but will have in mind the people who are referred to elsewhere in the book as "our enemies," Sanballat, Tobiah, Geshem, and other representatives of the surrounding peoples.

Leviticus 25 also makes the way people deal with the poverty of their neighbors an aspect of how they live in reverence for God, and Nehemiah does the same. You can't separate your economic policy from the way God expects people to treat each other.

NEHEMIAH 6:1–19

Don't Trust Anybody

¹When it was reported to Sanballat, Tobiah, Geshem the Arab, and the rest of our enemies that we had built up the wall and that no breach remained in it (admittedly, up to that time I had not put in place doors in the gates), ²Sanballat and Heshem sent to me saying, "Come, let's meet together at Kephirim in Ono Valley." But these men were planning to do me harm, ³so I sent aides to them saying, "I am undertaking a big project. I cannot come down. Why should the project cease while I leave it and come down to you?" ⁴Sanballat sent to me in accordance with this message four times, and I sent back to them in accordance with this message. ⁵Sanballat sent his boy to me in accordance with this message a fifth time, but with an open letter in his hand. ⁶There was written in it: "Among the nations it is reported (and Gashmu says)—you and the Judahites are planning to rebel. That is why you are building the wall. You are going to be their king, according to these words, ⁷and you have also put in place prophets to proclaim in Jerusalem about you that 'There is a king in Judah.' It will now be reported to the king in accordance with these things. So come and let's meet together now." ⁸I sent to him saying, "Nothing in accordance with these things that you are saying has happened, because you are devising them out of your own mind," ⁹because they were all intimidating us, saying [to themselves] "Their hands will cease from the project and it will not be undertaken." So now strengthen my hands.

¹⁰I myself came to the house of Shemaiah son of Mehetabel when he was restricted. [Shemaiah] said,

Let us meet in God's house, inside [God's] palace,
Let us shut the doors of the palace, because they are
    coming to kill you.
By night they are coming to kill you.

¹¹I said, "Will a person like me flee? And who is there such as me who may go into the palace and live? I will not come." ¹²I realized: There, God had not sent him, because he had spoken the prophecy about me when Sanballat and Tobiah had hired him. ¹³To this end he had been hired—to the end that I would

be afraid and would act thus and commit an offense, and they would have a bad name with which to disgrace me. [14]My God, be mindful for Tobiah and Sanballat in accordance with these acts of his, and also for Noadiah the prophetess and the rest of the prophets who were intimidating me.

[15]But the wall was finished on the twenty-fifth of Elul, after fifty-two days. [16]When all our enemies heard, all the nations around us were afraid and fell greatly in their own eyes. They acknowledged that this work had been done by God. [17]Also in those days, the heads of the Judahites were sending many letters to Tobiah, and ones that were Tobiah's were coming to them, [18]because many people in Judah were under oath to him, because he was a son-in-law of Shecaniah son of Arah, and his son Jehohanan had married the daughter of Meshullam son of Berechiah. [19]Further, they were speaking before me of his good deeds, and they were transmitting my words to him when Tobiah sent letters to intimidate me.

I couldn't access my e-mail last weekend. It transpired that the problem was something to do with my cache, a component in the computer that stores data; its operation was designed to ensure the security of my e-mail, but in effect it was being overzealous. Over the same weekend, I was trying to use my physician's new Web site to make an appointment, which involved registering and providing lots of obscure information such as the city where my mother was born and devising a "strong" password, all to protect the security of my medical data; and when I had done all this, I still could not log on to the system, so I was reduced to making an old-fashioned phone call after the weekend. Is there really someone who wants to read my e-mail or view my medical information, and does it matter?

If I were Nehemiah, I would have had to be concerned about the question. Nehemiah has to have his wits about him. Ono Valley is half-way between Jerusalem and Samaria and thus a plausible place to suggest for a meeting between Sanballat and Nehemiah, but it is thus twenty miles north of Jerusalem and that means it would involve Nehemiah being away from the city for several days—if he ever came back. More likely he would mysteriously disappear, an event that might then be attributed to bandits or Bedouin, like the kidnappers who took Joseph. It's always dangerous to be on the road in the open country.

Sanballat's subsequent ploy is more subtle and more dangerous (the Gashmu he mentions is the Geshem who appeared earlier—it is another form of the same name). Everyone knows that people such as the **Judahites** would rather be independent than be under **Persian** control, or even rather have a nominal ruler of their own who had local authority while accepting Persian foreign policy and seeing that taxes got paid. Sanballat's allies in Jerusalem would know about Judahite leaders such as Zerubbabel, a descendant of the Judahite royal line who had been governor in Jerusalem and would know that people in Jerusalem kept track of Zerubbabel's descendants (a list appears in 1 Chronicles 3). People in Jerusalem would be hoping to see a Davidic ruler on the throne in Jerusalem again. God's promise to David implied that this would happen.

Okay, so Nehemiah was not born from the Davidic line as far as we know, though he has behaved in rather king-like fashion in proclaiming that debts should be cancelled. Indeed, maybe belonging to David's line is just the small print in God's promise, not needing to be taken too literally; certainly, three centuries later the next line of rulers in Jerusalem were priests rather than people from David's line. To designate Nehemiah as king, all that would be needed was a prophetic word like the ones that had come to Samuel about anointing Saul and then anointing David himself, a word declaring that God was now anointing Nehemiah.

In fact, prophecy is working the other way, to discredit Nehemiah. The reason why Sanballat or his collaborators in Jerusalem can imagine how Nehemiah might maneuver his way to the throne with the help of a prophet is that they have worked out how they might bring him into disrepute with the help of some prophets, if he won't fall into the trap of taking a trip to Ono. While Shemaiah's words are down-to-earth in content, they are cast into the rhythm of poetry, like Judah's complaint in chapter 4. In the Old Testament, the rhythm of verse is appropriate for words that purport to come from God, as it is appropriate for words addressed to God. It gives a veneer of plausibility to Shemaiah's implicit claim that God's intent lies

NEHEMIAH 6:1–19 *Don't Trust Anybody*

behind his invitation. It needs that veneer, because Shemaiah is proposing that Nehemiah should ignore the **Torah**'s rule that only priests go right inside God's house or palace, the temple. Lay people could go into the temple courtyards for worship and for the offering of sacrifice, but not into the sanctuary itself. To go there is to risk being struck dead, rather than to safeguard against being killed. Shemaiah is Sanballat's agent (the cause of his being "restricted," unable to go to the temple, might be some temporary defilement that could end with nightfall).

From the story in the opening chapters of Nehemiah we might have imagined that people in general cooperated with Nehemiah enthusiastically in the building project, though there have been a number of signs that this may not have been so. While the list of participants in chapter 3 might seem impressive, it promotes reflection on who does not appear in the list. What about people apart from goldsmiths, perfumers, and merchants? What about people from cities other than Tekoa, Beth-zur, and one or two others? Was Tekoa the only city whose important people saw no reason to imperil their own city's affairs by allocating resources to rebuilding in Jerusalem? The people's protests about the economic situation indicate displeasure with the project, and the action required of the well-to-do will not have helped Nehemiah's standing with them.

The last paragraphs of chapter 6 make more explicit the opposition to Nehemiah in the city. It was not merely a problem in connection with enemies in other sub-provinces. There is opposition and intrigue within as well as without. If Nehemiah had had e-mail or a Web site, it certainly would have been hacked. He needs to be shrewd as a snake as well as harmless as a dove. He is that kind of man, and it contributes to his success. The rebuilding is achieved only because "the work had been done by God." But in its context the statement deconstructs. The rebuilding is achieved only because the work had been done by Nehemiah and because he is as smart as he is. The building would not have been done without God, but it would not have been done without Nehemiah either. He can be discerning about which voices come from God and which from people who are working against God, even when they seem reasonable and/or spiritual and/or concerned for his well-being. And he can be discerning about politically tempting calls that invite him to meetings that might lessen the possibility of deterioration in the situation or help find the middle ground, but will actually mean, at best, distraction, and at worst the sabotage of the project.

NEHEMIAH 7:1–73A

Working in the Context of God's Promises

[1]When the wall was built up and I had put in place the doors, they appointed the gatekeepers, singers, and Levites. [2]I commissioned my brother Hanani, and Hananiah the officer in the fortress, over Jerusalem, because he was truly a trustworthy man and one who revered God more than most. [3]I said to them, "The gates of Jerusalem shall not open while the sun is hot; while those men are standing [on duty] they must shut the doors and secure them. And put in place the inhabitants of Jerusalem as watches, each man at his watch or opposite his own house." [4]Now the city was broad in width and large, but the body of people within it was small and there were no houses built up. [5]My God put it into my mind to assemble the heads, the overseers, and the people for enrolling. I found the document with the roll of the people who went up at the first, and found written in it:

[6]These are the people of the province who went up from among the captives in exile whom Nebuchadnezzar the king of Babylon exiled and who returned to Jerusalem and Judah, each to his city, [7]who came with Zerubbabel, Jeshua, Nehemiah, Azariah, Raamiah, Nahamani, Mordecai, Bilshan, Mispereth, Bigvai, Rehum, Baanah. The number of the men belonging to the Israelite people: [8]The descendants of Parosh, 2,172; [4]the descendants of Shephatiah, 372; [5]the descendants of Arah, 652; [11]the descendants of Pahath-moab (through the descendants of Jeshua and Joab), 2,818; [7]the descendants of Elam, 1,254; [8]the descendants of Zattu, 845; [14]the descendants of Zaccai, 760; [15]the descendants of Binnui, 648; [16]the descendants of Bebai, 628; [17]the descendants of Azgad, 2,322; [18]the descendants of Adonikam, 667; [19]the descendants of Bigvai, 2,067; [20]the descendants of Adin, 655; [21]the descendants of Ater (through Hezekiah), 98; [22]the descendants of Hashum, 328;

114

[23]the descendants of Bezai, 324; [24]the descendants of Hariph, 112; [25]the descendants of Gibeon, 95; [26]the people of Bethlehem and Netophah, 188; [27]the people of Anathoth, 128; [28]the people of Beth-azmaveth, 42; [29]the people of Kiriath-jearim (Chephirah and Beeroth), 743; [30]the people of Ramah and Geba, 621; [31]the people of Michmas, 122; [32]the people of Beth-el and Ai, 123; [33]the people of the other Nebo, 52; [34]the people of the other Elam, 1,254; [35]the descendants of Harim, 320; [36]the descendants of Jericho, 345; [37]the descendants of Lod, Hadid, and Ono, 721; [38]the descendants of Senaah, 3,930.

[39]The priests: the descendants of Jedaiah (through the household of Jeshua), 973; [40]the descendants of Immer, 1,052; [41]the descendants of Pashhur, 1,247; [42]the descendants of Harim, 1,017. [43]The Levites: the descendants of Jeshua (through Kadmiel, through the descendants of Hodaviah), 74. [44]The singers: the descendants of Asaph, 148. [45]The gatekeepers: the descendants of Shallum, the descendants of Ater, the descendants of Talmon, the descendants of Akkub, the descendants of Hatita, the descendants of Shobai, altogether 138. [46]The assistants: the descendants of Ziha, the descendants of Hasupha, the descendants of Tabbaoth, [47]the descendants of Keros, the descendants of Siah, the descendants of Padon, [48]the descendants of Lebanah, the descendants of Hagabah, the descendants of Shalmai, [49]the descendants of Hanan, the descendants of Giddel, the descendants of Gahar, [50]the descendants of Reaiah, the descendants of Rezin, the descendants of Nekoda, [51]the descendants of Gazzam, the descendants of Uzza, the descendants of Paseah, [52]the descendants of Besai, the descendants of Meunim, the descendants of Nephishesim, [53]the descendants of Bakbuk, the descendants of Hakupha, the descendants of Harhur, [54]the descendants of Bazlith, the descendants of Mehida, the descendants of Harsha, [55]the descendants of Barkos, the descendants of Sisera, the descendants of Temah, the descendants of Neziah, the descendants of Hatipha. [57]The descendants of Solomon's servants: the descendants of Sotai, the descendants of Sophereth, the descendants of Perida, [58]the descendants of Jala, the descendants of Darkon, the descendants of Giddel, [59]the descendants of Shephatiah, the descendants of Hattil, the descendants of Pochereth-hazzebaim, the descendants of Amon. [60]All the assistants and the descendants of Solomon's servants, 392.

⁶¹These are the people who went up from Tel-melah, Tel-harsha, Cherub, Addan, and Immer, but who were unable to show their ancestral household and origin, whether they were from Israel: ⁶²the descendants of Delaiah, the descendants of Tobiah, the descendants of Nekoda, 642. ⁶³Of the priests: the descendants of Habaiah, the descendants of Hakkoz, the descendants of Barzillai (who had married a woman from among the daughters of Barzillai the Gileadite and was called by their name). ⁶⁴These looked for their record among the people enrolled but it was not found, and they were disqualified from the priesthood. ⁶⁵So the administrator told them that they should not eat of the most holy things until the emergence of a priest for Urim and Thummim.

⁶⁶The entire assembly altogether was 42,360, ⁶⁷besides their male and female servants; these were 7,337, and they had 245 male and female singers. ⁶⁸Their horses, 736; their mules, 245; ⁶⁹camels, 435; donkeys, 6,720. ⁷⁰Some of the ancestral heads gave for the work. The administrator gave to the treasury gold, 1,000 drachmas; basins, 50; priests' robes, 530. ⁷¹Some of the ancestral heads gave to the work treasury gold, 20,000 drachmas; and silver, 2,200 minas. ⁷²What the rest of the people gave: gold, 20,000 drachmas; silver, 2,000; and priests' robes, 67. ⁷³ᵃThe priests, the Levites, the gatekeepers, the singers, some of the people, the assistants, and all Israel settled in their cities.

At a dinner party, we were discussing the difference it made being married. One wife appreciated having a protector (she's not an old-fashioned girl in other ways). She once hesitated to park in dark streets. She once worried if there were noises in the apartment that might herald a burglar. She once worried about shadows in the night that might mean the presence of a monster. She once worried about whether she could pay the rent. Now she doesn't worry about any of those things. She feels protected. Yet like me she prays the Episcopal morning devotions that involve asking, "Father, you have brought us to the beginning of this new day: Preserve us with your mighty power, that we may not fall into sin, nor be overcome by adversity." In the evening in these devotions we ask God to "visit this place, and drive far from it all the snares of the enemy" and to "preserve us in peace." What's the relationship between divine protection and human protection—or fear, sensibility, paranoia, or strategic planning?

We have seen that one way Nehemiah's story raises such questions is by the way it speaks of the building of the wall as having been done by God. His story also does so by interweaving reference to prayer and to action. The community and Nehemiah himself need protection from their adversaries. He doesn't assume that some people's gift is action and other people's gift is prayer; he takes responsibility for both. He doesn't discuss the interrelationship of action and prayer or give any indication that he has reflected on the relationship. Instinctively, he just gives himself to both. The seamless way he moves between reporting things that have happened or things that he has done and reporting his prayers may even suggest that he did not distinguish between prayer and action the way Western people do. He would be unlikely to distinguish prayer and conversation in the way Western people do, because for Israelites (as for many modern Jews) prayer, like reading Scripture, is something one does aloud. It doesn't happen just inside our head.

Nehemiah's story also raises the question of the relationship between divine protection and human protection by offering a contrast with some words of Zechariah, who appeared back in Ezra 5. Zechariah 2 relates a vision of a man engaged in measuring the size of Jerusalem. One of God's supernatural aides appears and declares that Jerusalem is going to be an open, unwalled city like a village, and there will be so many people and cattle in it. **Yahweh** will be a firewall around it and will be splendor inside. What is Nehemiah doing rebuilding Jerusalem's wall of brick if God has promised to be its wall of fire? Yet the Old Testament implies that Nehemiah was indeed doing the right thing. If Nehemiah was aware of Zechariah's prophecy, perhaps he assumed that the promise that God will be your protector doesn't mean that you have no responsibility for protecting yourself. (The point about shutting the gates when the sun is hot is not to leave the city vulnerable when everyone is having a siesta.)

Saying there were no houses built up will not imply that the city is totally undeveloped; the story has mentioned people building the part of the wall near their houses. Rather the implication is that many other houses have not been rebuilt after the devastation of the recent calamity and/or the destruction of the previous century, and remain unoccupied. Perhaps many of their occupants were people who had been taken off into exile and have not returned. Nehemiah's starting point in recruiting families to come and live in the city is an existing roll of people who had come from Babylon, which is a variant of the one included in Ezra 2. The total number is the same as in that list but there are many differences of detail, perhaps mostly because elements such as names and figures easily get accidently changed as a manuscript is copied.

NEHEMIAH 7:73b–8:8

How to Teach without Packaging

^{73b}When the seventh month arrived, with the Israelites in their cities, $^{8:1}$the entire people assembled as one person at the square in front of the Water Gate and said to Ezra the scholar that he was to bring the scroll of Moses' teaching that Yahweh had commanded Israel. ^{2}Ezra the priest brought the scroll in front of the congregation (men and women and all who could understand when they listened) on the first day of the seventh month. ^{3}He read from it in front of the square in front of the Water Gate from dawn until midday before the men and women and the people who could understand, as the ears of the entire people were directed to the teaching scroll. ^{4}Ezra the scholar stood on a wooden tower that they made for the purpose. There stood next to him Mattithiah, Shema, Anaiah, Uriah, Hilkiah, and Maaseiah on his right, and at his left Pedaiah, Mishael, Malchijah, Hashum, Hashbaddanah, Zechariah, Meshullam. ^{5}Ezra opened the scroll before the eyes of the entire people, because he was above the entire people; and as he opened it, the entire people stood. ^{6}Ezra worshiped Yahweh, the great God, and the entire people answered, "Amen, amen" with their hands up, then bowed and prostrated themselves to Yahweh with their faces on the ground. ^{7}Jeshua, Bani, Sherebiah, Jamin, Akkub, Shabbethai, Hodiah, Maaseiah, Kelita, Azariah, Jozabad, Hanan, Pelaiah, the Levites, helped the entire people understand the teaching, with the people in their places. ^{8}So they read from the scroll from God's teaching, explaining and giving insight, so that they understood the reading.

A usually mild-mannered, placid member of our Bible study group blew a fuse the other week when we were discussing the story of David's last days in 1 Kings, which describes the ineptitude of those last days in failing to take action about who should succeed him and relates the way he encouraged Solomon to kill various people against whom David had a grudge, even while exhorting him to live in obedience to God. She was indignant that she had been brought up to revere David as the man after God's heart and that the ambiguity of his character had been concealed from her. That had been possible because she belonged to a church that paid great attention to teaching people the Bible and preaching from the Bible but that packaged the Bible's teaching, and did so selectively. It did not read the Bible with people; it told them what the Bible said (except that it did not do so; it told them what it thought the Bible said, or what the Bible should have said). As a church that honored the Reformation, with terrible irony it did what the Reformation faulted the church of its day for doing. I commented that as she is now in the position of being a teacher in a church, she needs to avoid the same practice.

I would like to think that Ezra's approach to teaching avoids that mistake. The beginning of the seventh month is the beginning of the New Year. This will seem odd, but it reflects the fact that one way of counting the months involved starting from Passover in the spring, which Exodus 12 told the Israelites to treat as the beginning of months because it marked the beginning of their life as a people freed by God. This way of counting the months was assumed in Ezra 6. But another way involved starting in September/October with the end of the old agricultural year and the beginning of the new agricultural year. In this sense the new year came in the seventh month.

Deuteronomy 31 in fact prescribes a reading of "this teaching" (presumably Deuteronomy itself) at Sukkot once every seven years. It would be a reminder to Israel of the terms of their covenant relationship with **Yahweh**—of what Yahweh had done for them and of the response Yahweh looked for,

which the **Torah** as a whole and Deuteronomy in particular
expound. In general terms, this gathering in the seventh month
fits into this framework, though the chapter doesn't make clear
whether it was a one-time event associated with Ezra's bringing
his Torah scroll from **Babylon**, or a later one-time event, or
a septennial event like the one Deuteronomy envisages, or an
annual event.

Nor can we be clear about the nature of the scroll that Ezra
read. The chapter later tells us that Ezra read from the scroll
every morning for a week, which might be just enough time
to read the whole of Deuteronomy and for this reading to be
interspersed with the **Levites**' small-group work. It would take
several weeks to read the entire Torah and teach people about
it. Maybe it's significant that Ezra read *from* the scroll (literally, *in* the scroll). We must imagine him reading selectively.
We don't know the significance of the thirteen men who stood
with him, but they were evidently supporting him or lending
authority to the reading in some way, and they might prevent
the people from getting the impression that there was something so uniquely authoritative about Ezra himself.

At least he both read the Torah itself and had the Levites do
their small-group teaching in the first-ever Bible study groups
in the Bible. We need to remember that every family would not
have a Bible in its house, let alone several copies in different
translations. It fits with this fact that the teaching event comes
about not because Ezra summons the people but because they
summon him. They want to hear the Torah read. "The ears of
the entire people were directed to the teaching scroll." Perhaps another implication would be that people are more used
than modern Westerners to learning by listening rather than
by reading (silently), and thus that they retain more of what
they hear than we do. They are able to listen to Ezra read a few
chapters and then listen to the Levites teaching them about the
implications of the chapters and clarifying things. But having
listened to Ezra do the actual reading, they might also be able
to ask sharp questions if the Levites do too much packaging. It
is worth remembering that the reason the Levites are the teachers is not that they have been identified as people with a gift
of teaching. They are the teachers because they belong to the

clan of Levi. The members of other clans who were listening to them would include people who were intellectually sharper than their teachers (like a seminary professor who has people in the class who are sharper than the professor).

The entire people are involved in listening to the Torah and participating in the group work. As the Old Testament emphasizes from time to time, especially in Deuteronomy, women as well as men are part of the people of God that have the privilege and responsibility of taking part in Israel's worship, and of knowing what the Torah says and seeing that it is implemented in family life. Deuteronomy also emphasizes that this is not just the privilege and responsibility of parents as the senior generation in the family but also of their sons and daughters. Nehemiah 8 spells out the point in terms of its being the privilege and responsibility of everyone who is old enough to understand. (It doesn't reveal what were the baby care arrangements for infants too young to fall in that category! But one might guess that the community followed the practice of other traditional peoples whereby the babies were left in the care of the children who were only a little bit older, and that they were all not far away from the gathering where the parents were.)

The teaching groups are not divided by sex or age. Learning is a family business, partly because the implementation of what people learn is a family business. Beyond that fact, learning is a whole-community business. Like the gathering to set up the altar (Ezra 3), the people gather as one person to listen to the Torah. They are one in connection with worship and one in connection with listening.

NEHEMIAH 8:9–18

Mourning or Celebration?

⁹Nehemiah (he was the administrator), Ezra the priest-scholar, and the Levites who were helping the people understand, said to the entire people, "Today is holy to Yahweh your God. Do not mourn or weep," because the entire people were weeping as they heard the words of the teaching. ¹⁰He said to them, "Go, eat rich food, drink sweet drinks, and send helpings to those who

have nothing prepared, because today is holy to our Lord. Do not be sad, because your strength lies in rejoicing in Yahweh." [11]The Levites were silencing the entire people, saying "Hush, because today is holy. Don't be sad." [12]So the entire people went to eat and drink and send helpings and make great celebration because they understood the things that they had made known to them. [13]On the second day, the ancestral heads of the entire people, the priests and the Levites, gathered to Ezra the scholar to study the words of the teaching. [14]They found written in the teaching that Yahweh had commanded by means of Moses that the Israelites should live in bivouacs in the festival in the seventh month [15]and that they should cause to be heard and should pass on an announcement in all their cities and in Jerusalem: "Go out into the mountains and bring branches of olive, pine tree, myrtle, palm, and other leafy trees to make bivouacs, as it is written." [16]So the people went out and brought them, and made themselves bivouacs, each person on his roof or in their courtyards or in the courtyards of God's house or in the square at the Water Gate and the square at the Ephraim Gate. [17]The entire congregation of people who had come back from the captivity made bivouacs and lived in the bivouacs, because the Israelites had not done so since the days of Jeshua son of Nun until that day, and there was a very great celebration. [18]So [Ezra] read from the scroll of God's teaching day by day, from the first day to the last day, and they made festival for seven days, and on the eighth day there was an assembly, in accordance with the rule.

In connection with the first chapter in Nehemiah I mentioned our congregational discussion of the Gospel for the day, which was the beginning of the Sermon on the Mount, Jesus' "Blessings" in Matthew 5. For a while we talked about the kind of expectations Jesus has of us as the potential recipients of his blessings, but eventually saw that the odd thing about his promises is that they are mostly promises concerning people who don't *do* anything. They are simply poor in spirit, sorrowful, meek, and so on. We realized that we didn't really like that idea. We wanted to divert into passages that tell us what to do, not to be told that Jesus' blessing comes to people who can't do. The aspect of this occasion that comes back to me now is the fact that the person who read the Gospel had said, "This is the Gospel of Christ" and we had responded, "Praise be to you, O Christ," but the subsequent discussion suggested that we hadn't meant it.

There's an amusing parallel in people's reactions to Ezra's reading from the **Torah**. As he opened the scroll, he worshiped God and the people answered, "Amen, amen" with hands raised, and then they bowed down in submission to God. Yet it seems that when they heard what the Torah has to say, they were much less enthusiastic, they needed to be told to stop weeping and mourning and to start to see that rejoicing in God was their strength, and they needed to enjoy a celebratory meal together. What is going on?

If Ezra read a cross-section of material from the Torah this would fit both the people's reaction and his corrective. The accounts we have read of intermarriage within the community and of the well-to-do making a profit off the less fortunate conflict with the Torah's teaching. Reading the Torah would make people aware of other ways their community life fell short of the Torah. Perhaps they didn't know what the Torah said about these matters. The Torah had been widely ignored in the period up to the exile; that is why the exile happened. Ezra came to Jerusalem in order to get the community there to start living by it, and the implication would be that as far as they were concerned, his scroll said things they had never heard before. They do not make ignorance an excuse. On the contrary, awareness of the contrast between the Torah's expectations and the nature of their community life was presumably the reason for their weeping. In the worship calendar in Leviticus 23, the Day of Atonement comes on the tenth day of the seventh month, just after this week's reading and teaching. There is no reference to its being observed in connection with the events in Nehemiah 8, though that might simply link with the fact that the Old Testament describes it as an observance that requires only the activity of priests; the whole people does not directly take part. But one can see how its theme would fit with a response of grief at the community's failure.

123

You might then expect Ezra to be pleased at the people's reaction, yet he is not pleased. His reaction links with another aspect to the nature of the Torah. In the Torah, God's expectations of people are set in the context of a description of what God has done for them, in creation, in making promises to Israel's ancestors, in the exodus, in appearing to them at Sinai, and in leading them through the wilderness to the edge of the promised land. It fits with this aspect of the Torah that it commissions festivals of rejoicing in these acts of God's grace, such as Passover and Sukkot or Tabernacles. Unless we are reminded to rejoice in such events, we are inclined to forget to do so, and to forget the events themselves.

Paradoxically, we might think, Ezra points out to them that they have no business being mournful, because it is a holy day. We might assume that the holiness of the day makes for solemnity and that mourning over one's sins would fit. Ezra's assumption is the opposite. The holiness of the day issues from its being a reminder of what God has done for the people, which makes for rejoicing. The holiness of God lies in being a God of grace and mercy, which makes for celebration. So they ought to go and eat and drink after a hard day's listening to the Torah. The eating and drinking will be the kind of celebratory fellowship meal associated with an occasion such as Passover and with the offering of a thanksgiving sacrifice, when people who come to worship together also share in the part of the sacrifice that the Torah allocates to them. It again fits with the Torah's teaching that when they celebrate, they do not just go home and forget about other people, but think about whether there are people they need to invite into their celebration, like families in the United States who do not treat Thanksgiving as merely a family gathering but ask who are the needy or lonely that they can invite in. The people who have nothing prepared might be in that position because of their own inefficiency, but that is no reason to leave them out of a celebration of God's generosity.

It is in this same seventh month that the Jewish people celebrate Sukkot, and in the course of their reading, the people, not surprisingly, discover the Torah's prescription for this celebration. Actually there are several passages in the Torah that describe Sukkot and only one, in Leviticus 23, makes a link with the idea that the Israelites had to live in bivouacs on the way from Egypt to the promised land. Maybe this is the point about the comment that the festival had not been celebrated this way before (Ezra 3 recorded a celebration). This is the moment when Sukkot gains its link with God's bringing people out of Egypt. That development in turn would fit with the specific reference to people having come back from the captivity. That new exodus was itself a reenactment of the first exodus.

In origin, however, Sukkot was a harvest festival and the bivouacs were a practical aid to the harvest process in the way we noted in connection with Ezra 3. But whether people thought about the harvest or about the exodus, Sukkot was an occasion for rejoicing in what God had given them. Suppose you have not had to live in real bivouacs, because (for instance) you live in the city and work as a goldsmith or merchant, or you are a priest in the temple. Then you still need to let yourself be drawn into the rejoicing at God's giving that is involved in Sukkot. So you make your own bivouac on your flat roof or in your yard or in a public place. Indeed, we are perhaps to assume that the community as a whole took part only in the first day of the reading and teaching; once they had gone home for their festive meal, maybe they had to get on with the harvesting. It would be the people who actually lived in the city who could take part in the alternative, substitute Sukkot. Maybe other people came back for the final community celebration on the eighth day.

Our congregation's reaction to Jesus' Blessings reflected our instinct to want to make our relationship with God depend on what we do. We don't care for the idea that God blesses us just because we are poor in spirit. The **Judahites'** instinct was likewise to assume that their relationship with God depended on what they did by way of living by the Torah. It would be amusing if it were not perilously misguided that Christians often think that this is in fact the regular Jewish view. Ezra knows, and the Old Testament knows that our relationship with God depends first on God's generosity. Of course living according to the Torah is vital as a response to that generosity. But if we get God's generosity and our obedience in reverse relationship, we are in trouble.

NEHEMIAH 9:1–19
How to Make Your Confession

[1]On the twenty-fourth day of this month the Israelites assembled with fasting and with sackcloth, and dirt on them. [2]The offspring of Israel separated themselves from all foreigners and stood and confessed their offenses and the wayward acts of their ancestors. [3]They stood up in their place and read out from the scroll of the teaching of Yahweh their God for a quarter of the day, and for a quarter they were confessing and prostrating themselves before Yahweh their God. [4]On the Levites' stairway Jeshua and Bani, Kadmiel, Shebaniah, Bunni, Sherebiah, Bani, and Chenani stood up and cried out in a loud voice to Yahweh their God. [5]The Levites Jeshua and Kadmiel, Bani, Hashabniah, Sherebiah, Hodiah, Shebaniah, and Petathiah said, "Stand up, worship Yahweh your God from eternity to eternity: 'May people worship your glorious name, though exalted above all worship and praise. [6]You are Yahweh, you alone. You made the heavens, the highest heavens, and all their army, the earth and all that is on it, the seas and all that is in them. You give life to all of them, and the army in the heavens prostrate themselves to you. [7]You are Yahweh, the God who chose Abram and brought him out from Ur of the Chaldeans, and made his name Abraham. [8]You found his mind true before you and sealed a covenant with him to give the country of the Canaanite, the Hittite, the Amorite, the Perizzite, the Jebusite, and the Girgashite—to give it to his offspring. You established your words because you are faithful. [9]You saw our ancestors' affliction in Egypt and you heard their cry at the Red Sea. [10]You did signs and marvels against Pharaoh and all his staff and all the people of his country because you acknowledged that they acted arrogantly against them, and you made a name for yourself this very day. [11]You split the sea in front of them and they passed through the midst of the sea on dry ground, but you threw their pursuers into the depths, like a stone into powerful waters. [12]With a cloud column you led them by day, and with a fire column by night, to lighten for them the way in which they were to go. [13]On Mount Sinai you came down and you spoke with them from the heavens. You gave them upright rulings and true teachings, good statutes and commands. [14]Your holy Sabbath you made known to them, and you ordained for them

commands, statutes, and teaching by means of Moses your servant. [15]Bread from the heavens you gave them for their hunger, and you made water go out from a rock for them, for their thirst. You told them to go and take possession of the country that you had raised your hand [to swear] to give them. [16]But they—our ancestors—acted arrogantly, stiffened their neck, and did not listen to your commands. [17]They refused to listen and were not mindful of your wonders, which you had done with them. They stiffened their neck and appointed a leader so as to go back to their serfdom, in their rebelliousness. But you are a pardoning God, gracious and compassionate, long-tempered and big in commitment, and you did not abandon them. [18]Even when they made themselves a figurine of a calf and said, "This is your God who brought you up from Egypt." They committed great acts of contempt. [19]But you in your great compassion you did not abandon them in the wilderness. The cloud column you did not remove from them by day, nor the fire column by night, to lighten for them the way in which they were to go.'"

In our church each Sunday we say a creed in which we "confess our faith" in who God is as Father, Son, and Holy Spirit, though the creed is dominated by the middle section in which we proclaim the basic facts of Jesus' story—he is God's Son, he was born a human being, was crucified, rose from the dead, and will come back as judge. We go on to confess our wrongdoings against God and one another. These are both forms of confession—we publically acknowledge what God has done and we publically acknowledge what we have done. But in our worship they are not connected; in between the two confessions we pray for the world and the church and one another, and if anything, our confession of our sin links more with those other prayers.

The dynamic of the **Levite**-led confession has some overlapping dynamics. It, too, incorporates some declaration of who God is: **Yahweh** alone is God (the heavenly "army" is the stars and planets, which other peoples might see as gods in their own right, entities that decide what happens in the world). But it focuses on what God has done for us, even more than Christian creeds do. Old Testament faith is a gospel, a message of good news concerning what God has done; in the Levites' confession these declarations come before the timeless statements about God and they are more fundamental than those statements. Christian faith is a gospel in a similar way, a further declaration concerning what God has done, a continuation of the same message of good news. To the report as it existed by Jesus' day it adds later news items bringing the story to a climax and throwing the previous news into new light. It's thus odd that Christian creeds ignore the earlier stages in the story of which the good news about Jesus is a continuation. The Christian Church made the Old Testament into Part One of its Scriptures, recognizing that you understand Jesus only if you see his story in light of the story of creation and God's involvement with Israel, but the creeds neglect that fact.

The Levites' double confession then also makes a link between what God has done and what the people have done, the link missing in Christian liturgy. Their confession of what God has done is not just a declaration of the objective facts but a story in light of which they look at their own lives. They ask, what kind of response have we given to what God has done? Conversely, when they make their confession of their own waywardness, they do so in terms of the way they have responded to what God has done. (There is also a further converse point, which is that it becomes possible to tell our story with its shameful elements when it is set in the context of God's acts in restoring us, so that the story does more to glorify God than to shame us.) A Christian equivalent would be to frame our understanding of and our confession of our sin in light of God's action in Jesus' becoming a human being, letting himself be crucified, rising from the dead, and future coming. A further feature of the Levites' confession that makes it stand out from our usual practice is that (like the prayer in Ezra 9) it assumes that the present generation needs to express its identification with the wrongdoing of previous generations because it is bound up with previous generations in all sorts of ways.

When the beginning of Nehemiah 9 refers to "this month," we would assume it refers to the same month in the same year as the celebration described in the previous chapter, but it isn't clear why this further reading from the **Torah** and the confession of sin follows the celebration. Nor is it clear what is the significance of alluding to the twenty-fourth day of the month,

128

though often the concreteness of dates in Scripture has the effect of making the scene and the events seem truly real. The provision of people's names has the same effect. These are real people. The reference to separating themselves from foreigners suggests a link with the kind of action on intermarriage reported in Ezra 9–10; that comparison at least reminds us that the point about this separation isn't ethnic but religious. There would be foreigners in the community, as was always the case, but they would be people like Ruth who had made a commitment to Yahweh the God of Israel.

The arrangement of the chapters suggests that while there are situations in which the people of God properly give priority to celebration, not to mourning for their sins (Nehemiah 8), such sorrow has a proper place in the life of the people of God as a response to its reading of Scripture. So there needs to be a balance in the life of the people of God between celebration and sorrow. Sorrow at sin such as is expressed here is a characteristic of Judah's life in the **Second Temple** period; Ezra 10 was an earlier illustration. Elsewhere in the Old Testament, "crying out" is an expression of pain at what other people have done to us, or what God has done to us. Here, it is an expression of pain at what we have done.

As usual the Old Testament models for us the natural way in which a response to God is not just one that involves inner feelings and spoken words. Because we are bodily people relating to other bodily people, we express ourselves in bodily ways. (I went to a great concert last night and have just been looking online for a t-shirt to commemorate it; further, today I am wearing a t-shirt that commemorates a great concert I went to years ago.) So sorrow at sin is expressed in fasting (when you are grieving over something, you don't feel like eating). It's expressed in wearing basic clothes (the point about sackcloth is not that it's uncomfortable but that it's everyday or work clothing, and when you are grieving over something, you don't feel like dressing up). It's expressed in a disheveled appearance (when you are grieving over something, you don't feel like bothering to shave or clean yourself up). It's expressed in prostration before God (when you are full of enthusiasm or shame, you express it in the way you hold yourself). It's then

also expressed in standing up straight, because when our confession is done, God takes over and forgives, and we are not
expected to wallow in self-pity over our feebleness or to lie in
the dirt like worms forever.

NEHEMIAH 9:20-37

Serfs and Servants

20"'You gave them your good spirit to instruct them and you
did not withhold your manna from their mouth, and you gave
them water for their thirst. 21Forty years you sustained them
in the wilderness, where they did not lack, while their clothes
did not wear out and their feet did not swell. 22You gave them
kingdoms and peoples, and allocated these as a border; thus
they took possession of the country of Sihon, which was the
country of the king of Heshbon, and the country of Og, king
of Bashan. 23You made their descendants as many as the stars
in the heavens and brought them to the country that you told
their ancestors to go in to possess. 24Their descendants came
and took possession of the country. You subdued before them
the Canaanites, the inhabitants of the country, and gave them
into their hand, both their kings and the peoples of the country,
to do with them in accordance with their wish. 25They took for-
tified cities and rich land and took possession of houses filled
with every good thing: hewn cisterns, vineyards, olives, and
fruit trees in quantities. They ate, were full, grew stocky, and
reveled in your great goodness.

26But they defied and rebelled against you and threw your
teaching behind their back. They slaughtered your prophets
who testified against them to get them to come back to you,
and committed great acts of contempt. 27You gave them into
the hand of their adversaries and they oppressed them. In their
time of distress they cried out to you and from the heavens you
yourself would listen. In accordance with your great compassion you gave them deliverers and they delivered them from
the hand of their adversaries. 28But when there was relief for
them, they again did what was displeasing in your sight, and
you abandoned them into the hand of their enemies. They
subjugated them, so they again cried out to you, and from
the heavens you yourself would listen. You rescued them in

accordance with your great compassion, time after time. [29]You testified against them to get them to come back to your teaching, but they themselves acted arrogantly and did not listen to your commands and offended against your rules, which a person should keep, and live by them. They offered a stubborn shoulder, stiffened their neck, and did not listen. [30]You extended [commitment] to them for many years and testified against them by your spirit by means of your prophets, but they did not pay attention, so you gave them into the hand of the peoples of the countries. [31]But in your great compassion you did not make an end of them and you did not abandon them, because you are a God gracious and compassionate.

[32]So now, our great God, mighty and awe-inspiring, who keeps covenant and commitment, may all the suffering not seem small that has fallen upon us, our kings, our officials, our priests, our prophets, our ancestors, and all your people, from the days of the Assyrian kings until this day. [33]You are in the right over everything that has come upon us, because you have acted truly, but we have been faithless. [34]Our kings, our officials, our priests, and our ancestors did not keep your teaching and did not pay heed to your commands and your declarations that you testified against them. [35]In spite of their kingship and your great goodness that you gave them and the broad and rich country that you put before them, they did not serve you and did not turn from their ways. [36]Now: today we are serfs. The country you gave our ancestors to eat its fruit and its goodness, now: we are serfs on it. [37]Its great produce belongs to the kings you have put over us because of our offenses. They rule over our bodies and our animals in accordance with their wish. We are in great distress.'"

In Britain at Christmas I was struck by the way a couple of people from the Indian subcontinent and the Caribbean were running a branch of my British bank with relaxed confidence; it was the most natural thing in the world. Last night I had dinner with an Indian American, a former student who is also the wife of a British jazz musician who was playing at the restaurant. She had moved to the United States in her twenties a couple of decades ago, and it was evident from the conversation how at home she feels in the United States. Yet for many people from the Caribbean and the Indian subcontinent, life in Britain, at least, feels like the life of second-class citizens; within their lifetime (or that of their parents) they were part of the British Empire. Britain had built up its position in the world on the backs of earlier generations of their peoples.

The **Judah** of Nehemiah's day is a colony of the **Persian** Empire. As the **Levites'** prayer implies, it has been a colony of someone (**Assyria, Babylon,** Persia) for centuries; over the next few years, the masters will change (Greece, Rome) but the status will not. "We are serfs," they say. As was the case in chapter 5, translations use the word *slaves*, which is misleading. We have seen that the Persians were not too oppressive. They did not treat the Judahites as property that they were free to treat as they wished, and they were quite capable of behaving in ways that encouraged the restoration of the community; but human communities have a deep-seated desire to run their own lives. The creation stories in the Old Testament say nothing about God having an intention that some human beings should rule over other human beings, and certainly nothing about whole nations ruling over other nations. The exercise of rule came about as a result of human disobedience. It is now inevitable, but it's an expression of the human waywardness of nations when they try to control other nations—and when they justify it on the grounds that they are bringing benefits to these nations.

While the Persians did support Judah's restoration, the Levites are more aware of what they took from Judah in taxes. You don't have to be very cynical to assume that the Persians' support is designed to encourage subservience and docile payment of taxes. God gave the country to Israel so that they could eat its fruit, but its produce in effect belongs to the Persian kings. Serfs are people who have no choice but to spend much of their time working on the land of its owners in return for their protection. Judah was in a similar position, in that much of their labor did not benefit them but benefited only their imperial overlords—as the story in Nehemiah has already shown.

The parallel between the relationship of Judah with Assyria, Babylon, and Persia and that of the Indian subcontinent or the Caribbean with Britain breaks down when the Levites acknowledge that Judah's position results from God's putting these kings over Judah "because of its offenses." The Levites' prayer continues the twofold confession that began in the chapter's earlier verses. It is a confession of the good things that God has done and a confession of the wayward fashion in which Israel has responded to God. A prayer like this one has been called "an act of praise at the justice of the judgment of God." It declares, "This is the way you have treated us, and we cannot complain." As the Levites put it, God is in the right over what has come upon the people, because God has acted truly but they have been faithless.

The reason why the Levites are praying the prayer of confession is that the leadership of worship is their business. The Psalms include many prayers of protest at the way God has treated people when they cannot see any reason for it, and on other occasions the Levites would be involved in praying those prayers of protest on behalf of the community or of families or of individuals. But the Levites evidently understood the need to exercise discernment over whether a calamity that came from people was something they had to accept as an act of justified chastisement or something they could protest.

Yet perhaps that puts the antithesis too sharply, because it is typical of the Old Testament's prayers of confession that they do not assume that we simply have to accept God's judgment until God decides to bring it to an end. That would be to forget who God is, and to hold back from urging God to be mindful of who God is. Earlier stages in the story of God's grace and Israel's waywardness have demonstrated that **Yahweh** is "a pardoning God, gracious and compassionate, long-tempered and big in **commitment**." The Levites thus remind God of the aspects of God's character that God drew attention to back at the beginning of Israel's story at Sinai (see Exodus 34). These aspects of God's character were the basic reason why Israel continued existing through the Old Testament story, and the reason why Jesus' coming and his death were the logical end of that story. They are the basic reasons why God remains committed to the Jewish people and to the church.

They mean that even when you are acknowledging that you deserve the trouble that has come to you, it is possible to urge God to bring the trouble to an end. Even then, God may say

"I think it will be good for you to stew in your own juice for a while yet." But the Levites know it is always worth asking. They know Yahweh is a loving Father. They do not use that word, but it sums up the nature of God as Israel knows God, as one who is prepared to chastise, but who has a hard time saying that enough is not yet enough.

NEHEMIAH 9:38–10:29

Putting Your Life Where Your Mouth Is

[38]"In accordance with all this, we are confirming a pledge and putting it in writing, and on the sealed document are [the names of] our officials, our Levites, and our priests." [10:1]So on the sealed documents are Nehemiah son of Hacaliah, the administrator, and Zedekiah, [2]Seraiah, Azariah, Jeremiah, [3]Pashhur, Amariah, Malchijah, [4]Hattush, Shebaniah, Malluch, [5]Harim, Meremoth, Obadiah, [6]Daniel, Ginnethon, Baruch, [7]Meshullam, Abijah, Mijamin, [8]Maaziah, Bilgai, Shemiah: these are the priests. [9]The Levites: Jeshua son of Azaniah, Binnui of the sons of Henadad, and Kadmiel. [10]Their brothers: Shebaniah, Hodiah, Kelita, Pelaiah, Hanan, [11]Mica, Rehob, Hashabiah, [12]Zaccur, Sherebiah, Shebaniah, [13]Hodiah, Bani, and Beninu. [14]The heads of the people: Parosh, Pahath-moab, Elam, Zattu, Bani, [15]Bunni, Azgad, Bebai, [16]Adonijah, Bigvai, Adin, [17]Ater, Hezekiah, Azzur, [18]Hodiah, Hashum, Bezai, [19]Hariph, Anathoth, Nebia, [20]Magpiash, Meshullam, Hezir, [21]Meshezabel, Zadok, Jaddua, [22]Pelatiah, Hanan, Anaiah, [23]Hoshea, Hananiah, Hasshub, [24]Hallohesh, Pilha, Shobek, [25]Rehum, Hashabnah, Maaseiah, [26]and Ahiah, Hanan, Anan, [27]Malluch, Harim, Baanah. [28]"The rest of the people, the priests, Levites, gatekeepers, singers, assistants, and everyone who separated from the peoples of the countries to God's teaching, their wives, sons, and daughters, everyone who knows how to understand, [29]are holding fast to their brothers, their nobles, and are entering into a curse and an oath to walk by God's teaching that he gave by means of Moses, God's servant, and to keep and do all the commands of Yahweh our Lord, and his rules and statutes."

A friend of mine once lived in an area in the Pacific Northwest where most of her daughter's friends were Jewish. She had no idea what would happen when all these young people turned thirteen, but discovered that she should have put about a million dollars in her budget for Bat Mitzvah and Bar Mitzvah gifts because all her friends had elaborate celebrations of these events with receptions that were as expensive as weddings. But the most striking aspect of the events was the all-day readings of the **Torah** in the synagogue that preceded the reception and dominated the celebrations. My friend commented that this was when she became aware of how important the word of the Torah was to the Jewish community, which they kept "alive" by each generation learning Hebrew and reading it out loud.

The books of Ezra and Nehemiah have illustrated how important reading the Torah aloud became in the **Second Temple** community, and how important the congregational response was to the reading. To become Bat Mitzvah or Bar Mitzvah means agreeing to become a daughter or son of the commandment. It would be no use if those Jewish young people made their commitment in a ceremony but did not put their lives where their mouths were. The same applied to the Second Temple community. Its response had to involve commitment in life. In the present context in Nehemiah, the implication is that the **Levites**' impassioned appeal for God to look at their downcast circumstances can only hope to get anywhere if confession is accompanied by repentance in the sense of a change in the people's ways. If they don't want to be serfs (of the **Persians**) they have to be prepared to be servants (of God).

They have already indicated that this is their intention by gathering as people who have separated from foreigners. Their pledge-making after their confession makes explicit that this separation does not have an ethnic or political basis: it is a separation "to God's teaching," to the Torah. By implication, that phrase would cover people distinguishing themselves from Moabites and Ashdodites who did not acknowledge **Yahweh** at all, and also from Samarians who acknowledged Yahweh but whose commitment was questionable to the **Judahite** community. In connection with Ezra 4 we noted that in later times the Samarians were stricter in their adherence to the Torah than the Judahites, in the sense that they accepted only the Torah as Scripture and did not accept the Prophets and the Writings (see the Introduction for some explanation of these terms). But if the community in Nehemiah's day was using the question of adherence to the Torah as an excuse for ethnic prejudices or political policies, then its statement about the Torah nevertheless shows that it recognizes the proper basis for separation.

The people indicate that they are prepared to accompany confession with repentance by putting their commitment in writing. The Levites' prayer identified God as one who made a covenant with Abraham and as one who keeps covenant, and, in effect, the people now make their covenantal response to God. They "confirm" it, taking up the odd use of a verb that literally means "cut" and is a common way to speak of confirming a covenant (see **covenant**). Yet they do not use the actual word *covenant*, as Shekaniah did in Ezra 10. Instead they use a different word meaning a pledge or true commitment, one related to words in the Levites' prayer that described God as acting truly and that described Abraham as true. Not using the word *covenant* preserves the distinctiveness of the commitment that God makes to them, a commitment that is not conditioned by them or conditional on their response but that issues from God's grace (as the prayer emphasized). Yet using this novel word for "pledge" means they recognize that they are not let off the hook by the uniqueness of God's commitment to them. They are saying they will be like God and like Abraham. Their commitment is underlined by the talk of a curse and an oath. The oath is a solemn promise made in God's **name**; the curse is a prayer for trouble to come on them if they fail to keep their pledge.

Once again the community as a whole is involved. They are "holding fast" to one another in making their pledge. But this also implies the participation of every individual—men and women, and not only the heads of families but everyone in the family who is old enough to understand what is going on. Judah relates to God as a corporate entity but also as a collection of individuals. The political, administrative, and religious leaders of Judah are mostly men, but the relationship with God belongs to everyone. The list of names hints at another sense in which this is true. The names are familiar from other parts of Ezra and Nehemiah and form a kind of illustrative cross-section of names from the two books, and some are the names of families, not of individuals. The list thus sets up links between individuals both horizontally (the present members of families) and vertically (the members of families through the generations). Yes, the whole community makes this commitment.

NEHEMIAH 10:30–39

On Being Specific

[30]"[We are confirming a pledge] that we will not give our daughters to the peoples of the country and we will not take their daughters for our sons. [31]The peoples of the country who bring their wares or any grain on the Sabbath day to sell, we will not take it from them on the Sabbath, or on a holy day. We will forgo the seventh year and the usury on every signature. [32]We have imposed upon ourselves commands to put upon ourselves one-third of a shekel per year for the service of our God's house, [33]for the bread in the row, for the regular grain offering, and for the regular burnt offering, Sabbaths, new moons, for appointed occasions, holy offerings, and purification offerings, to expiate for Israel, and all the work of our God's house. [34]We have cast lots for the wood offering (the priests, the Levites, and the people) to bring it to our God's house by ancestral households at set times year by year to burn on the altar of Yahweh our God, as it is written in the teaching. [35][We undertake] to bring the first fruits of our ground and of every fruit of every tree year by year for Yahweh's house, [36]and the firstborn of our sons and our animals, as it is written in the teaching, and to bring the firstborn of our cattle and our flocks to our God's house to the priests who minister in our God's house. [37]We will bring the first of our dough, our contributions, and of the fruit of every tree, wine and oil, to the priests, to the store chambers in our God's house, and the tithe of our ground to the Levites; the Levites are the ones who collect tithes in all the cities where we serve. [38]The priest, the son of Aaron, is to be with the Levites when the Levites are collecting tithes, and the Levites are to bring up a tithe of the tithe to our God's house, to the store chambers of the treasury, [39]because the Israelites and the Levites are to bring to the store chambers the contribution of

> grain, wine, and oil. The utensils belonging to the sanctuary, the priests who minister, the gatekeepers, and the singers are there. We will not abandon our God's house."

I missed our congregational meeting three weeks ago because I was sick, and while this didn't exactly make it worthwhile to be sick, it was a kind of consolation, because I can't say I enthuse over the congregational meeting. I apologize to fellow members of St. Barnabas, and I know this lack of enthusiasm is my problem and that I should be glad to go to the meeting. It's the occasion when we review what we have been doing over the past year and discuss priorities and goals for the next year. Some of these priorities and goals are spiritual—they concern the way we seek to identify what is God's vision for us as a congregation and what are ways in which we might seek to reach out into our community. Some are practical. We have to agree on a budget and determine how we are going to finance the ministry for the next year as well as do something about the leak in the church roof. Some priorities live at the interface between the spiritual and the practical—to which category do you allocate a plan to serve a dinner for homeless people once a month? Some of the questions we need to ask vary from year to year; some are distinctive to a particular year.

Something similar is true of the detailed pledge that the **Judahites** make, and this explains the random-looking nature of the areas it covers. The problem of intermarriage with other communities that were not committed to the **Torah** is one peculiar to the **Second Temple** period. While kings such as Solomon were involved in such marriages for political reasons, as far as we can tell intermarriage was not an issue for ordinary people. So the community makes a specific commitment in relation to marriage. The problem of Sabbath observance has a similar background; if you live your life in an Israelite or Jewish community, there is little pressure to ignore the Sabbath or other holy days, but in a more pluralist context the temptation rises. So the community makes a specific commitment in relation to these. We know from Nehemiah 5 and other passages about the economic pressures on the community. These pressures made it tempting to ignore the Torah's rule about not charging interest on loans to people and would also make it tempting not to keep the Torah's rules about letting the land have its Sabbath every seven years. So the community makes a commitment about these.

The same economic pressures would make it tempting to hold back from supporting the work of the temple, and the bulk of the pledge concerns this obligation. Before the exile the support of the temple might work more smoothly because the king had responsibility for the matter. It was still the ordinary people who ultimately footed the bill, but the king's heavies went around collecting taxes that then paid for the temple's support. The abolition of the Judahite monarchy did not mean the end of taxation any more than the termination of the British monarchy's rule in the American colonies (the latter event was the context of Benjamin Franklin's observation that "in this world nothing can be said to be certain, except death and taxes"). People now paid taxes to the imperial government rather than to the Judahite monarchy. We have seen that the imperial government did finance special projects in Jerusalem and maybe provided more regular subventions, but evidently the local community was responsible for most of the temple's costs. So now the community had to commit itself to the giving that would meet these needs, rather than having no choice in the matter—which in terms of their relationship to God would be a step forward. The last line of the pledge says it all: "We will not abandon God's house." It was an undertaking they needed to think hard about before they made it. Commitments of all kinds (building projects, relationships, getting married, having children, being church, following God's call) all seem to cost more than we think when we make them. The community's commitment to the temple is going to cost them on an ongoing basis.

The pledge refers a couple of times to its involving undertakings that are in accordance with what is written in the Torah. At the same time it illustrates the way every generation has to work out how the Torah applies in new contexts. The Torah says nothing about what you do when foreign merchants are offering their wares on the Sabbath. The Sabbath is not binding on foreigners, and for a Judahite the Sabbath's ban relates to working not buying, so no transgression of the Sabbath commandment is involved when a Judahite buys on the Sabbath. Yet a moment's reflection generates the intuition that there is something wrong with that conclusion, and the pledge knows it is necessary to go beyond the letter of the law in order to get to the spirit of what God is asking of Israel. As it might be put theologically, the Judahite community knows that the reading of Scripture needs to be done in light of insight offered by the spirit of God whose work lies behind the Scriptures' coming into being. We need to live in a way that keeps with Scripture, but also in a way that reflects the context in which we live. Such living means not feeling free to leave scriptural imperatives aside because they are contextual, but seeing how these contextual imperatives apply in our context. There is no method for doing that; it requires intuition, or spiritual discernment, something exercised by the community together to safeguard against our blind spots as individuals and then to offer us support as we pay the price for our commitment to what we perceive God expecting.

Christian communities in the West might also need to think about the pledge they should make for the coming year, doing so in light of the Torah and the rest of the Scriptures, asking where lie the concrete challenges of the Scriptures for them. Their members would also need to do so. Whereas U.S. English uses the word *pledge* to describe the commitment we make in connection with giving, British English uses the word covenant, but a Californian church I know expects its members to draw up and sign a covenant with regard to what they will do as individuals in the next year as they seek to identify the concrete challenges that the Scriptures issue to them and as they seek to grow in faith, hope, and love.

We will discover that a number of the areas covered by this pledge are matters of concern in Nehemiah 13. The implication might be that people simply didn't keep the pledge or soon found other ways of sidestepping God's expectations. But we have already noted that there is some unevenness about Nehemiah 8–10 and about its relationship to its context, and more likely these three chapters sum up the dynamic of events in the time of Ezra and Nehemiah as a whole. Maybe an aspect of this

dynamic is that a community commitment to the elements in
a pledge of this kind might counteract the divisive effect of the
rift within the community threatened by awareness of what the
building project was costing families, implied by Nehemiah 5.

NEHEMIAH 11:1–36

The Holy City

¹The officials of the people settled in Jerusalem, but the rest of
the people cast lots to bring one out of ten to settle in Jerusalem,
the holy city, while nine tenths were in the cities. ²The people
blessed all the individuals who volunteered to settle in Jerusalem. ³These are the heads of the province who settled in Jerusalem, while in the cities of Judah they settled, each individual on
his property in their cities: Israel, priests, Levites, assistants, and
the descendants of Solomon's servants, ⁴and some of the Judahites and Benjaminites settled in Jerusalem. Of the Judahites:
Athaliah son of Uzziah son of Zechariah son of Amariah son
of Shephatiah son of Mahalel of the descendants of Perez,⁵and
Maaseiah son of Baruch son of Col-hozeh son of Hazaiah son
of Adaiah son of Joiarib son of Zechariah son of the Shilohite.
⁶All the descendants of Perez who settled in Jerusalem: 468 able
men. ⁷These are the Benjaminites: Sallu son of Meshullam son
of Joed son of Pedaiah son of Kolaiah son of Maaseiah son of
Ithiel son of Jesaiah, ⁸and after him Gabbai, Sallai: 928. ⁹Joel
son of Zichri was supervisor over them and Judah son of Has-
senuah was second-in-command over the city. ¹⁰Of the priests:
Jedaiah son of Joiarib, Jachin, ¹¹Seraiah son of Hilkiah son of
Meshullam son of Zadok son of Meraioth son of Ahitub, ruler
of God's house, ¹²and their brothers responsible for the work
in the house: 822; and Adaiah son of Jeroham son of Pelaliah
son of Amzi son of Zechariah son of Pashhur son of Malchijah, ¹³and his brothers, the ancestral heads: 242; and Amishai
son of Azarel son of Ahzai son of Meshillemoth son of Immer,
¹⁴and their brothers, able warriors: 128. Zabdiel son of Hagged-
olim was supervisor over them. ¹⁵Of the Levites: Shemaiah son
of Hasshub son of Azrikam son of Hashabiah son of Bunni,
¹⁶and Shabbetai and Jozabad of the heads of the Levites over the
external work for God's house, ¹⁷Mattaniah son of Micah son of
Zabdi son of Asaph, the head (the beginning of thanksgiving

for the prayer), Bakbukiah, one of his brothers, second-in-command, and Abda son of Shammua son of Galal son of Jeduthun. [18]All the Levites in the holy city: 284. [19]The gatekeepers: Akkub, Talmon, and their brothers who watched at the gates: 172. [20]The rest of Israel, the priests, the Levites in all the cities of Judah, each settled on his property. [21]The assistants settled on the Ophel; Zipha and Gishpa were over the assistants. [22]The supervisor of the Levites in Jerusalem was Uzzi son of Bani son of Hashabiah son of Mattaniah son of Micha, of the Asaphite singers, for rule over the work of God's house, [23]because there was a command of the king concerning them, namely a pledge concerning the singers, each day's requirement. [24]Petahiah son of Meshezabel, of the descendants of Zerah son of Judah, was the king's right hand man with regard to every matter relating to the people. [25]With regard to the villages, with their fields: some of the Judahites settled in Kiriath-arba and its dependencies, Dibon and its dependencies, and Jekabzeel and its villages, [26]Jeshua, Moladah, Beth-pelet, [27]Hazar-shual, Beer-sheba and its dependencies, [28]Ziklag, Meconah and its dependencies, [29]En-rimmon, Zorah, Jarmuth, [30]Zanoah, Adullam and their villages, Lachish and its fields, and Azekah and its dependencies. So they camped from Beer-sheba to the Hinnom Canyon. [31]The Benjaminites: from Geba, Michmash, and Aija, and Bethel and its dependencies, [32]Anathoth, Nob, Ananiah, [33]Hazor, Ramah, Gittaim, [34]Hadid, Zeboim, Neballat, [35]Lod, Ono, Ge-harashim. [36]Some of the Levites who were allocated to Judah belonged to Benjamin.

The first time I went to Jerusalem, I drove up the highway from the west, as most visitors do. The three-thousand-foot climb into the mountains is impressive, though when you reach the top of the ridge, the approach does not give you an awe-inspiring first sight of the modern city; you could be anywhere. Yet my heart was thrilled. This was Jerusalem, the holy city. The approach from the east, from across the Jordan River, below sea level, climbs four thousand feet more spectacularly through the desert and past the Inn of the Good Samaritan, until the rooftops of an ancient city appear over the skyline. It is Jerusalem, the holy city (though like other perspectives, now scarred by the wall dividing Israel from the West Bank). From the south, near Bethlehem, you can stand on a plaza with a panoramic

142

view of the ancient city, the Dome of the Rock glinting in the sunlight. This is Jerusalem, the holy city. From the north, you follow the road along the crest of the ridge in the way Isaiah imagines the **Assyrians** coming, and the way Titus led the Roman army in 70 AD, and eventually you can look down from Mount Scopus and get the opposite version of that panoramic view of the ancient city, with the Dome of the Rock gleaming in the sunlight (or covered in snow, like the last time I looked from that angle). This is Jerusalem, the holy city.

The expression "the holy city" comes twice in Nehemiah 11; it appears only three more times in the Old Testament: twice in Isaiah, once in Daniel. Jerusalem is the holy city because the holy place, the temple, is there; the holiness of the sanctuary flows over into the city. The city is identified with the holy God in a distinctive way. In a sense there is then not much difference between describing Jerusalem as the holy city or the chosen city, the much more common expression. "Chosen" is the term Nehemiah used in his prayer when he heard about its devastation (Nehemiah 1), and he makes the link with its being the place where the temple is, the place where **Yahweh** has made his **name** dwell. Jerusalem being the holy city then links with the awareness in Ezra and Nehemiah of a need to preserve the holiness of that which Yahweh has taken hold of. The need applies to the people, to the temple, and to the city.

In this chapter, the implication of Jerusalem's being the holy city is that it needs a population, and a population of a particular kind, a population of **Judahites**. There will be the practical consideration that it will be vulnerable to attack by those hostile neighboring peoples; a population throbbing with life is as important as walls in this connection. Yet the deeper consideration is that it seems inappropriate for the holy city to be an impressively walled ghost town. That was not what God had in mind when promising that after the exile the city would be transformed. In connection with Nehemiah's wall-building project and the initial talk there of repopulating the city, we noted God's promise in Zechariah 2 that Jerusalem was destined (figuratively speaking, at least) to be an open, unwalled city, like a village, because there will be so many people and cattle in it. Nehemiah 7 could describe the city as indeed broad and large, yet as lacking sufficient population. If the Judahite leadership is aware of Zechariah's prophecy, they again assume that when God makes a promise you don't necessarily just sit around waiting until God fulfills it in a miraculous way. On the contrary, the promise encourages you to take action because you know you are involved in an undertaking that fits into God's purpose and that God might therefore prosper. You're a bit like the little boy giving Jesus his loaves and fish.

Describing Jerusalem as the holy city implies an incentive to people to come and live there even though for years they have been used to living in, say, Ziklag or Lachish. There is indeed some ambiguity about the basis on which it was determined who would move to Jerusalem. If this was decided by lot, why are the people commended for volunteering? Did they jump or were they pushed? Are they commended because they willingly accepted their selection when the lot fell that way? Or perhaps there were some who volunteered and this lessened the number who had to be selected. The list of the people who made the sacrifice involved in going to live in Jerusalem (whether under pressure or voluntarily) further honors them as people of faith, love, pride, and dedication in their relationship with the city. It might be further significant that volunteering is a term that can be used of people offering themselves to take part in a battle when one is imminent, and people who go to live in Jerusalem may well find themselves having to defend the city.

In the New Testament, Revelation three times uses the phrase *holy city* to designate the new Jerusalem. One might think that the physical Jerusalem ceases to be the holy city after Jesus' coming, yet decades after Jesus' death and resurrection, Revelation 11 and Matthew 4 and 27 also speak of the physical place as the holy city. Human nature has a built-in awareness of there being a holy place, a material place where we can be sure of meeting with God. It is part of God's making us physical creatures. God meets that God-given need in providing such a place. Yet there is a more specific reason why Jerusalem in particular continues to be the holy city. It is not surprising that Jews at Passover say, "Next year in Jerusalem."

As a Christian who lives in the Old Testament, I find it awe-inspiring to approach Jerusalem from any direction, but it is not surprising if any Christians find Jerusalem awe-inspiring. Jerusalem became part of the story of God's involvement with Israel, and that involvement continued with the birth, death, and resurrection of Jesus in the holy city, and the way the holy city is the place from which the message about Jesus goes out to the world. Neither Rome nor Canterbury nor Geneva is the holy city. Jerusalem is.

NEHEMIAH 12:1–43

Our Achievement, God's Enabling

[1]These were the priests and Levites who went up with Zerubbabel son of Shealtiel and Jeshua: Seraiah, Jeremiah, Ezra, [2]Amariah, Malluch, Hattush, [3]Shecaniah, Rehum, Meramoth, [4]Iddo, Ginnethoi, Abijah, [5]Mijamin, Maadiah, Bilgah, [6]Shemaiah, Joiarib, Jedaiah, [7]Sallu, Amok, Hilkiah, Jedaiah. These were the heads of the priests and their brothers in the days of Jeshua. [8]The Levites: Jeshua, Binnui, Kadmiel, Sherebiah, Judah, and Mattaniah over the thanksgivings, he and his brothers, [9]with Bakbukiah and Unni, their brothers, opposite them for the duties. [10]Jeshua was father of Joiakim, Joiakim of Eliashib, Eliashib of Joiada, [11]Joiada of Jonathan, Jonathan of Jaddua. [12]In the days of Joiakim, the priests who were ancestral heads were: for Seraiah, Meriaiah; for Jeremiah, Hananiah; [13]for Ezra, Meshullam; for Amariah, Jehohanan; [14]for Melicu, Jonathan; for Shebaniah, Joseph; [15]for Harim, Adna; for Meraioth, Helkai; [16]for Iddo, Zechariah; for Ginnethon, Meshullam; [17]for Abijah, Zichri; for Miniamin; for Moadiah, Piltai; [18]for Bilgah, Shammua; for Shemaiah, Jehonathan; [19]for Joiarib, Mattenai; for Jedaiah, Uzzi; [20]for Sallai, Kallai; for Amok, Eber; [21]for Hilkiah, Hashabiah; for Jedaiah, Nethanel. [22]The Levites in the days of Eliashib, Joiada, and Johanan, and Jaddua, were written down as ancestral heads, also the priests, in the reign of Darius the Persian. [23]The Levites, the ancestral heads, were written down in the annals up to the days of Johanan son of Eliashib. [24]The heads of the Levites: Hashabiah, Sherebiah, Jeshua son of Kadmiel, and their brothers opposite them, in praising, in giving thanks, by the command of David the man

of God, duty corresponding to duty; ²⁵Mattaniah, Bakbukiah, Obadiah, Meshullam, Talmon, and Akkub, keeping the watch as gatekeepers at the stores by the gates. ²⁶These were in the days of Joiakim son of Jeshua son of Jozadak, and in the days of Nehemiah the governor and Ezra the priest-scholar.

²⁷At the dedication of the Jerusalem wall, they sought out the Levites from all their places to bring them to Jerusalem to carry out the dedication celebration with thanksgivings and with song, cymbals, banjos, and guitars. ²⁸The singers gathered both from the area around Jerusalem and from the villages of the Netophathites, ²⁹from Beth-hagilgal, and from the country around Geba and Azmaveth, because the singers built themselves villages around Jerusalem. ³⁰The priests and Levites purified themselves and purified the people, the gates, and the wall. ³¹I got the officials of Judah to go up onto the wall and I put in place two large thanksgiving [choirs]. They went, one to the right on the wall to the Trash Gate, ³²and Hoshea and half the officials of Judah went behind them, ³³as did Azariah, Ezra, and Meshullam, ³⁴Judah, Benjamin, Shemaiah, Jeremiah, ³⁵some of the priests with trumpets, Zechariah son of Jonathan son of Shemaiah son of Mattaniah son of Micaiah son of Zaccur son of Asaph, ³⁶his brothers Shemaiah and Azarel, Milalai, Gilalai, Maai, Nethanel, Judah, and Hanani, with the musical instruments of David the man of God, Ezra the scholar being at the front of them. ³⁷Above the Spring Gate, straight ahead of them they went up the ascent to David's city by the ascent to the wall, above David's house, as far as the Water Gate on the east. ³⁸The second thanksgiving [choir] went the opposite way, with me behind it, and half the people, on the wall above the Ovens Tower to the broad wall, ³⁹and above the Ephraim Gate, the Jeshanah Gate, the Fish Gate, Hananel's Tower, the Hundred Tower, to the Sheep Gate, and stopped at the Guard Gate. ⁴⁰The two thanksgiving [choirs] stopped at God's house, as did I and half the overseers with me, ⁴¹and the priests Eliakim, Maaseiah, Miniamin, Micaiah, Elionai, Zechariah, Hananiah, with trumpets, ⁴²and Maaseiah and Shemaiah, Eleazar, Uzzi, Jehohanan, Malchijah, Elam, and Ezer. The singers made proclamation, with Jezrahiah as the supervisor. ⁴³They offered great sacrifices that day and celebrated, because God had enabled them to celebrate greatly. The women and children also celebrated. The celebration in Jerusalem was heard from afar.

From whichever of the four directions you approach Jerusalem, which I described in connection with Nehemiah 11, you are sooner or later struck by the medieval walls of the "Old City," though they impress you most if you are arriving from the east after that long climb from the Jordan River because there is much less modern development of the city on its east side. The walls tower above you as you draw near the city. In introducing people to the city, I take them on a walk around the walls because this gives a perspective on the city as a place teeming with life. On the north-south axis the medieval walls are located some hundreds of yards north of the walls of biblical times, and on the west they cover a broader area than Nehemiah's wall. Yet in any age it is easy to imagine the sense of security that walls give to a city in an age that lacks cannons or rockets or bombs (though attackers scaled them in order to take the city on a number of occasions).

It is therefore easy to imagine the rejoicing at their completion. The walls are also dedicated; during the building the priests had consecrated their section. It is usually altars or temples that are dedicated (see Ezra 6), though the verb can also be used in connection with children or a house, but then it means something like "initiate." One could say that the ceremony on the walls is their initiation, the moment when they come into use. Yet the thanksgiving, sacrifice, and purification do parallel the ceremony practiced when a temple is brought into use. The ceremony involves more than what happens when a couple start living in their house or when they educate a child. Maybe there is a link with the unusual designation of Jerusalem as the holy city in the preceding chapter. The walls mark the bounds of its holiness and thus fulfill a function in serving its holiness.

The people could congratulate themselves on their achievement. They had bought into Nehemiah's vision, done the work, made the sacrifice involved in neglecting their regular work and imperiling their livelihood, and been ready to fight against opponents if necessary. Yet the dedication ceremony is one of thanksgiving, led by the **Levites** in their capacity as worship-leaders and involving marshaling Levites from a wide area to generate choirs big enough to match the occasion's importance. Two thanksgiving choirs process around the city on the wall, starting from the Canyon Gate on the west and then going in opposite directions until they meet again on the east, at the temple. There they offer thanksgiving sacrifices of the kind that God and people share as they rejoice in what God has done. Like the account of the completion of the work in chapter 6, the account of the dedication presupposes the coming together of human effort and divine enabling. When we attempt something and it comes off, we may have a sense that we should not merely be pleased with ourselves but be grateful to God. You can work very hard at building and keeping watch yet not succeed unless God is involved (see Psalm 127). Things may go wrong despite your best efforts. The same was true about building the walls. If the people do nothing, the walls will not get built. If God does nothing, the walls may also not get built. So there is reason to be thankful. God had enabled them to celebrate in the sense that God had given them reason to celebrate.

The dedication also involves the purification of the Levites leading the worship and of the people offering it, and of the gates and walls themselves. The dedication ceremony involves people drawing near to God, so they have to make sure that they are not affected by defilement. Further, in requiring purification, this ceremony parallels the dedication of the temple in Ezra 6. The community is defiled by the worship of other deities that sparked the judgment that led to the fall of the city, the destruction of its walls, and then by their having to live cheek-by-jowl with foreigners who worshiped other deities and by their own involvement in that worship. The community has been further defiled by its intermarriages with people who did not live by the **Torah** but worshiped other deities. It cannot claim to have walked in a very different way from the community before the **exile**. But God's enabling it to complete the walls is another testimony to God's grace and mercy. So is God's providing it with means of eliminating these defilements. God, the offended party, provides them with the means of starting over in the relationship.

In the lists of the priests and Levites, the duties opposite each other or corresponding to each other imply a link with the way Israel's worship involves antiphonal singing; one choir sings the first half of a verse, the other responds with the second half in a way that corresponds to the parallelism in the verses. The lists begin with people who came from **Babylon** nearly a century previously and thus point to the continuity between present and previous generations. Indeed, they point toward our seeing the building of the wall and its dedication as the final completion of the story that began in Ezra 1–6, the final completion of the restoration of the community and the city after the exile. The only Jaddua we otherwise know about was senior priest in the next century when the **Persian** Empire fell to Alexander, so if this Jaddua is the same person, the list extends down a century beyond Nehemiah's day as well as extending back a century from his day, and points to the ongoing continuity of Judahite life.

NEHEMIAH 12:44–13:14

The Pastor's Frustration

[44]On that day they appointed people over the store chambers for the contributions, first fruits, and tithes, for collecting in them (with regard to the fields belonging to the cities) the portions specified by the teaching for the priests and Levites, because Judah's rejoicing was over the priests and the Levites who stood in attendance [before God] [45]and kept the duty of their God and the duty of purity, and the singers and gatekeepers, in accordance with the command of David and his son Solomon [46](because in the days of David and Asaph of old, there were heads of the singers and of the song of praise and thanksgiving to God). [47]In the days of Zerubbabel and Nehemiah all Israel would give the portions of the singers and gatekeepers, the amount for each day, and consecrate [contributions] for the Levites, while the Levites would consecrate [contributions] for the Aaronites.

[13:1]On that day there was a reading from Moses' scroll in the ears of the people and it was found written in it that an Ammonite or Moabite should not come into God's congregation, in perpetuity, [2]because they did not meet the Israelites with bread and water but hired Balaam to belittle them—though our God turned the belittling into blessing. [3]When they heard the teaching, they separated the entire mixed crowd from Israel. [4]Before this, Eliashib the priest had been placed over a chamber in our God's house; he was close to Tobiah, ⁵and he had prepared for him a large chamber where previously they were putting the grain offering, the incense, the accoutrements, the tithe of grain, wine, and oil that was commanded for the Levites, the singers, and gatekeepers, and the contribution for the priests. ⁶During all this time I was not in Jerusalem because in the thirty-second year of Artaxerxes king of Babylon I came to the king. After a period of time I asked leave of the king ⁶and came to Jerusalem. I learned about the wrong that Eliashib had done for Tobiah in preparing a chamber for him in the courtyards of God's house. ⁸It was very displeasing to me. I threw all the accoutrements of Tobiah's household out of the chamber ⁹and said they should purify the chamber, and I put back there the accoutrements of God's house, the grain offering, and the incense.

¹⁰I got to know that the portions for the Levites had not been given, so that the Levites and the singers who were responsible for the work had fled each of them to his field. ¹¹I contended with the overseers and said, "Why has God's house been abandoned?" I assembled [the Levites] and put them in place at their post, ¹²and all Judah brought the tithe of grain, wine, and oil into the stores. ¹³I appointed as storekeepers over the stores Shelemiah the priest, Zadok the scholar, and Pedaiah from the Levites, and at their right hand Hanan son of Zaccur son of Mattaniah, because they were reckoned trustworthy, and it was up to them to make allocations to their brothers.

¹⁴Be mindful of me, my God, because of this. Do not blot out my acts of commitment, which I have performed for God's house and for its duties.

Last night I was talking to a group of pastors about what they found discouraging about their ministry. It seemed that often they had a vision for something but they couldn't sell the vision to their congregation. A trivial example (in a way) was one pastor's one-time attempt to raise money to buy sleeping bags for twelve homeless people during the cold snap we had last month. He ended up buying the sleeping bags himself. A bigger example was a pastor who had watched his congregation grow from a few hundred to more than a thousand but who feared he had merely encouraged the development of a religious social club. His proposal that they reshape their life in order to reach out to the substantial Hispanic population in their city led to a substantial reduction in the congregation's size. Admittedly pastors can be insensitive in the way they seek to share their vision and maybe need to pay more attention to letting the vision arise from the congregation.

I imagine Nehemiah tearing his hair out as a pastor. He thinks he has got the community on board with his reforms, but he turns his back and things are on their way back to the way they were previously. One area where this is so is the need for practical arrangements for the support of the people involved in ministry in the temple. The problem isn't merely one of persuading people to give. Indeed, maybe this is only where the problem starts. In our own world there can be an outpouring of public generosity toward the victims of a natural disaster, but how do you get the gifts to the people who need them (and without their being siphoned off by people who can make money out of the generosity)? Here, too, the community is touchingly enthusiastic about supporting the ministry of the temple, and the administrative task is further increased because the giving has to be in kind not in cash (imagine the vast number of bags of grain, dried fruit, and so on). But the community does make practical arrangements for the storage of the tithes and other contributions so that they can be properly distributed among the priests, **Levites**, singers, and **gatekeepers**, who are responsible for offering the people's sacrifices, for other aspects of leading in worship, and for making sure that the sanctuary stays pure by advising people about possible causes of defilement and how to deal with them, and for keeping it secure in other ways.

So far so good. But Nehemiah is absent, reporting back to the emperor who had commissioned him (we don't know if this was a routine procedure). A priest called Eliashib (who might or might not be the senior priest of that name) coolly provided rooms in the temple area for no one other than Tobiah the Ammonite, who seems to have been Sanballat's man in Jerusalem and thus someone opposed to Nehemiah's rebuilding work in the city. It was surely obvious that the temple should not be defiled by an action such as this. Maybe Eliashib's action is another indication that not everyone in Jerusalem supported

Nehemiah's work, even if they kept quiet about their opinions when he was around. Or maybe Eliashib felt unable to resist pressure from Tobiah. The rooms are the very ones that were supposed to be used for storing the provisions that were to go to the people involved in the temple ministry. Either Tobiah's occupying of the rooms then caused a breakdown in the distribution arrangements, or people's enthusiasm about supporting the ministry had waned and the rooms were no longer needed in this connection.

The inclusion of the passage about not accepting Moabites or Ammonites into the congregation relates to the priest's giving accommodation in the temple precincts to an *Ammonite*, for goodness' sake. The relevant passage from the **Torah** comes in Deuteronomy 23. Neither that rule nor Nehemiah's appeal to it implies that an Ammonite or Moabite can't become a worshiper of **Yahweh** and join the congregation in that sense. At least, the story of Ruth presupposes that a Moabite can become a worshiper of Yahweh, and the community that accepted Ruth into its Scriptures made the same assumption. Likewise there was an Ammonite and a Moabite among David's crack troops. On the other hand, a Moabite or an Ammonite like Tobiah who lives in Jerusalem but wants to stay loyal to his traditional god and his people can't be a full member of the community. That rule applies to any foreigners, though there was a particular reason for antipathy to such Ammonites and Moabites because of the stance they took in relation to Israel when the people were on their way to Canaan.

Nehemiah has to sort all this out when he gets back to Jerusalem, making Tobiah find offices elsewhere and ensuring that the Levites could be provided with support so they could fulfill their ministry by putting them back in their proper position where they could superintend the tithes. It would be more of an issue for the Levites and other temple ministers than for the priests because the priests received a share from the people's sacrifices and they were not reliant on tithes and other offerings. As long as people continued to bring sacrifices, they and their families would not starve. For all the ministers in the temple, whether people did bring tithes and offerings was a matter of life and death.

NEHEMIAH 13:15–31

Desecration and Trespass

¹⁵In those days I saw people in Judah treading winepresses on the Sabbath, and bringing grain and stacking it on donkeys, and also wine, grapes, figs, and every sort of load, and bringing them into Jerusalem on the Sabbath day. I testified on the day when they sold the provisions ¹⁶and when the Tyrians who had settled there were bringing fish and every sort of merchandise and selling on the Sabbath before Judah and in Jerusalem, ¹⁷and contended with the nobles of Judah. I said to them, "What is this wrong thing that you are doing, and desecrating the Sabbath day? ¹⁸Didn't our ancestors act like this, and our God brought all this trouble on us, and on this city? You are increasing wrath against Israel by desecrating the Sabbath." ¹⁹When the gates of Jerusalem grew dark before the Sabbath, I said that the doors should shut, and said that they should not open them until after the Sabbath. I put in place some of my boys at the gates so that no load should come in on the Sabbath day. ²⁰The merchants and the people selling every sort of merchandise spent the night outside Jerusalem once or twice, ²¹but I testified to them and said to them, "Why are you spending the night opposite the wall? If you do it again, I will lay hands on you." From that time they did not come on the Sabbath. ²²I said to the Levites that they should purify themselves and come guard the gates to consecrate the Sabbath day. Be mindful of this for me, too, my God, and spare me in accordance with the greatness of your commitment.

²³In those days I also saw the Judahites were bringing home Ashdodite, Ammonite, and Moabite women. ²⁴Half their children were speaking Ashdodite and none of them knew how to speak Judahite, but [spoke] in accordance with the tongue of one people or another. ²⁵I contended with them and belittled them, and struck some of them down and pulled out their hair, and swore by God: "If you give your daughters to their sons or if you take some of their daughters for your sons or for yourselves. . . . ²⁶Was it not in these things that Solomon the king of Israel offended? Among the many nations there was no king like him. He was cared for by God, and God made him king over all Israel. Foreign women caused even him to offend. ²⁷Are we to listen to you doing this great wrong, trespassing against

our God by taking foreign women home?" ²⁸One of the sons of Joiada son the senior priest Eliashib was son-in-law to Sanballat the Horonite. I drove him away from me. ²⁹Be mindful with regard to them, my God, because they polluted the priesthood, the covenant of the priesthood and the Levites.

³⁰I purified them of everything foreign and put in place the duties for the priests and Levites, each one in his work, ³¹and for the wood offering at designated times and for the first fruits.

My God, be mindful for me for good.

One weekend in December my new wife and I flew to London for a first meeting with my sons and their families and for a marriage thanksgiving service at the American Church in London. The occasion meant new frocks all around, and on the day of the service my elder son was ironing his daughter's frock when he realized he had burnt a large hole in the front. The family rushed down to Oxford Street, London's premiere shopping thoroughfare, to buy another dress, knowing that the store opened at 11:00. Everything should have been fine; they could still be on time for the wedding lunch at noon. Except that the store was indeed open for people to look at merchandise from 11:00, but they couldn't sell anything until noon because that is how the Sunday trading laws in England work. So they showed up an hour late; but a good time was had. The rules about Sunday trading had changed from what they were when I was a child, though not without eliminating arcane rules. My parents kept a mom and pop store, and on Sunday they could sell fresh produce (say, fresh peas) but not canned produce (say, a can of peas), which was reasonable enough because the former were perishable and the latter not. So which category do frozen peas come in? Presumably the latter. Wrong! They could sell frozen peas. The rules were designed as a compromise attempt to let stores open but still offer some protection to family life, church attendance, and the rights of the people who work in the stores.

The first and last of these considerations are likely implicit in the fourth commandment, especially in the version in Deuteronomy 5. The whole family stops work on the Sabbath, and the head of the family is to make sure that servants and animals also take part. The middle of the three considerations (that people be free to go to church) does not apply to the Sabbath, which is not especially a worship day, even though one might guess that it would be a natural day for families to be involved in learning from the **Torah** in the way Deuteronomy also describes. Yet a related consideration does apply. In the Ten Commandments the Sabbath is the last of the commandments concerned with relationships with God as well as leading into the commandments covering relationships with other people. The Sabbath is a day people have to treat as holy. It belongs to God. God has claimed this day and it is sacred ground. They have to keep off it.

Nehemiah makes that assumption and is thus concerned with the "desecrating" of the Sabbath. People are treating it as just an ordinary day instead of as a day that God has made sacred and has a special claim on. It parallels the holiness of the sanctuary and the offerings. People have to treat them as holy by using them in the way God says.

In connection with Nehemiah 10 we noted that the question of buying and selling on the Sabbath is a new one over against the Ten Commandments. The way the fourth commandment is expressed reflects the fact that most Israelites lived in villages and were engaged in farming so that the temptation to treat the Sabbath as ordinary finds expression in a temptation to work on the farm on that day. Maybe the crops are ripe and it seems vital to harvest them quickly (milking cows might be a different matter, as it is hardly kind to them to leave them unmilked). Can people really afford to take a day off from work in these circumstances?

In Jerusalem the dynamics of life were different. Some people would be involved in farming outside the city, but many others are occupied in the affairs of the city such as trade, diplomacy, crafts, administration, and the work of the temple. In the city the temptation to treat the Sabbath as ordinary thus takes the different form of declining to be involved in shopping. The fact that the people who are doing the actual selling are foreigners highlights another significance of the Sabbath, which gained increasing significance in the **Second Temple** period as **Judahites** were living cheek-by-jowl with people from other communities. The Sabbath becomes a marker of Israel's distinctiveness. Everyone would agree with most of the Ten Commandments. But stop work one day a week? That's weird. So it becomes a distinctive feature of Israel's covenant commitment to God. The deployment of the **Levites** to safeguard the Sabbath and the expectation that they will purify themselves for this task reflects the sense that this is a matter that affects Israel's own holiness. If Western Christians don't feel they need to observe a Sabbath, we need to ask whether the Sabbath principles are embodied in our lives (probable answer—no). Indeed, observing a Sabbath can still be a way we embody and witness to the reality of God.

The last main paragraph in the book again covers a matter about which we have read more than once in Ezra–Nehemiah. Here Nehemiah is not merely tearing out his own hair as a pastor but tearing out the hair of the people he is confronting. "Tearing out" may give the wrong impression; perhaps he simply "tore at" their hair, perhaps the hair in their beards. The point of the action is that it is a gesture of shaming.

With the miscellaneous list of actions in this closing chapter, Ezra–Nehemiah comes to a puzzling, anti-climactic end, though that makes it like some other books in the Bible such as Jonah and Mark's Gospel. The effect in Nehemiah is to set up a tension between the decisive action of Ezra and Nehemiah, affirmed by the Judahite community, and the need for them to continue to handle issues that they have handled before. It is a characteristic feature of life that we do not finally solve problems. It is not a reason to hold back from taking action. It is a reason not to be depressed when what we think are solutions turn out not to be final. We have to pull ourselves together and take action again.

In that context, the three prayers for God to be mindful gain particular significance. It is impossible for Nehemiah to know whether his work has been worthwhile or whether it will have an effect on the future. Perhaps his reforms will all unravel. The prayers suggest some anxiety about whether God will be mindful of him and of the egregious nature of some of the actions of other people. There is a limit to what our best efforts can achieve and we cannot know what they will in fact achieve. Nehemiah is free to express that anxiety to God and then leave things with God.

ESTHER 1:1-22

The Woman Who Won't Play Ball

[1]In the days of Xerxes (it was the Xerxes who reigned from India to Sudan over a hundred and twenty-seven provinces), [2]in those days, when King Xerxes sat on the royal throne in the fortress of Susa, [3]in the third year of his reign, he made a banquet for all his officials and staff. The army officers of Persia and Media, the nobles, and the officials of the provinces were before him [4]while he displayed the riches of his royal glory and the honor of his great splendor for many days—one hundred and eighty days. [5]At the completion of these days the king made a banquet for all the people to be found in the fortress of Susa, high and low, for seven days, in the courtyard of the king's palace garden, [6]with white cloth, fine linen, and purple cloth, fastened with bands of white linen and purple wool to silver rods and alabaster pillars, couches of gold and silver on a pavement of porphyry, alabaster, marble, and mosaic, [7]the giving of drinks in gold vessels (vessels differing from one another) and much royal wine in accordance with the king's liberality, [8]and drinking in accordance with the rule "There is no one restraining," because that was how the king had established it with every steward in his house, to act in accordance with the wishes of each individual. [9]In addition Queen Vashti made a women's banquet at the royal house of King Xerxes.

[10]On the seventh day, when the king was in good spirits because of the wine, he said to Mehuman, Bizzetha, Harbona, Bigtha, Abagtha, Zethar, and Carcas, the seven eunuchs who attended on the presence of King Xerxes, [11]to bring Queen Vashti before the king in her royal crown, to show the peoples and officials her beauty, because she was lovely in appearance. [12]But Queen Vashti refused to come at the king's word by means of the eunuchs. The king was very angry. His fury burned in him. [13]The king said to the experts who knew the times (because this was the practice of the king in relation to all those

who knew law and judgment; ¹⁴near to him were Carshena, Shethar, Admatha, Tarshish, Meres, Marsena, and Memucan, the seven officials of Persia and Media who had access to the king's presence and sat in first place in the realm), ¹⁵"According to the law, what should be done with Queen Vashti because she has not obeyed the word of King Xerxes by means of the eunuchs?" ¹⁶Memucan said in the presence of the king and the officials, "It is not against the king alone that Queen Vashti has done wrong, but against all the officials and all the peoples in all the provinces of King Xerxes. ¹⁷Because the queen's action will get out to all the women so as to make them despise their husbands in their eyes when they say, 'King Xerxes told Queen Vashti to come before him, and she did not come.' ¹⁸This day the ladies of Persia and Media who have heard of the queen's action will say it to all the king's officials, with quite enough scorn and provocation. ¹⁹If it seems good to your majesty, a royal word should issue from the king and it should be written into the laws of Media and Persia and not pass away, that Vashti is not to come before King Xerxes. The king should give her royal position to another woman who is better than her. ²⁰The king's proclamation that he makes will be heard in all his realm (because it is great), and all the women will give honor to their husbands, both great and small." ²¹The thing was pleasing in the eyes of the king and the officials, and the king acted in accordance with Memucan's word. ²²He sent documents to all the king's provinces, province by province in accordance with its script and people by people in accordance with its language, for every man to be ruler in his household and speak in accordance with the language of his own people.

"Stand by your man," Tammy Winette urged, even if he has done things that you can't understand and that are hard to forgive. Every few months some governor or senator or mayor or pastor is exposed for having an affair or seeing a prostitute, and the exposure is followed by tearful scenes on TV where the man declares how repentant he is and how he intends to focus on mending relationships with his family, and his wife stands there by her man looking gray but supporting him. And you wonder how on earth things can be mended. But then from time to time you hear that a woman who might (or might not) have appeared in those tearful scenes isn't standing by her man

158

after all but has said "I'm outta here." It was the premise of a whole TV series about *The Good Wife*.

Vashti has reached that point. Of course we don't know what has preceded the king's summons at this banquet. Has she been paraded this way before? Her husband has quite a harem; we should not assume a loving exclusive personal relationship between the king and his queen modeled on the ideals of Western marriage. Perhaps it would be quite natural for the king to parade one or two of his dancing girls in this way; but the queen? One reason why the king holds a six-month drinking party (the etymological meaning of the word for "banquet") is to keep his (male) staff loyal and hard-working. Parading the queen is another means to that end. Some further assumptions about marriage surface as the chapter unfolds. It's the job of a wife to obey her husband. That obviously applies to the wife of a king, and the men in the **Persian** court assume it applies to all wives.

An Israelite couple might laugh. There is nothing in the Old Testament that says wives have to obey their husbands, and stories like those of Abraham and Sarah or Isaac and Rebekah don't give the impression that Old Testament wives could be ordered around. The terms the Persians use to refer to husbands and wives are telling in this connection. They literally suggest that the man is the "master" or "owner" and the women is the "mastered" or "owned." Usually the Old Testament itself does not use these words to refer to husbands and wives but rather uses the ordinary words for "man" or "woman." "His wife" is literally "his woman." "Her husband" is literally "her man." There is a sense in which a married couple own each other, but the ownership is mutual. The man stands by his woman and the woman stands by her man. That was how things started, at creation. Of course things then went wrong and human disobedience to God led to husbands starting to exercise authority over wives. Many of the rules in the **Torah** accept that this is how things work, but the stories about marriages in the Old Testament also show that the creation ideal survived.

At least, that was so among ordinary people. When you become a king, like Saul or David or Solomon, the ideal goes out of the window. It had done so at the Persian court. And the men in the Persian court are in a panic about what will follow if men's authority is questioned.

The opening of the story throws into sharper light the rather pathetic nature of their reaction to Vashti's taking her stand. This is the royal court of Persia, which rules all those provinces! This is a king who can throw a drinking party lasting six months! This is a banquet that takes place in the setting of the splendid parks decorated with the most splendid hangings, and one that of course involved drinking without limit! (We should assume some hyperbole throughout the book of Esther; we are not to take every detail literally.) But the king who can manage all this self-indulgence cannot manage his wife?! Men know that women have sexual power and that they are in control of what they do with their sexual power, so they (we) fear women's sexual power and try to control it, but often do so in vain. And the king's dilemma results in a monumental over-reaction as all the resources of the famed Persian legal system are brought to bear on his domestic crisis. The trouble is that a man and a system that make such a mess of a domestic crisis don't look as if they are likely to work very well in connection with more serious matters. We will not be surprised that the great king later walks into the crisis that will form the focus of the book.

Confronted by sexism like that of Xerxes, women have a number of possible reactions open to them. One is to accept it in the way Xerxes expects. Another is to accept it in a formal way (maybe letting the men think they are in control) but to exploit their sexual power to get their way. Another is to work with sexism but to subvert it in more subtle ways; this is what Esther will do. Another is simply to say "No"; that is what Vashti does. In theory one might picture these as choices, as if a woman decides which kind of woman to be, but I am not sure this is really the dynamic of what happens. I doubt if Vashti has much choice. She does what she has to do in order to be her own person and be able to look at herself in the mirror, even though the price she pays is being deposed from her position as queen and wife.

Xerxes was king of Persia from 485 to 465, so chronologically this story fits in between the move of **Judahites** to rebuild

160

the temple in the time of Cyrus and Darius (Ezra 1–6) and the missions of Ezra and Nehemiah in the time of Artaxerxes (Ezra 7–Nehemiah 13). Many translations give a more literal translit-eration of the Hebrew name as Ahasuerus, which is the Hebrew version of the Persian name; the English name Xerxes is the Greek version of that Persian name.

ESTHER 2:1–18

The Girl Who Pays a Price

[1]After this, when King Xerxes' fury had subsided, he was mind-ful of Vashti and what she had done and what had been deter-mined against her. [2]The king's boys who attended on him said, "Young girls of beautiful appearance should be sought out. [3]The king should appoint representatives in every province of his realm so that they can assemble every young girl of beautiful appearance to the fortress of Susa, to the women's household to the control of Hege, the king's eunuch, the women's guard-ian, and they should be given their cosmetics. [4]The girl who is pleasing in the king's eyes should reign instead of Vashti." The thing was pleasing in the king's eyes, and he did so.

[5]Now there was a Judahite in the fortress of Susa named Mor-decai son of Jair son of Shimei son of Kish, a Benjaminite, [6]who had been exiled from Jerusalem with the group of exiles that had been exiled with Jeconiah king of Judah, which Nebuchad-nezzar king of Babylon had taken into exile. [7][Mordecai] was looking after Hadassah (that is, Esther), his uncle's daughter, because she had no father or mother. The girl had a lovely figure and was beautiful in appearance. When her father and mother died, Mordecai took her as his daughter.

[8]When the king's word and decree was made known and many girls assembled to the fortress of Susa to the control of Hegai, Esther was taken into the king's household into the control of Hegai, the women's guardian. [9]The girl was pleasing in his eyes and she gained commitment before him. He hurried to give her her cosmetics and her allowance of food, and to give her the seven girls who had been looked for from the king's household, and he moved her and her girls to the best part of the women's household. [10]Esther did not disclose her people or her fam-ily, because Mordecai had commanded her not to disclose it.

[11]Every day, day-by-day, Mordecai used to walk about in front of the courtyard of the women's household so as to know about Esther's welfare and what was happening to her.

[12]When each girl's turn arrived to come to King Xerxes at the end of her being treated for twelve months in accordance with the decree for the women (because thus were the days of their cosmetic treatment fulfilled: six months with oil of myrrh and six months with perfumes and women's cosmetics) [13]in this way the girl went to the king: everything she said would be given her to go with her from the women's household to the king's household. [14]In the evening she went and in the morning she came back to the second women's household, to the control of Shaashgaz, the king's eunuch, guardian of the secondary wives. She would not come again to the king unless the king wanted her and she was summoned by name. [15]When the turn arrived for Esther daughter of Abihail (uncle of Mordecai, who had taken her as his daughter) to come to the king, she did not request anything except what Hegai the king's eunuch, the guardian of the women, said. Esther found favor in the eyes of everyone who saw her.

[16]Esther was taken to King Xerxes in his royal household in the tenth month (that is, the month of Tebeth) in the seventh year of his reign. [17]The king liked Esther more than all the women. She found favor and commitment from him more than all the young girls, and he put a royal crown on her head and made her queen instead of Vashti. [18]The king made a great banquet for all his officials and his staff, "Esther's Banquet." He made a remission of taxes for the provinces and gave gifts in accordance with the power of the king.

I write just after the Super Bowl and I have been reading that wherever it happens, the Super Bowl is a magnet for sexual exploitation. The Texas Attorney general called it one of the biggest human trafficking events in the United States. According to more general news reports, the George W. Bush administration set up forty-two task forces to investigate the problem of sexual exploitation in the United States; sexual exploitation means forced involvement of people (usually women, and especially young girls) in sex. While there seemed to be widespread agreement that sexual exploitation is a serious issue here as in other parts of the Western world, involving both the abuse of nationals of the country and trafficking across borders, the task forces were unable to gain traction in dealing with the problem.

From time to time I show my classes a clever and amusing animated version of the Esther story and get them to think about how far the animated version communicates the significance of the Bible story faithfully and effectively. In a number of ways the retelling of the story has to adapt it to the needs of children and risk enfeebling it, though it does make clear that Esther has no option but to submit herself to the beauty contest organized by Xerxes' henchmen. Of course this is no ordinary beauty contest, but one that leads to a harem in which young girls are prepared for a night of involuntary sex with the king, then to the night of involuntary sex itself, then to another harem. The two harems are naturally in the charge of eunuchs, men who in one way or another have been rendered incapable of sexual activity, or at least of fathering children. They may have volunteered for this mutilation in order to get jobs in the administration, though nevertheless it means the young girls are not the only ones subjected to sexual oppression. (Hege and Hegai are variants on the same name for one of the eunuchs.)

While it is possible to laugh at the opening chapter of Esther with its account of the pathetically and stupidly self-indulgent king and his court, we might remind ourselves that the background to this self-indulgence is the suffering of ordinary people, the kind of suffering that Nehemiah 5 witnesses to. If the government in Susa had not been living so well, the people in Jerusalem who paid the taxes that financed its indulgence would not be falling into servitude. The same issue arises in this chapter. The king's beauty contest is pathetic and laughable. But its victims are a series of young teenage girls who have their first sexual experience in the bed of this older man and are then shunted off into his post-coital harem as people with the status of **secondary wives** but never to be seen again.

Now many Israelite women, perhaps most Israelite women, had their marriages arranged for them, as may have been the case in most cultures. Arranged marriage does not mean the boy and girl have no choice in who they marry, as is evident in a number of Old Testament stories; it does mean that they are not the only ones involved in the process of decision-making.

It doubtless also means that if love is part of the story, this love develops as much after the marriage as before it. So many Israelite girls might spend their marriage night hoping and praying that sex may lead to love. Maybe the girls in Xerxes' harem cherished this hope, but statistically their chances were poor.

The way the story of Esther starts is the way it intends to continue. First there is the outrageous banquet, then the sexual abuse. There will follow the horrifying plot to annihilate the **Judahite** people, and eventually the appalling slaughter of over seventy-five thousand **Persians**. The story gives us no explicit clue as to whether it intends us to be horrified as we read; it is like much of Scripture in that it leaves us to draw conclusions of that kind. Scripture does put its stories in the context of teaching that suggests the moral framework with which to read its stories, even as the stories give concrete content to the moral and theological generalizations. It can hardly be the case that the Scriptures as a whole expect us to be amused at the Esther story. Yet at the same time the story is told in such a way as to entertain and amuse. Maybe that is partly because humor takes the edge off horror and makes it possible to read a story we would not otherwise be able to read. To put it another way, humor is often grounded in anger, so humor gives anger a means of finding expression.

There is another aspect to the matter-of-factness running through the book. Gross self-indulgence for which other people pay the price, sexual oppression and abuse, anti-Semitism, and slaughter are facts of the world in which we live. One of the great characteristics of the Bible is that it faces those facts. It does not deal with issues of a merely spiritual kind. It deals with how things are in our world. It invites us to face the fact of what happens to young girls in the United States, Europe, and elsewhere. Then, most scandalously, it invites us to assume that God is involved in this world, even in its wickedness. The Persian king is about to seek to eliminate the Jewish people, and the means whereby God will avoid the fulfillment of that intention is the sexual abuse of the teenage Esther. Esther pays a price and her entire people lives. It might seem disturbing that God is prepared to use such means to bring about the defeat of evil. It would be even more disturbing if such horrors happened and were incapable of having any significance. It is also because of considerations such as this that the story does not dwell on the moral offense or religious irregularity (sex with and marriage to a foreigner) that Esther is sucked into. The issues are bigger than these.

ESTHER 2:19–3:11

Amalek Redivivus

[19]When the young girls assembled a second time, Mordecai was sitting at the king's gate. [20]Esther had not disclosed her family or her people, as Mordecai had commanded her; Esther did as Mordecai said, as when she was being brought up with him. [21]At that time, when Mordecai was sitting in the king's gate, Bigthan and Teresh, two of the king's eunuchs who guarded the threshold, became angry and sought to lay hand on King Xerxes. [22]The thing became known to Mordecai. He disclosed it to Queen Esther, and Esther told the king in Mordecai's name. [23]The thing was inquired into and found [to be so], and the two were hanged on a gallows. It was written in the annals in the king's presence.

[3:1]After this, King Xerxes promoted Haman son of Hammedatha the Agagite. He elevated him and put him on a seat higher than all the officials who had been with him. [2]All the king's staff at the king's gate would kneel and bow low to Haman, because the king had commanded this with regard to him. But Mordecai did not kneel and did not bow low. [3]The king's staff at the king's gate said to Mordecai, "Why are you transgressing the king's command?" [4]But when they said it to him day after day, he did not listen to them. They told Haman, to see whether Mordecai's words would prevail, because he had told them he was a Judahite. [5]When Haman saw that Mordecai was not kneeling or bowing low to him, Haman filled with rage, [6]but in his own eyes he despised laying hand on Mordecai alone, because they had disclosed Mordecai's people to him and Haman sought to destroy all the Judahites in all Xerxes' kingdom, Mordecai's people.

[7]In the first month (that is, the month of Nisan) in Xerxes' twelfth year, *pur* (that is, the lot) was cast before Haman concerning each day and each month: the twelfth (that is, the

month of Adar). [8]Haman said to King Xerxes, "There is a single people, spread about but kept separate among the peoples in all the provinces in your kingdom, and their laws are different from every people. They do not keep the king's laws, and it is not appropriate for the king to let them alone. [9]If it seems good to your majesty, let it be decreed to destroy them, and I will pay ten thousand talents of silver into the hands of those responsible for works to bring into the king's treasuries." [10]The king removed his ring from on his hand and gave it to Haman son of Hammedatha the Agagite, the Judahites' adversary. [11]The king said to Haman, "The silver is given to you, and so is the people, to do with it as seems good in your eyes."

The last few weeks have seen "days of rage" in Middle Eastern countries, the overthrow of more than one government, and a sense that this unrest might spill over into greater vulnerability for the state of Israel. Coincidentally, last Friday saw the United States vetoing a U.N. Security Council resolution condemning Israel for continuing to build settlements in the West Bank, and Saturday saw Palestinians calling for a "day of rage" there this coming Friday. This Monday morning I received an e-mail prayer request, forwarded from a society committed to being Christian friends of Israel. It urged prayer for Israel's protection in this context and referred to the promise in Zechariah 2 that God would be a firewall around Jerusalem, the promise we considered in connection with Nehemiah's wall-building project. Whatever one thinks of the rights and wrongs of the Israeli-Palestinian conflict, the sense that the Jewish people in general has been vulnerable to schemes for its annihilation does not issue from Jewish paranoia. Haman's scheme marks its beginning.

The opening reference to a second assembly of girls seems to refer to the gathering of the next batch of potential victims for Xerxes. It reminds us again of the ongoing significance of the way men will seek out attractive women (or girls) to bolster their own position ("Isn't my assistant glamorous, so aren't I important?"). And what is one to think of the girls in Susa who don't make the cut? Beauty creates a kind of prejudice that differs from ethnic prejudice (everyone would like to be beautiful; not everyone wants to belong to another ethnic group) but resembles it in some ways (everyone wants to be valued for what they are, not for their ethnic identity or looks). In Susa the beautiful girls are vulnerable because of their beauty and the Judahites are vulnerable because of their ethnic identity.

The gate of a city is its place of meeting; in an Israelite city it is where the elders meet. Mordecai's being at the gate literally and/or metaphorically suggests that he is involved in the city's administration and the service of the king, like Nehemiah and like Daniel and his friends in **Babylon**. **Judahites** have come a long way since their transportation nearly a century prior; like the families of Ezra and Nehemiah, Mordecai's family has not seized the chance to move "back" to Jerusalem. They are doing well. Yet they know that they are vulnerable, not merely because they are foreigners but because they are Jews. Still, Mordecai knows how to use his position. He knows how to take advantage of his capacity to "use" Esther, who is at the mercy of the men's direction for ill or for good, though she will gain some self-determination or independence of action as the story unfolds. And he knows how to use information he comes across.

The words *Judahite, Judean, Jew,* and *Jewish,* all go back to the Hebrew word *Yehudi.* In other words, *Yehudim* can be an ethnic term, referring to members of the clan of Judah (which can become, in effect, a synecdoche for Israel itself as a people), whether or not they are religiously Jewish. Or it can be a religious term, referring to people who are committed to Jewish religion and life whether or not they are ethnically Jewish. Within the Old Testament, Esther marks when *Yehudim* comes to have religious implications. In Susa, being *Yehudim* can suggest the distinctive way people live as well as the distinctive ethnic group they belong to.

Haman is scandalized not by Mordecai's belonging to a different ethnic group, but by his belonging to an ethnic group that keeps itself separate from other peoples and has laws different from those of other people. Human beings are often threatened by people who are different. Food is one area where this unease manifests itself; many British people are uneasy about people who eat snails or frogs or horse meat. Haman's generalization perhaps presupposes this instinct, but we know something that

Xerxes does not know. Haman's real concern is the fact that Mordecai will not bow down to him as the top dog in the royal administration. But he correctly recognizes that this is not just a personal issue between him and Mordecai. Mordecai is just behaving as a Jew. It is the objectionable nature of this deviant behavior that makes the Judahites vulnerable, and it is this that lies behind Mordecai's instruction to Esther to keep her Jewish identity secret. Haman's casting of the lot will be designed to discover what will be an auspicious day either for approaching Xerxes about destroying the Jewish community or for actually implementing the plan. Ironically, it will transpire that his lot-casting is entirely unreliable. The fact that the festival celebrating his failure will be called *purim*, "lots," reflects the fact that decisions about such questions are being made elsewhere than where Haman thinks.

Ironically, too, there is nothing in the Torah that would forbid Mordecai from bowing down to Haman. Prostration before a superior appears in both Testaments without its implying that one is treating the person as a deity. Thus the king's requirement that people bow down before Haman was not outlandish, and the puzzlement of Mordecai's peers at his apparent perversity was natural enough. The rest of the portrayal of Mordecai makes it unlikely that we are to infer that he gets everyone into trouble because of his human pride. More likely the clue to his refusal lies in the pointed identification of Haman as an Agagite. Agag was the Amalekite king whose sparing from execution cost Saul his position as a servant of God and chosen king of Israel, while the Amalekites as a group were the epitome of a people irrationally and inhumanly hostile to Israel (see 1 Samuel 15). As a Persian, Haman is not literally an Amalekite or a descendant of Agag, though maybe one of his forebears had a name that was sufficiently like Agag to suggest the link. Spiritually, we might say, Haman was an Agagite. The way the story unfolds shows that the designation was apposite. Whatever was in Mordecai's mind when he declined to bow down to Haman, events will show that Haman's designation as an Amalekite was appropriate; and Mordecai knew from the way Amalek had treated Israel in the past that an Israelite did not bow down to an Amalekite.

There are Israelis who see the Palestinians as the contemporary embodiment of the Amalekites just as there are Arabs who would like to see Israel removed from the map. There are also hate groups in a country such as the United States who would like to eliminate Jews all over the world.

ESTHER 3:12–4:17

The Possibility of a Non-miraculous Miracle

[12]So the king's scribes were summoned in the first month, on the thirteenth day of it, and a decree was made in accordance with all that Haman had commanded to the king's satraps and to the governors over each province and to the officials of each people, province by province in accordance with its script and people by people in accordance with its language, written in the name of King Xerxes and sealed with the king's ring. [13]Documents were sent by means of runners to all the king's provinces with orders to destroy, slaughter, and eliminate all the Judahites from young to old, little ones and women, on one day, on the thirteenth day of the twelfth month (that is, Adar), and to plunder their [property as] spoil. [14]A copy of the document was to be given out as a law in every individual province, shown to all the peoples so that they would be ready for this day. [15]The runners went out, driven by the king's word, and the law was given out in the fortress of Susa. While the king and Haman sat down to a banquet, the city of Susa was perplexed.

[4:1]When Mordecai got to know all that had happened, Mordecai tore his clothes and put on sackcloth and dirt. He went out into the midst of the city and cried out with a loud and bitter cry. [2]He came as far as before the king's gate because people could not come into the king's gate in sackcloth. [3]In every individual province, each place where the king's word and his law arrived, there was great mourning on the part of the Judahites, fasting, weeping, and lamenting; sackcloth and dirt were laid on many people. [4]Esther's girls and her eunuchs came and told her, and the queen trembled. She sent Mordecai clothes to put on so that he could put off the sackcloth on him, but he would not accept them. [5]So Esther summoned Hathach, one of king's eunuchs whom he had put in place before her, and charged him to go to Mordecai to get to know what this [was about] and why this [was happening]. ⁶Hathach went out to Mordecai in the city square in front of the king's gate ⁷and Mordecai told him everything that had happened to him and about the details of the silver that Haman said he would pay to the king's treasuries in connection with the Judahites, to eliminate them. ⁸[Mordecai] gave [Hathach] a copy of the document containing the law that had been given out in Susa for their destruction to show Esther and tell her, and to charge her to come to the king and seek favor with him and inquire of him concerning her people. ⁹Hathach came and told Esther Mordecai's words, ¹⁰but Esther said to Hathach and charged him [to say] to Mordecai, ¹¹"All the king's staff and the people of the king's provinces know that any man or woman who comes to the king in the inner courtyard who has not been summoned—he has one law, execution, unless the king extends to him the gold scepter, and he lives; and I have not been summoned to come to the king these thirty days." ¹²When they told Mordecai Esther's words, ¹³Mordecai said to take back word to Esther, "Do not imagine within yourself that you will escape in the king's household, of all the Judahites, ¹⁴because if you indeed stay silent at this time, relief and deliverance will arise for the Judahites from one place, but you and your father's house will perish. Who knows if it was for this time that you reached royal position?" ¹⁵Esther said to take back word to Mordecai, ¹⁶"Go, assemble all the Judahites to be found in Susa and fast for me. Do not eat or drink for three days, night or day. I, too, will fast, and my girls, in this way, and in this way I will come to the king, which is not in accordance with the law. And if I perish, I perish." ¹⁷Mordecai went his way and did in accordance with everything that Esther charged him.

A month ago I was dizzy for several days and spent two days in the hospital having tests to make sure I didn't have a brain tumor or wasn't having a stroke. All the tests came out clear; so whence the dizziness? The vagaries of the health insurance system meant that to try to resolve the puzzle I had to see a different neurologist, a young guy without the hospital neurologist's reputation. Within five minutes he had identified the problem. Some crystals in my ears had got out of alignment, and there was a simple maneuver that could put this right, which my wife and I could use if the dizziness recurs. The doctor recognized the problem because he and his mother had both experienced it; and the fact that by using the maneuver he could at will make me dizzy and then resolve the dizziness showed he was not simply projecting his problem onto me. My wife and I left his office marveling that God had done something miraculous. Yet it was a behind-the-scenes, non-miraculous miracle, a miracle of timing and coincidence.

The book of Esther is about that sort of miracle, but it never mentions God, never mentions Israel or the **covenant**, and never mentions prayer, as it did not mention the reason for Mordecai's refusing to bow down to Haman. You can compare and contrast it with the story of Joseph in Genesis or with the story of the Israelites' deliverance from Egypt in Exodus or with the story of Daniel and his friends in **Babylon** itself. The Joseph story illustrates the way God can be at work through human decision making, taking of responsibility, and coincidences, yet in the end Joseph makes the point explicit to his brothers in Genesis 50: "Whereas you yourselves intended wrong for me, God intended it for good, so as to act today to keep alive a numerous people." The book of Esther leaves the matter unarticulated. The exodus story goes on to illustrate the way God works spectacularly to rescue God's people and bring judgment on oppressors and on people who set themselves up over against God, but in Exodus God works miraculously; without a special act of God, there would be no Red Sea deliverance and judgment. In Esther, God works to the same end, but without the miracle. Daniel 3 is explicit in its talk of God's capacity to deliver the three young men from the burning furnace in Babylon. Here, Mordecai declares that relief and deliverance will similarly arise for the Jews in Susa, but he does not say what will be its source. His declaration is an outrageous one. He himself has shown his capacity to use information that comes to him and to use the potentials of his position, his relationship with Esther and his position at the king's gate, but the story makes no mention of God's directing him in this connection. He does what he sees he must and can do. He has torn his clothes, put on sackcloth and dirt, and cried out loudly and bitterly, and it seems that taking such actions means he now knows that there will be deliverance.

The story takes for granted that it is God who will be the source of the Jews' deliverance, that this deliverance is certain because God is committed to the Jewish people, that Mordecai's certainty issues from his having prayed and heard God's answer, and that the fasting that Esther also urges on her fellow Jews is the accompaniment of prayer; indeed, it has been suggested that the book's declining to make explicit any of these assumptions puts even more emphasis on them. It also takes for granted that being *yehudim* is a religious commitment as well as an ethnic identity, but neither does it make this fact explicit (and thus I continue to use the translation "Judahites" rather than "Jews").

Yet the refusal to refer to God makes a significant point. Our characteristic human experience of God's extraordinary involvement in our lives is anticipated more in the Esther story than the Exodus story, as will have been the case for Jews in Susa. God's deliverance comes about because human beings accept responsibility to use the position they are in. They act in faith and with courage, as Esther commits herself to doing. They take the risk of doing so even though they know that the risk is genuine; Daniel's three friends know that God can rescue them (though they know they cannot expect the king to agree) but they do not know *whether* God will do so. Acceptance of our responsibility does not guarantee that deliverance will come to us.

Paradoxically, Mordecai goes further in this connection than Daniel's three friends, while Esther, with her hesitation, manifests more realism about the situation. Mordecai, of course, has nothing to lose. Not having disclosed her Jewish identity, if Esther also keeps her head down she may escape with her life, though Mordecai seeks to close off the temptation to think so. Indeed, maybe the reason she finds herself in the position she has reached is that she has a role to play in ensuring that other people escape from the threat to their lives. Once again, there is no reference to God's having brought her to that position.

That is presupposed but not stated because it illustrates the way things often work out without one being able to see the hand of God. It will transpire that the survival of the Jewish people hinges on the decision, courage, and cleverness of a beautiful Jew and her guardian.

Esther's hesitation and fear make her faith and courage even more remarkable, and the more real to us. She is not a super-hero with special powers but an abused girl put in a horrible position because of what she is, a beautiful Jew. Being beautiful does not mean having overwhelming special advantages because of one's beauty. Often beauty puts a person in the position of becoming a tragedy (Marilyn Monroe, Princess Diana) even while people attribute to them a kind of super-humanity. They were just candles in the wind. Esther illustrates the way that courage and faith are not incompatible with fear and hesitation; indeed, they come into their own in the context of fear and hesitation. If there is none of these latter, who needs faith or courage?

There is a difference in reactions in Susa city from those in the fortress. As in other ancient cities, the fortress or citadel is a development within the city, a mound on which the king has his palace and thus his administrative center, and a place that provides an extra level of defense if the city itself should be overcome by attackers. (It would thus be possible for Mordecai to appear in the city in informal dress and a disheveled state, but not in the fortress at the king's gate.) The fortress is directly implicated in Haman's edict. The ordinary people are bewildered at what has been determined for the Jewish family next door. There can be a difference between the tough policies that a government is prepared to adopt and the way ordinary human values prevail among ordinary people, like the people in the city of Susa. Indeed, even the other members of the king's staff are not so much hostile to Mordecai as curious about whether he will get away with not bowing to Haman on the basis of his being a Judahite (it is not clear whether they mean that the basis for his refusal is his being a foreigner or that his religion forbids him). There is an even bigger contrast between the people's perplexity and the cool way

Xerxes and Haman sit down for dinner and drinks, a good day's work done.

ESTHER 5:1-14

The Girl Who Knows How to Work Her Man

[1]On the third day, Esther dressed royally and stood in the inner courtyard of the king's house, facing the king's palace, while the king was sitting on his royal throne in the royal house facing the entrance to the house. [2]When the king saw Queen Esther standing in the courtyard, she found favor in his eyes and the king extended to Esther the gold scepter in his hand. Esther drew near and touched the head of the scepter. [3]The king said to her, "What do you have [on your mind], Queen Esther? What is your request? Up to half the kingdom, it will be given you." [4]Esther said, "If it is pleasing to the king, may the king and Haman come today to the banquet I have made for him." [5]The king said, "Get Haman to hurry to do what Esther says." So the king and Haman came to the banquet that Esther had made. [6]The king said to Esther at the wine banquet, "What is your petition? It will be given you. What is your request? Up to half the kingdom, it will be done." [7]Esther replied, "My petition, my request: [8]If I have found favor in the king's eyes and if it is pleasing to the king to grant my petition, to do my request, may the king and Haman come to the banquet I will make for them, and tomorrow I will act in accordance with the king's word." [9]Haman went out that day rejoicing and happy in heart, but when Haman saw Mordecai at the king's gate and he did not get up or tremble because of him, Haman filled with rage at Mordecai. [10]But Haman controlled himself and came to his house. He sent and brought his friends and his wife, Zeresh. [11]Haman recounted to them the splendor of his wealth and the number of his sons and all about how the king had promoted him and elevated him above the officials and the king's staff. [12]And Haman said, "Indeed, Queen Esther did not bring anyone to the banquet with the king that she made, except me. Tomorrow, too, I am summoned to her with the king. [13]But all this is not the same to me every time I see Mordecai the Judahite sitting at the king's gate." [14]His wife Zeresh said to him, with all his friends, "A gallows should be made, fifty cubits high, and in the

> morning say to the king that they should hang Mordecai on it, and go with the king to the banquet happy." The words seemed good to Haman and he made the gallows.

In describing the possibility of a non-miraculous miracle, I spoke of an experience of my own, an experience on the part of a gentile Christian. A Jewish scholar I know has described his interaction with Esther in quite different terms, because the story is a story directly about his own people. I can see the book as illustrating ways in which God might show faithfulness to me and expect faithfulness from me, but my relationship with the book is not as direct as that of this Jewish writer. Christians may also see it as illustrating ways in which God might show faithfulness to individual Christians and churches under persecution and ways in which they are called to faithfulness. But our being able to appreciate the story in that way emerges from our relationship with a Jew who was a descendant of the Jews of Esther's day and our being adopted into his people.

There is then a terrible irony in the fact that the pogroms of the late nineteenth and early twentieth centuries, and the holocaust of the mid-twentieth century, were undertaken by Christians, and that these events were but the climactic episodes in the history of Christian anti-Semitism over the centuries. The holocaust's location in Western Europe, its temporal proximity to people living in the twentieth and twenty-first centuries, and above all its nature as an attempt finally to eliminate the Jewish people, gave the book of Esther new significance in the twentieth century. I do not imply that the book's meaning changed; its meaning issued from what its author wrote for the community to which he (or she) belonged. But what it came to signify for other people in other contexts changed. Perhaps a better way to put it is to note that we now have grievously easy access to the book's own meaning as a story about the attempt actually to eliminate the Jewish people. Admittedly there have been a number of Christian stances in relation to the book. As well as seeing it as providing models for the way their own relationship with God worked, Christians have seen it as unworthy of a place in Scripture. One great Old Testament scholar declared that a Christian preacher could never take his (or her) text from Esther. But he made that declaration before the issues that the Holocaust poses for Christian and Jewish faith came to be perceived.

When Haman became the first person we know of who dreamed of a final solution to the Jewish problem, his dream was frustrated because a Jewish man emboldened a Jewish girl to take seriously her solidarity with her people and her special position with the responsibility and potential it had given her. It was then Adolf Hitler who explicitly spoke of this dream that there should be a "final solution of the Jewish problem." In his "Speech to the Reichstag" on January 30, 1939, he declared, "In the course of my life I have very often been a prophet, and have usually been ridiculed for it. During the time of my struggle for power it was in the first instance the Jewish race which only received my prophecies with laughter when I said that I would one day take over the leadership of the State, and with it that of the whole nation, and that I would then among many other things settle the Jewish problem. Their laughter was uproarious, but I think that for some time now they have been laughing on the other side of their face."

Where Haman failed, Hitler almost succeeded. While one could not attribute that near-success to the presence of someone like Esther in Hitler's circle who failed to act in the way she did, the message of the book includes a challenge to her descendants to be prepared to take seriously her solidarity with her people and her willingness to take the risk of making use of her special position with the responsibility and potential it gave her. It also includes a challenge to gentiles who care about her descendants and who, in some sense, identify with her people because they have been grafted into this olive tree (as Romans 11 puts it). There were indeed such "righteous gentiles" in Europe who took action that saved Jews, some of whom paid with their own lives for doing so. Jews have no reason to assume that anti-Semitism died with Hitler, and gentiles who care about the Jewish people need to be ready to follow Esther rather than Haman.

Esther's having won Xerxes' favor made her initiative less dangerous than it would be for some people, but she was not wrong when she pointed out to Mordecai the risk involved in her approaching Xerxes given the conventions of imperial protocol. She had no way of being sure that her approach would issue in his extending the scepter to her rather than taking offense and ordering her execution. Her petition and request is not merely that Xerxes and Haman should come to dinner. In issuing that invitation, she is observing the proper standards of Middle Eastern graciousness rather than rushing straight into a shopping list of requests. "Let's have dinner first—we can talk about that later." (Xerxes is doing something similar in offering to give her up to half of his kingdom; she would be wise not to take that offer too literally.) At the same time, working in this way and then repeating the strategy the next day encourages the development of a relationship with the king that will surely, in due course, make it impossible for him to resist her actual request. Indeed, her words in issuing the second invitation invite him to recognize that fact. In effect she says, "If you would like to come to dinner again tomorrow, I will tell you my request then, and you will grant it then, won't you?" And by accepting the dinner invitation, he has made an even more explicit commitment to doing so.

Maybe Xerxes recognizes this fact, and is fine with it because he is a bit besotted with Esther. Maybe poor Haman perceives it, too, but he has no idea of its implications for him. Ironically, his pleasure is spoiled only by another experience of having Mordecai fail to recognize his importance; he does not realize that he has a much bigger problem looming. He focuses rather on trying to restore his wounded pride by reminding himself and his family how much he has to be proud of; but they have no more insight than he does.

So that evening before going to bed he makes a gallows (or a pole for the exposure of a body after an execution; literally it is a "tree"). Fifty cubits is seventy-five feet or thirty-five meters, the height of a five- or six-story building, so it's quite a gallows and quite an indication of Haman's determination to shame Mordecai to get his revenge for Mordecai's dishonoring of him, whether or not it is what Haman actually intends and whether or not this is another indication that the book of Esther delights in hyperbole.

ESTHER 6:1–11

Do-Right Man

¹That night the king's sleep fled and he said to bring the book of records (the annals), and they were read before the king. ²It was found written that Mordecai had reported about Bigthana and Teresh, two of the king's eunuchs among the guards of the threshold, who had sought to lay hands on King Xerxes. ³The king said, "What honor or promotion was there for Mordecai on account of this?" The king's boys, his attendants, said, "Nothing was done with him." ⁴The king said, "Who is in the courtyard?" Now Haman had come into the outer courtyard of the king's house to say to the king to hang Mordecai on the gallows that he had set up for him. ⁵The king's boys said to him, "There—Haman is standing in the courtyard." The king said, "He is to come in." ⁶Haman came in and the king said to him, "What's to do with a man whom the king wants to honor?" Haman said to himself, "For whom would the king want to do honor more than me?" ⁷So Haman said to the king, "A man whom the king wants to honor—⁸they should bring royal apparel that the king has worn and a horse on which the king has ridden and on whose head a royal crown has been put, ⁹and put the apparel and the horse in the charge of one of the king's noble officials. They should clothe the man whom the king wants to honor, have him ride on the horse through the city square, and proclaim in front of him, "This is what is done for the man whom the king wants to honor!" ¹⁰The king said to Haman, "Quick—get the apparel and the horse, as you spoke, and do so for Mordecai the Judahite, who sits in the king's gate. No word of all that you spoke should drop." ¹¹So Haman got the apparel and the horse, clothed Mordecai, had him ride through the city square, and proclaimed in front of him, "This is what is done for the man whom the king wants to honor."

I acknowledge that there won't seem to be much link between Mordecai and Eric Cantona, the French soccer star who played for Manchester United, but I was thinking about the link in bed last night after watching the movie *Looking for Eric*. The movie is about a Manchester fan called Eric Bishop whose life is sliding into calamity. Cantona appears to him and helps him find a way out of the mess he is in. Cantona talks about the way part of his inspiration in a game was "to do something for the fans," to make something magical happen for them when he managed to score an amazing goal. The way soccer and some other spectator sports work is by fans identifying with the team so fully that they share in the team's achievements, and one can see this sense at work when Cantona scores and throws up his arms at the crowd, and the crowd roars with him. Bishop asks Cantona about his best-ever moment, expecting him to say it was some spectacular goal, but Cantona identifies it as a pass he once offered a colleague that enabled this other player to score. The semblance of a link with Mordecai is that part of the background to Cantona's achievements and fame (so he claims, anyway) is thus not his desire to serve himself but his concern about other people.

Back in chapter 2 we were told a story about Mordecai, the significance of which was not clear at the time. There was a plot against the king's life, and as a loyal member of the administration Mordecai ensured that Xerxes got to know, by telling Esther. If he did it to serve himself, he failed; the incident was recorded but forgotten. To set Aretha Franklin alongside Eric Cantona and Mordecai the Benjaminite, "if you want a do-right, all days, woman, you've got to be a do-right, all-night man." But of course it doesn't necessarily work, as it hasn't for Mordecai. Indeed his faithful action (his second faithful action—the first was his adopting of Esther) was soon followed by the disastrous royal edict.

Then one night the king can't sleep. To judge from what follows, the problem isn't that he can't get to sleep but that he wakes up early and can't drop off again, and the image of his sleep fleeing fits with that idea. Understandably he thinks that some reading from the royal archives may solve the problem and send him back to sleep, but the result is actually that he is reminded of Mordecai's action and of the fact that it never received its appropriate reward. The king's sleeplessness thus becomes the crucial turning point in the story. In the destiny of the Jewish people in the context of the **Persian** Empire— everything depends on the king's sleepless night. It is the crucial coincidence.

People sometimes speak of God orchestrating events behind the scenes of our lives, but the image is a misleading one. An orchestrator decides what happens and gets the orchestra to play together in accordance with the score or the chart. The Bible can certainly portray God doing so; the beginning of Ezra portrays God in this way, making it possible for **Judahites** to move to Jerusalem to rebuild the temple. But this is not the way it sees all God's involvement in events. While there is some sense in which God is sovereign in all events, sometimes its picture is more of God doing something creative with independent human actions and with events after they happen. The original building of the temple was emphatically not God's idea but an idea of David's that God was not keen on, yet God did something creative with it. You could call this harnessing rather than orchestrating. The distinctive feature of the Esther story is that omitting to mention God means one makes an overstatement even by talking in terms of harnessing. All you have is coincidence and people courageously taking responsibility. We may infer that the book assumes God's involvement in taking up the potential of Mordecai's doing the right thing and of Xerxes' sleeplessness, but the point the book overtly makes is that we have to assume that truth or infer it. In experience, all we see is a coincidence.

Haman gets caught by a further coincidence, this time laced with irony. He just happens to show up at this moment, presumably soon after the time when nighttime (when the king could not sleep) has given way to morning. As the senior member of the king's staff he is the natural person to ask for advice on how to honor someone. Haman not only misunderstands the question but turns it into a question whose implications are the exact opposite to what he would want and the exact opposite to the concerns about Mordecai with which he comes to the king. He ends up indeed elevating Mordecai, but not in the sense he desired.

ESTHER 6:12–8:2

Realism about Empire Becomes Execution Farce

[12]Mordecai went back to the king's gate, but Haman hurried to his house, mourning and head covered. [13]Haman told his

wife Zeresh and all his friends everything that had happened to him. His counselors and his wife Zeresh said to him, "If Mordecai, before whom you have begun to fall, is of Judahite origin, you will not overcome him, because you will surely fall before him." [14]While they were still speaking with him, the king's eunuchs arrived and hastened to bring Haman to the banquet that Esther had made. [7:1]When the king and Haman came to drink with Queen Esther, [2]the king said to Esther again on the second day at the wine banquet, "What is your petition, Queen Esther? It will be granted you. What is your request? Up to half the kingdom, it will be done." [3]Queen Esther replied, "If I have found favor in your eyes, your majesty, and if it seems good to your majesty, may my life be given me as my petition, and my people as my request, [4]because I and my people have been sold to be destroyed, slaughtered, and eliminated. Had we been sold as male and female servants, I would have kept silent, because the distress would not be worthy of the king's trouble." [5]King Xerxes said—he said to Queen Esther, "Who is this? Where is this man who is so full of himself to act like this?" [6]Esther said, "The man of distress and the enemy is this bad man Haman." As Haman panicked in front of the king and queen, [7]the king got up in his fury from the wine banquet, into the palace garden, while Haman stayed to petition for his life with Queen Esther, because he saw that trouble was certain for him from the king. [8]When the king came back from the palace garden into the wine banquet hall, Haman was falling on the couch where Esther was. The king said, "Is he also to violate the queen, with me in the house?" When the words came out from the king's mouth, they covered Haman's face. [9]Harbonah, one of the eunuchs in attendance on the king, said, "In addition, there—the gallows that Haman made for Mordecai, who spoke for the benefit of the king, are standing in Haman's house, fifty cubits high." The king said, "Hang him on it." [10]So they hanged Haman on the gallows that he had set up for Mordecai, and the king's fury subsided.

[8:1]That day King Xerxes gave Queen Esther the house of Haman, the Judahites' adversary. Mordecai came before the king because Esther had disclosed what he was to her. [2]The king took off his ring, which he had removed from Haman, and gave it to Mordecai, and Esther put Mordecai over Haman's household.

At the end of *Looking for Eric*, Cantona urges Bishop to take action about the situation that is threatening final calamity. Bishop's son had been compelled to hide a local drug baron's gun in his house. If the police discover it, it will mean five years in prison. So Bishop gathers three coachloads of Manchester fans wearing Cantona masks and they confront the drug baron at his own home. As a reviewer said, social realism becomes revenge farce. So there is some similarity between the two Erics and Xerxes. (Another reviewer was troubled at the way the movie saw vigilante justice as the way to solve a problem that ought to have been the business of the police.)

Haman's ironically described counselors (more literally, "wise men" or "experts"), the friends who had set him up for his reversal, now express an extraordinary insight about the danger of getting into conflict with Jews. It anticipates Hitler's Jewish paranoia, but that is a particularly dangerous version of a paranoia that has often manifested itself in the gentile world. But the counselors' wisdom does not lead to their responding like Hitler and others who have attacked the Jewish people. Rather, they unwittingly agree with Mordecai's earlier declaration to Esther that deliverance will arise for the Jews from one place or another. Their own declaration about Haman's danger seems odd, but we will soon learn that they are dead right. What on earth can explain their being right? It is the fact that the Jewish people are God's people. It is because of God's commitment to them that an adversary like Haman is bound to fall before them. Yet once again, the narrative leaves that reality unstated. The story goes that the eighteenth-century Prussian king, Frederick the Great, asked a member of his court for one compelling proof of God's existence. (It's one of those stories told of a number of people; the questioner is usually Frederick, but the interlocutor's identity varies.) The reply was, "The existence of the Jews." Their survival against all odds could not be explained except on the basis of God's involvement with them. If this were the book of Daniel, Daniel or his friends would make explicit to the **Babylonian** authorities that it is the God of Israel who lies behind the survival and success of **Judahites** in Babylon. The book of Esther refrains from including this explanation and leaves it between the lines, inviting us merely to marvel at the empirical fact of Jewish survival. In addition, it invites its Jewish readers to take its claim seriously. The Jewish people will survive in a manner that is mysterious but certain. They can be encouraged and can live in hope when the situation looks deadly.

The farcical element in the story is enhanced by the king's perception that Haman is setting about raping the queen when Haman is actually trying to get her to take his side. Covering the face is referred to only here, but in the previous chapter, as elsewhere, Haman's covering his head was a sign of distress and/or shame, so the expression perhaps indicates that people somehow covered Haman's appearance with the marks of distress or shame preparatory to his death.

Is one to feel sorry for him? The story does not imply so. Is the execution of the would-be executioner right? The story also does not ask that question. Back in Genesis, God declared that people who shed blood would find their own blood being shed. Maybe God was declaring that it was the business of human authorities to execute murderers, but God may as easily be declaring something similar to the words Jesus will later utter, that people who wield the sword will die by the sword. It is part of the way life works, and while not commissioning that it should be so, God seems content that it should be so. So the man who prepared gallows for an unjustified hanging finds himself hanged on his own gallows. It is typical of the Old Testament that it often looks at such events from the perspective of the victim. It does not ask what you should do if you are Xerxes. It frees its readers to be encouraged by the fact that justice is done to the Hamans of this world, and that this happens through an abused girl with few cultural choices, using the power that culture has handed her.

The poetic justice, the irony, and the redress continue as Mordecai comes to be head of Haman's household in Haman's place, instead of Haman and his kind being able to appropriate the property of Mordecai and his compatriots, having killed their households.

183

ESTHER 8:3–17

The Right to Self-Defense

³Esther again spoke before the king, and fell down before his feet and wept. She sought favor from him in order to remove the evil of Haman the Agagite, the plan he had devised against the Judahites. ⁴The king extended to Esther the gold scepter and Esther arose and stood in front of the king. ⁵She said, "If it is pleasing to the king, if I have found favor before him, if it seems proper before the king and I am pleasing in his eyes, may it be written to reverse the documents, the plan of Haman son of Hammedatha, the Agagite, which he wrote to eliminate the Judahites who are in all the king's provinces, ⁶because how can I look upon the harm that will come on my people? How can I look upon the destruction of my family?" ⁷King Xerxes said to Queen Esther and Mordecai the Judahite, "There: I have given to Esther the house of Haman and they have hanged him on the gallows because he laid his hand on the Judahites. ⁸You yourselves—write as it seems pleasing in your eyes concerning the Judahites in the king's name and seal it with the king's ring" (because a document that has been written in the king's name and sealed with the king's ring cannot be reversed).

⁹So they summoned the king's scribes at that time, in the third month (that is, the month of Sivan), on the twenty-third of it, and a letter was written in accordance with all that Mordecai commanded to the Judahites and to the satraps, the governors, and the officials of the provinces from India to Sudan, one hundred and twenty-seven provinces, province by province in accordance with its script, and people by people in accordance with its language, and to the Judahites in accordance with their script and language. ¹⁰He wrote in King Xerxes' name, sealed it with the king's seal, and sent the documents by the hand of runners on horses riding royal relay steeds, the offspring of racehorses, ¹¹that the king gave [permission] to the Judahites in every individual city to assemble and stand up for themselves, to destroy, slaughter, and eliminate the entire force of a people or province that attack them, little ones and women, and to plunder their [property as] spoil ¹²on one day in all King Xerxes' provinces, on the thirteenth of the twelfth month (that is, the month of Adar). ¹³A copy of the document was to be given out as a law in every individual province, shown to all

the peoples, so that the Judahites would be ready for this day to take redress from their enemies. [14]The runners went out riding royal relay steeds, hurrying and driven by the king's word, and the law was given out in the fortress of Susa.

[15]Mordecai went out from the king's presence in royal apparel of blue and white, a large gold diadem, and a robe of white linen and purple wool, and the city of Susa shouted and celebrated. [16]For the Judahites there was light and celebration, rejoicing and honor. [17]In every individual province and every individual city, each place where the king's word and his law arrived, there was celebration and rejoicing for the Judahites, a banquet and a good time. Many of the peoples of the country professed to be Judahites, because fear of the Judahites had fallen upon them.

So last night's movie was another British combination of social comment and humor, *Cemetery Junction* (yes, you can assume that we watch a couple of movies in bed each week), which incorporates a number of fist fights. If someone throws a punch at you personally, do you throw one back? Presumably not, especially if it is persecution; you turn the other cheek. What if one ethnic group attacks another ethnic group? Some Jews today might wonder if the Jews could have done with a little less turning the other cheek in the Second World War. What if someone attacks your family?

There is a sense in which Mordecai and Esther's new Persian law reverses Haman's law, and a sense in which it does not. It does not give the Jews authority to attack other ethnic groups. In this respect it corresponds to the Old Testament's widespread stance. There are one or two spectacular occasions when God commissions them to take action against other peoples because of their wickedness, but God is not in the habit of commissioning them to take action against people just because they are their enemies. More often, God is telling them to knuckle down under the authority of the empire of the day until the time comes when God decides to do something about it. There are occasions when foreign powers are acting against them as the agents of God's chastisement; they certainly have to knuckle down then. Haman and his edict are a different question.

Now for the first time since chapter 3 Haman is described as an Agagite, and one might not have been surprised if this designation provided a lead in to commissioning the Judahites to set about eliminating Haman's people in keeping with one of those rare commissions to take action against wickedness, the one in 1 Samuel 15. In fact, the new edict simply gives them the right to stand up for themselves. In Daniel 6 it is explicit that a Persian king can sometimes get caught out by his own edicts. In issuing an edict in an especially formal fashion, he sacrifices the right to change it later; hence the phrase "the law of the Medes and Persians." While this may be a joke at the Persians' expense that deliberately misunderstands the Persian law in question (underdogs make jokes at the expense of the authorities over them), the Esther story may presuppose the same understanding. The king cannot change the Haman-inspired edict; what he has to do is authorize another edict that reverses the first one in effect, though it cannot do so formally. Although the new edict makes a point of using the exact language of Haman's edict, in content it is not a mirror-image of it. It does not authorize Judahites to attack members of other ethnic groups. It does give them the right to self-defense, and it thus implicitly acts as a deterrent to other ethnic groups. They cannot attack with impunity.

When Haman had his edict drawn up, the city was perplexed; now it is relieved. Whereas Mordecai had put on mourning clothes, now he is robed in honor. Whereas the Jews likewise mourned, now they celebrate. Whereas Mordecai had feared that Queen Esther would want to continue to hide her Judahite identity, now people want to share that identity. People have been able to join Israel in making a commitment to **Yahweh** and to the **Torah** since the beginning of Israel's story, but they do not exactly become Israelites; Ruth (for instance) is still called a Moabite after she has made her commitment. Here alone the Old Testament refers to people becoming Jewish/Judahite or professing to be Jewish/Judahite. Admittedly, there is some ambiguity about the meaning of this expression. Do people want to become Jewish because they have come to respect the Jews? Are they like Ruth? Or do they pretend to be Judahite because they are scared of the Judahites? This ambiguity aligns with the way the story steadfastly refuses to refer to God, Israel, the covenant, prayer, or faith.

But for Judahites/Jews in Persia, either fear or respect will do, thank you very much.

ESTHER 9:1–22

Boxing Day

[1]So in the twelfth month (that is, the month of Adar) on the thirteenth, the day when the king's word and his law were due to be enacted, on the day when the Judahites' enemies expected to be in power over them, that was turned around so that the Judahites—they were in power over the people who repudiated them. [2]The Judahites in their cities in all King Xerxes' provinces assembled to lay hand on people who sought their harm, and no one withstood them, because fear of the Judahites had fallen on all the peoples, [3]and all the king's provincial officials, satraps, governors, and people responsible for works were elevating the Judahites, because fear of Mordecai had fallen on them, [4]because Mordecai was important in the king's house. So his reputation was going about all the provinces, because the man Mordecai was getting more and more important.

[5]So the Judahites struck down all their adversaries with the edge of the sword, with slaughter and elimination, and acted in accordance with their wishes to the people who repudiated them. [6]In the fortress of Susa the Judahites slaughtered and eliminated five hundred people, [7]and Parshandatha, Dalphon, Aspatha, [8]Poratha, Adalia, Aridatha, [9]Parmashta, Arisai, Aridai, and Vaizatha, [10]the ten sons of Haman son of Hammedatha, the Judahites' adversary. They slaughtered, but they did not lay their hand on the plunder. [11]That day the number of people slaughtered in the fortress of Susa reached the king, [12]and the king said to Queen Esther, "In the fortress of Susa the Judahites have slaughtered and eliminated five hundred people, and Haman's sons. In the rest of the king's provinces, what have they done? But what is your petition? It will be given you. What else is your request? It will be done." [13]Esther said, "If it is pleasing to the king, may it be granted tomorrow also to the Judahites in Susa to act in accordance with today's law, and may they hang Haman's ten sons on the gallows." [14]The king said this was to be done, and a law was given out in Susa and they hanged Haman's ten sons. [15]The Judahites in Susa assembled

187

again on the fourteenth day of the month of Adar and slaughtered three hundred people in Susa, but they did not lay their
hand on the plunder.

[16]The rest of the Judahites, in the king's provinces, assembled
and stood up for their lives and got relief from their enemies.
They slaughtered seventy-five thousand people but they did
not lay their hand on the plunder, [17]on the thirteenth day of the
month of Adar. They rested on the fourteenth of it, and made it
a day of banquet and celebration, [18]while the Judahites in Susa
assembled on the thirteenth of it and the fourteenth of it, and
rested on the fifteenth of it and made it a day of banquet and
celebration. [19]That is why the rural Judahites, who live in the
rural cities, make the fourteenth day of the month of Adar one
of celebration and banquet, a good time and one of sending
portions of food to one another.

[20]Mordecai wrote down these things and sent documents to
all the Judahites in all King Xerxes' provinces, near and far, [21]to
lay upon them to keep the fourteenth day of the month of Adar,
and the fifteenth day of it, every individual year, [22]as the days
when the Judahites got relief for themselves from their enemies
and the month that turned for them from sadness to celebration and from mourning to a good time, and to make them
days of banquet and celebration, and sending portions of food
to one another and gifts to the poor.

When Americans ask me about the significance of Boxing Day,
the day after Christmas Day and a public holiday in Britain,
they are inclined to make the reasonable guess that it is a day
for boxing matches. Actually it is a day for giving and receiving Christmas boxes or gifts. Nowadays Christmas is a time
when families and friends give gifts to one another, largely on
a transactional basis that means we are really giving gifts to
ourselves. It's really pretty pathetic. The explanation of Boxing Day that I like most is that it was when the poor boxes in
church were opened and their contents distributed, and in this
connection I like the legend about King Wenceslas, a tenth-
century Duke of Bohemia, which is told in a doggerel-verse
Christmas carol. On the Feast of Stephen (the day after Christmas Day is St. Stephen's Day) in the freezing cold, Wenceslas
goes out and gives meat, wine, and fuel for a fire to a poor

man, thus embodying the ideal of the good king. So St. Stephen's Day, the day when the king acted in this way according to the story, became the day for opening the poor boxes and giving to needy people.

The celebration of the Jews' deliverance combines the ancient and the modern ideal of Boxing Day. It is an occasion of celebration and gift-giving, and the gift-giving benefits both the family and the needy. One might have thought that the commemoration of the people's deliverance would just be an occasion for self-indulgence, but this is not so. One can certainly imagine that the commemoration would be an occasion of praise and thanksgiving to God, like an event such as the building of Jerusalem's walls for the protection of the Judahite community. But to the end, the Esther story resolutely avoids reference to God, and alongside fasting, giving to the poor becomes another cipher for a grateful recognition that we have been blessed.

The collocation of giving to one another and to the poor suggests that the poor need not be members of the Jewish community. It fits with the Judahites' declining to take plunder from the people who attack them. The story again makes clear that in important ways the permission Xerxes gives the Judahites is the reverse of the edict Haman had sought. The same language recurs: they are allowed to destroy, slaughter, and eliminate people. Yet it is also a more limited permission, apparently because the edict was drafted by Mordecai rather than by Haman or Xerxes. We have noted that what they are given is the right to self-defense—permission to stand up for themselves—not permission to take the initiative in attacking other people. The first paragraph in the section then summarizes events and the rest of the section gives the detail in order to explain differences in the way the deliverance was celebrated in different parts of the community.

What is then surprising is the number of people who attack them when they know that the Jewish community is not going to be a pushover. The attackers are not going to be able to withstand the Jewish community—either to overcome them, or to stand firm when they fight back. It seems that some people just can't stop themselves, when it comes to racial hatred. Are they so threatened or afraid or cocky, or do they not know who they are without someone to fight against? Modern people are inclined to be offended at the Judahites killing so many people, despite (or because of) the fact that our lives are so violent; the difference is that we can send other people (the police or the army) to take violent action for us without our being directly involved, though we like to watch it on television.

One Jewish approach to the story sees the point of this motif as consisting in the stupidity of the people who attack the Jews. Yet elsewhere the book is friendly toward the ordinary people of Persia as opposed to leaders such as Xerxes and Haman, who are the fools in the book. It would not be surprising if Haman's sons were as stupid as he, and if they wanted to get redress for their father's execution. Here it is clear that their hanging involves the public display of their corpses as an act of shaming, a known practice in parts of the ancient world. It would act as another disincentive to people inclined to violence.

Another Jewish approach sees the Jews' act of slaughter as the book's ultimate irony. It reminds Jewish readers that they are no more peace-loving and gentle than anyone else. Such an understanding certainly fits with the nature of the book as a whole with its liking for humor and irony, and irony at one's own expense would be a plausible Jewish motif. Of course the trouble with irony is that people often fail to get it (as any Brit lecturing in the United States knows), and people's failure over the millennia to perceive this irony in Esther may make such an understanding implausible.

One should perhaps not take the numbers too literally, though compared with the numbers in the books of Chronicles from the same period of time, they are rather small. In Chronicles, even Sudan can muster an army of a million. Compared with such numbers, seventy-five thousand people in the entire Persian Empire is a tiny number. If the number of deaths is intended to suggest restraint, this would fit with the similar implication of the note about not taking plunder. Judahites were not killing in order to make a profit. Yet in light of the way Esther proceeds by making theological comments covertly rather than overtly, maybe it is most likely that the numbers are there to underline the dimensions of the deliverance that had come to the Jewish people. Even seventy-five thousand attackers are not going to overwhelm them.

ESTHER 9:23–10:3

A True Story, a Law That Will Last

⁹:²³So the Judahites accepted what they had begun to do and what Mordecai had written to them, ²⁴because Haman son of Hammedatha the Agagite, the adversary of all the Judahites, had planned to eliminate the Judahites and had cast the *pur* (that is, the lot) for crushing them and eliminating them. ²⁵But when [Esther] came before the king, he said with a document [that Haman's] evil plan, which he had devised against the Judahites, should reverse onto his own head, and they hanged him and his sons on the gallows. ²⁶On account of this they called these days Purim, after the word *pur*. On account of this, on account of all the words in this letter and what they had seen on account of such, and what had happened to them, ²⁷the Judahites established and accepted for themselves and for their offspring and for all who would join them, so that it should not pass away, to observe these two days in accordance with the document about them and in accordance with their time each year, ²⁸these days being commemorated and observed in every generation, generation by generation, family by family, province by province, and city by city. These days of Purim are not to pass away from the Judahites, and their commemoration is not to cease from their offspring. ²⁹Queen Esther daughter of Abihail and Mordecai the Judahite wrote with all force to establish this second letter about Purim. ³⁰Documents were sent to all the Judahites in the one hundred and twenty-seven provinces in Xerxes' realm, words about well-being and truthfulness, ³¹to establish these days of Purim at their time as Mordecai the Judahite and Queen Esther established for them, and as they had established for themselves and for their offspring statements about fasts and their lament. ³¹Esther's word established these statements about Purim and it was written down in a document.

¹⁰:¹King Xerxes imposed conscript labor on the country and the distant shores. ²All his powerful and mighty acts, and details of the importance of Mordecai, which the king conferred on

191

> him, are indeed written down in the annals of the kings of
> Media and Persia, ³because Mordecai the Judahite was second
> to King Xerxes and important to the Judahites and admired by
> his many brothers, seeking the good of his people and speaking
> of well-being for all its offspring.

A Jewish scholar who wrote an academic book on Esther also
described his personal interaction with its story; I alluded to
his account in connection with chapter 5 of Esther. However
historical one thinks the Esther story is, he comments, he
knows when he hears it read in the synagogue at Purim that
it is indeed a true story. When he reads the story, he relives its
truth and its actuality. It does not take much imagination for
him to sense the anxiety that seized the Jews in Persia when
they heard of Haman's threat to their lives, and to join in the
exhilaration at their deliverance. "Except," he says, "that I do
not think 'their' but 'my.'" He then refers to the pogroms in
southern Russia at the beginning of the twentieth century,
to the killing of a hundred thousand Jews in the Ukraine in
1919–1920, and then to Hitler's wiping out of one third of the
Jews in the world, through which Haman's goal was nearly realized. The ease with which he identifies with the Jews in Esther
is facilitated by his sense of having had a narrow, accidental
escape. His grandfather left the scene of the pogroms just
before they took place and he happened to be born outside the
reach of Nazi power. (See Michael Fox, *Character and Ideology
in the Book of Esther*; Eerdmans, 2001.)

The modern Jewish experience of Purim fulfills Mordecai's
and Esther's prescription for its observance. The instructions
for the celebration may seem convoluted; they are concerned
both to show how the official regulations for Purim constitute
a formalizing of a celebration that the people had already initi-
ated, and to explain the rationale for the different way the festival is observed in different parts of the Jewish world.

Calling the festival Purim, "Lots," might remind people that
the lots that decide what happens in the world are not cast
where Haman thought. The reminder at Haman's expense is
complemented by another reminder at Xerxes' expense. We
have noted that the law of the Medes and Persians was supposed

to be irrevocable, and Memucan had urged Xerxes to make that kind of law, the kind that "does not pass away," in respect to the ban on Vashti's ever again coming before the king. The same expression is now used with respect to the observance of Purim; indeed, to make sure we get the point, the verb "pass away" comes twice here. And unlike Medo-Persian laws, the rule for the observance of Purim indeed has not passed away. Adolf Hitler did attempt to ban the observance of Purim (with some inconsistency, the festival was also an occasion for Nazi attacks on and slaying of Jews), but the everlasting Reich has also been outlasted by the observance of Purim.

In another contrast, Mordecai and Esther are able to write a document using words that signify well-being (*shalom*) and truthfulness. The document Haman had dictated spoke of death and destruction and led to fasting and outcry. Now Mordecai can dictate words that imply very different prospects and that make possible a move from fasting to praise for the gifts of well-being and truthfulness. The point about the closing account of Xerxes' greatness is the implications it carries for Mordecai's importance as his second-in-command. As happens in the stories in Daniel, not only do the Judahite leaders escape a threatened death because of their commitment as Judahites, but they prove it is possible to triumph in the imperial administration and to use one's benefit for the benefit of members of the community.

It is thus appropriate that Jews celebrate Purim with gusto and humor. The story is read in the synagogue with hissing, stamping, and the shaking of noisemaking rattles at each mention of Haman. Some forms of celebration have involved dressing up in costumes, wearing masks, comic dramatization, puppet shows, and the burning of an effigy of Haman in the manner of a British "celebration" of Guy Fawkes. But the instructions make clear that the observance is not ethnically based. It is also for people who choose to join the community. While it was not clear that the people who earlier "professed to be Judahites" were genuinely associating themselves with the community, people who "join them" are people who seriously identify with it; passages such as Isaiah 56 use the verb "join" to describe foreigners who choose to join themselves to Yahweh.

The presence of Esther in the Christian Scriptures corresponds to Paul's emphasis in Romans 9–11 on God's eternal commitment to the Jewish people and on the importance of that commitment to Christians. In Paul's day it could seem as if God had abandoned the Jewish people; they had failed to recognize their Messiah. Subsequently, Christians have often inferred that the church has replaced the Jewish people in God's purpose. Paul implies that this is a disastrous view for Christians to take, because if God could cast off the Jewish people and not treat the divine commitment to them as a commitment that lasts forever, then God could do the same with the church. Rather (Paul says) the church is a body of people grafted into a Jewish tree—it does not signify the planting of a second tree. The church is a parasite on Israel, and when we read the story of the Jewish people's deliverance in Esther's day, gentile Christians will appropriately breathe a sigh of relief as our Jewish brothers and sisters do.

GLOSSARY

altar

The word usually refers to a structure for offering a sacrifice by burning it (the word comes from the word for sacrifice), made of earth or stone. An altar might be relatively small, like a table, and the person making the offering would stand in front of it. Or it might be higher and larger, like a platform, and the person making the offering would climb onto it. The word can also refer to a smaller stand for burning incense in association with worship.

ancestral heads

The heads of the (very) extended families within the twelve clans of Israel, a family unit larger than the household.

assistants

These are the *nethinim*, people who played a support role in the temple. Etymologically their name implies that they are people who were "given," dedicated to the service of God or given to the priests and Levites as their assistants in fulfilling menial tasks. The Gibeonites (Joshua 9:27) are not called *nethinim*, but the role ascribed to them as water carriers and wood cutters for the sanctuary conveys an idea of these assistants' work. The assistants came to be treated as among the **Levites**.

Assyria, Assyrians

The first great Middle Eastern superpower, the Assyrians spread their empire westward into Syria-Palestine in the eighth century, the time of Amos and Isaiah, and made **Ephraim** part of their empire. When Ephraim kept trying to assert independence, they invaded, and in 722 they destroyed Ephraim's capital at Samaria, transported many of its people, and settled people from other parts of their empire in their place. They also invaded **Judah** and devastated much of the country, but they did not take Jerusalem. Prophets such as Amos and Isaiah describe how God was thus using Assyria as a means of disciplining Israel.

Babylon, Babylonians

A minor power in the context of Israel's early history, in Jeremiah's time they succeeded **Assyria** as the region's superpower and remained that for nearly a century until conquered by **Persia**. Prophets such as Jeremiah describe how God was using them as a means of disciplining **Judah**. They took Jerusalem and transported many of its people in 587. Their creation stories, law codes, and more philosophical writings help us understand aspects of the Old Testament's equivalent writings, while their astrological religion forms background to aspects of polemic in the Prophets.

commitment

The word corresponds to the Hebrew word *hesed*, which translations render by means of expressions such as steadfast love or loving kindness or goodness. It is the Old Testament equivalent to the special word for love in the New Testament, the word *agapē*. The Old Testament uses this word to refer to an extraordinary act whereby someone pledges himself or herself to someone else in some act of generosity, allegiance, or grace when there is no prior relationship between them and therefore no reason why she or he should do so. Thus in Joshua 2, Rahab appropriately speaks of her protection of the Israelite spies as an act of commitment. It can also refer to a similar extraordinary act that takes place when there is a relationship between people, but one party has let the other party down and therefore has no right to expect any faithfulness from the other party. If the party that has been let down continues being faithful, they are showing this kind of commitment. In their response to Rahab, the Israelite spies declare that they will relate to her in this way.

covenant

The Hebrew word *berit* covers covenants, treaties, and contracts, but these are all ways in which people make a formal commitment about something, and I have used the word *covenant* for all three. Where you have a legal system to which people can appeal, contracts assume a system for resolving disputes and administering justice that can be used if people do not keep their commitments. In contrast, a covenantal relationship does not presuppose an enforceable legal framework of that kind, but a covenant does involve some formal procedure that confirms the seriousness of the solemn commitment one party makes to another. Thus the Old Testament often speaks of *sealing* a covenant, literally of *cutting it* (the background lies in the kind of formal procedure described in Genesis 15 and Jeremiah 34:18–20, though such an actual procedure would hardly be required every time someone made a covenantal commitment). People make covenants sometimes *to* other people and sometimes *with* other people. One implies something more one-sided; the other, something more mutual.

Ephraim, Ephraimites

Initially Ephraim is the name of one of Joseph's sons, then the name of the clan that traces its origin to him. After Solomon's reign, the nation of Israel split into two. The northern nation was the larger of the two and kept the name Israel as its political designation, which is confusing because Israel is still also the name of the people as a whole as the people of God. So the name Israel can be used in both these connections. Even more confusing, Chronicles is especially inclined to continue to use the name Israel for the people of God, and thus for **Judah** itself, to mark the fact that Judah is the real expression of the people of God. The northern state can, however, also be referred to by the name of Ephraim, one of its central clans, so I use this term to refer to the northern kingdom to try to reduce the confusion. After the **exile**, the province of Samaria covers much of the area once occupied by Ephraim, and many of its people see themselves as successors to the Ephraimites.

exile

At the end of the seventh century **Babylon** became the major power in **Judah**'s world, but Judah was inclined to resist its authority. As part of a successful campaign to get Judah to submit to it, in 597 and in 587 the Babylonians transported many people from Jerusalem to Babylon, particularly people in leadership positions, such as members of the royal family and the court, priests, and prophets. These people were compelled to live in Babylonia for the next fifty years or so. Throughout this period, people back in Judah were also under Babylonian authority, so they were not physically in exile but were living in the exile as a period of time. After the exilic period, many Judahites stayed in places such as Babylon, not as exiles who had no alternative but as part of what was now the dispersed Judahite/Israelite/Jewish community.

gatekeepers

Like the **assistants**, the gatekeepers have an important adjunct role in the temple. In general terms, their name implies that their responsibility was to make sure that people who should not come into the temple area did not do so. This might cover excluding people who would bring defilement into the sanctuary, but also people who might want to steal its resources such as animals, gold, and silver. They came to be treated as among the **Levites**.

Greece

In 336 BC Greek forces under Alexander the Great took control of the **Persian** Empire, but after Alexander's death in 333 his empire split up. The largest part, to the north and east of Palestine, was ruled by one of his generals, Seleucus, and his successors. **Judah** was under its control for much of the next two centuries, though it was at the southwestern border of this empire and sometimes came under the control of the Ptolemaic Empire in Egypt, ruled by successors of another of Alexander's officers.

Israel, Israelite

Originally, Israel was the new name God gave Abraham's grandson, Jacob. His twelve sons were then forefathers of the twelve clans that comprise the people Israel. In the time of Saul, David, and Solomon these twelve clans became more of a political entity; Israel was then both the people of God and a nation or state like other nations or states. After Solomon's day, this one state split into two, **Ephraim** and **Judah**. Ephraim was far bigger and often continued to be referred to as Israel. So if one is thinking of the people of God, Judah is part of Israel. If one is thinking politically, Judah is not part of Israel, but once Ephraim has gone out of existence, for practical purposes Judah *is* Israel, as the people of God.

Judah, Judahites

Judah is one of the twelve sons of Jacob, then the clan that traces its ancestry to him, then the dominant clan in the southern of the two states after the time of Solomon. Later, as a **Persian** province or colony, it was known as Yehud. Later still, the Hebrew word *yehudim* becomes a religious designation, the term for people who live by the **Torah**; the translation *Jews* is then appropriate. In Esther, it has those overtones, though the book's avoidance of religious terms such as God and Israel makes it appropriate to keep the translation *Judahites* there, too, even though the people come under attack because of their distinctive Jewish religious commitment

Levites

Within the clan of Levi, the descendants of Aaron are the priests, the people who have specific responsibilities in connection with offering the community's sacrifices and helping individuals to offer their sacrifices by performing some aspects of the offering such as the sprinkling of the animal's blood. The other Levites fulfill a support and administrative role in the temple and are also involved in teaching the people and in other aspects of leading worship.

name

The name of someone stands for the person. The Old Testament talks of the temple as a place where God's name dwells. It's one of the ways it handles the paradox involved in speaking of the temple as a place where God lives. It knows this is nonsense: how could a building contain the God who could not be contained by the entire heavens? Yet Israel knows that God does in some sense dwell in the temple. They know they can talk with God when they go there; they are aware that they can talk with God anywhere, but there is a special guarantee of this freedom in the temple. They know they can make offerings there and that God will receive them (supposing they are made in good faith). One way they try to square the circle in speaking of the presence of God in the temple is therefore to speak of God's name being present there, because the name sums up the person. Uttering the name of someone you know brings home his or her reality to you; it's almost as if the person is there. When you say someone's name, there is a sense in which you conjure up the person. When people murmur "Jesus, Jesus" in their prayer, it brings home the reality of Jesus' presence. Likewise, when Israel proclaimed the name **Yahweh** in worship, it brought home the reality of Yahweh's presence.

Persia, Persians

The third Middle Eastern superpower. Under the leadership of Cyrus the Great, they took control of the **Babylonian** empire in

199

539 BC. Isaiah 40–55 sees God's hand in raising up Cyrus as the means of restoring **Judah** after the **exile**. Judah and surrounding peoples such as Samaria, Ammon, and Ashdod were Persian provinces or colonies. The Persians stayed in power for two centuries until defeated by **Greece**.

Second Temple

The First Temple was that built by Solomon, and the First Temple period was thus the time from his day to the **exile**. The Second Temple was that rebuilt by Zerubbabel and Jeshua after the exile, but vastly expanded by Herod. The Second Temple period is thus the time from the restoration after the exile until the temple's destruction in AD 70.

secondary wife

Translations use the word *concubine* to describe people such as some of David's wives and Xerxes' wives, but the Hebrew term used for them does not suggest that they were not properly married, as the word *concubine* may. Being a secondary wife rather means that a woman has a different status from other wives. It perhaps implies that her sons had fewer or no inheritance rights. It may be that a wealthy or powerful man could have several wives with full rights and several secondary wives, or just one of each, or just the former, or even just a secondary wife. A king like Xerxes could certainly have a number of wives.

Torah

The Hebrew word for the first five books of the Bible. They are often referred to as the "Law," but this title gives a misleading impression. Genesis itself is nothing like "law," and even Exodus to Deuteronomy are not "legalistic" books. The word *torah* itself means "teaching," which gives a clearer impression of the nature of the Torah. Often the Torah gives us more than one account of an event (such as God's commission of Moses), so that when the early church told the story of Jesus in different ways in different contexts and according to the insights of the different Gospel writers, it was following the precedent whereby Israel told its stories more than once in different contexts. Whereas Samuel–Kings and Chronicles keep the versions separate, as would happen with the Gospels, in the Torah the versions were combined.

trespass

This term to describe sin or wrongdoing suggests the idea that in varying ways we owe it to one another to respect the rights that another person has. So married people owe each other faithfulness, and unfaithfulness involves failure to respect that right. Unfaithfulness to Yahweh by serving other gods has similar implications; it fails to respect Yahweh's right to allegiance and trust. Thus in Ezra and Nehemiah, marrying the devotees of other religions is an act of trespass.

Yahweh

In most English Bibles, the word "LORD" often comes in all capitals, as sometimes does the word "GOD" in similar format. These represent Yahweh, the name of God. In later Old Testament times, Israelites stopped using the name Yahweh and started to refer to Yahweh as "the Lord." There may be two reasons. They wanted other people to recognize that Yahweh was the one true God, and this strange, foreign-sounding name could give the impression that Yahweh was just Israel's tribal god, whereas "the Lord" was a term anyone could recognize. In addition, they did not want to fall foul of the warning in the Ten Commandments about misusing Yahweh's name. Translations into other languages then followed suit in substituting an expression such as "the Lord" for the name Yahweh. The downsides are that this ignores God's wish to be known by name, that often the text is referring to Yahweh and not some other (so-called) god or lord, and that it gives the impression that God is much more lordly and patriarchal than actually God is. (The form *Jehovah* is not a real word but a mixture of the consonants of Yahweh and the vowels of the word for "Lord," to remind people in reading Scripture that they should say "the Lord," not the actual name.)